The Complete Idiot's Reference Card

Child Safety

1. Remember that the responsibility for your children's safety rests on your shoulders. If you don't take it seriously, your kids won't either.
2. For the training to be effective, you must always strive to make it fun for your kids.
3. Use role-playing techniques with your kids as often as you can so they will be prepared for real-life situations.
4. Call your local police department to see whether there are any convicted child offenders living in your neighborhood.
5. Take the time to have your children fingerprinted and make sure you always have a recent photograph of them.
6. Make your kids memorize their full name, address, and telephone numb...
7. Teach your children the definition of a stranger.
8. Create a family password that must be used by a... ...ing your home.
9. Teach your kids that they are not allowed to ke...
10. Talk to your children about the private parts of ... touch.
11. Before letting your child spend the night with a fr... ...get to know the host family.
12. If your child is being chased, teach him to use a car to shield him from the attacker.
13. Teach your child to never leave with a police officer unless two uniformed officers are present.
14. Encourage your children to practice staying in groups and to never stray off by themselves.
15. Don't let your children wear clothes or name tags that reveal their names to strangers.

Securing Your Home

1. Make sure your home always looks occupied, even when you're not there.
2. In the majority of all break-ins, the burglar kicks in the front door. Take extra care in securing this area.
3. Alarm systems are an invaluable tool for deterring criminals.
4. Criminals hate dogs. If you don't have an alarm, a dog is the next best thing.
5. Keep your windows covered so people walking or driving by can't see inside.
6. If you are not at home, be sure to leave a few lights on that can be seen from the street.
7. Buy a switch that automatically turns your porch light on and off at certain times. This will help give the impression that someone is at home.
8. It is good to invest in a motion sensor light. This will startle potential intruders and will alert you to what's happening outside your house.
9. Make sure your shrubbery does not hinder your view when looking out your windows or doors.
10. Avoid having large bushes close to entryways. This provides a good hiding place for a potential criminal.
11. Unsecured basement windows often are a criminal's first choice for entering a house.
12. Take an inventory of all the valuables in your home so you'll know exactly what is missing if your home is burglarized.
13. Be a good neighbor and get involved in your local neighborhood watch program. If there isn't one, team up with your neighbors to create a program.

alpha books

1. If a criminal approaches you, you should not consider staying and fighting unless it is your only option.
2. Criminals are turned off by people who show confidence.
3. Just as confidence is your strength, fear is your greatest weakness. Don't be afraid to confront your fears.
4. Don't be afraid to offend someone.
5. Don't ignore your internal alarm system. Trust your gut feelings.
6. A criminal is not identified by what is on the surface, so don't go by appearance.
7. One of the advantages of a good stance is that it reduces the number of available targets for your attacker to strike.
8. To execute a block properly, it is important that you use your forearm and elbow to stop the blow instead of your wrist or hand.
9. Don't ever comply with a criminal's request to relocate. Criminals won't commit a crime if they are uncomfortable with their surroundings.
10. The best hand strikes are the ones that protect your hand from injury while still generating a lot of power.
11. There are no rules for defending yourself in a life-or-death situation. Do whatever it takes.
12. A slight step in one direction could be the difference between being hit by an attacker or being missed. Footwork is key.
13. If you are ever grabbed from behind, throw the back of your head into the attacker's face repeatedly.
14. Regardless of how big, strong, or fast an attacker is, poking a finger in his eye will stop him every time.

Car Safety

1. Unless a child is with you, be quick to give a carjacker your vehicle without resistance.
2. The best deterrent to carjacking is to be aware and alert anytime you're driving, exiting, or entering your vehicle.
3. Removing valuable items from your car is a great way to prevent theft and vandalism.
4. The best vehicle antitheft devices are the ones that act as visual deterrents as well.
5. Try to avoid parking next to large vehicles that provide cover for a carjacker.
6. Get into the habit of surveying the area around your car as you approach it.
7. When approaching your vehicle, have your keys in hand and be ready to unlock the door so you can get into your vehicle much faster.
8. If someone suspicious is approaching your car, don't be afraid to lay on your horn to draw attention to yourself.
9. Having a panic button to enable your car alarm is also helpful in an emergency.
10. Sometimes a decal or sticker that advertises your vehicle's alarm system is enough to deter a criminal.
11. Properly maintaining your car greatly reduces your chances of being stranded.
12. Cell phones are one of the best investments you can make to ensure your safety when in your vehicle.
13. Road rage has cost many innocent people their lives, so make sure you do not provoke someone on the highway.
14. If you run out of gas, don't accept a ride from a stranger. Instead, ask them to bring back a container of gas while you stay with your car.
15. Keep a small container of mace in your vehicle at all times.

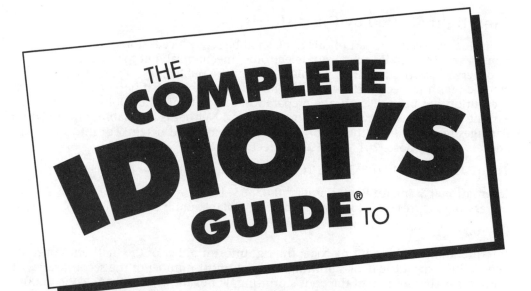

THE COMPLETE IDIOT'S GUIDE® TO

Self-Defense

By Chris Harris

alpha books

Macmillan USA, Inc.
201 West 103rd Street
Indianapolis, IN 46290

A Pearson Education Company

Alpha Books

Publisher
Marie Butler-Knight

Editorial Director
Gary M. Krebs

Associate Managing Manager
Cari Shaw Fischer

Acquisitions Editor
Randy Ladenheim-Gil

Development Editors
Phil Kitchel
Amy Zavatto

Production Team

Development Editor
Amy Bryant

Production Editors
M. Faunette Johnston
JoAnna Kremer

Copy Editor
Amy Lepore

Technical Editor
Floyd Powell

Research
David Coats

Cover Designer
Mike Freeland

Cartoonist
Brian Mac Moyer

Illustrator
Dan Nelson

Designer
Scott Cook and Amy Adams of DesignLab

Indexer
Nadia Ibrahim

Layout/Proofreading
Gloria Schurick
Donna Martin

Contents at a Glance

Contents

Part 2: Staying Safe While Out and About   61

6 Dangerous Places   63

24 Children: The World's Most Valuable Resource   289

25 Good-Old-Fashioned Safety for Seniors   301

Introduction

I'll never forget the hot summer night in 1989 that changed my life forever. It was the night a 10-year-old girl was abducted from her home, which was more than an hour's drive from where I was. She was riding her bicycle in front of her house while her dad was mowing the lawn when a strange man pulled up next to her in a white Chevy Blazer. He jumped out, grabbed the girl, and quickly drove away. A crime that took him only a few seconds to commit could have taken a family a lifetime to forget. Thankfully, I was at the right place at the right time, and the little girl was rescued from her abductor. I pulled the girl into my vehicle, followed the pedophile in a high speed chase, got close enough to get his license plate number, went to the police station, and turned over the girl and the abductor's info. He was apprehended at his house three hours later.

After testifying and seeing the man receive life without parole in prison and after watching the little girl be reunited with her family, I knew what I was meant to do.

I had been training in the martial arts since 1978 and loved every minute of it, but my interests were divided. Up until that point, I had been working toward a career in commercial aviation, but it always was competing with my passion for teaching people how to protect themselves. Not any more! After I helped the little girl, I knew where my heart was. I began to train in the martial arts even harder, and I started studying crime statistics, criminal behavior, and anything else I could get my hands on. My mind was made up; I was going to follow my heart and dedicate my life to self-defense.

I've been training in the martial arts for more than 20 years now, and I've been studying crime and violence prevention for more than a decade. My goal is simple. I want to help people get home safe at night, every night, regardless of their age, gender, size, strength, or ability. When I founded Harris Personal Safety in 1993, I set out to educate as many people as possible in one lifetime. Since then, I have taught people all over the world how to protect themselves, and I'm just getting started.

Teaching people how to reduce their chances of being targeted for crime and how to defend themselves against violence has to be the most rewarding job in the world. No one appreciates preventative medicine until an illness hits home. I've received nearly 500 letters in the past three years, many of them tear-stained, all of them thanking me. This is the greatest reward of all.

I would like to personally thank you for taking your safety seriously enough to buy this book. It could prove to be one of the smartest investments you've ever made. I'd also like to thank you for trusting me to teach you about such an important subject. I consider it an honor, and I don't take your trust lightly.

How to Use This Book

This book is divided into six parts, each one focusing on a particular area of self-defense. I wrote this book so it would be a great reference guide for someone who has a good understanding of the subject, as well as a fun and informative book to read straight through for beginners. If you want to brush up on a specific subject, just turn to that chapter and spend a few minutes arming yourself. If you're a novice and don't know anything about self-defense, take your time and read a few chapters at a time. Either way, I'm sure you'll find the chapters very thorough and informative.

In **Part 1, "The Scoop on Safety,"** I'll walk you through the differences between the martial arts and self-defense, and then I'll take you on a tour through the mind of a criminal. To finish this section off, I'm going to teach you what the law has to say about defending yourself. This information is good to know if you ever have to get physical.

In **Part 2, "Staying Safe While Out and About,"** I'm going to show you how to play it safe whenever you're out of the house. If you do any traveling for business or pleasure, you definitely don't want to miss this section. Dating can be tricky business where your safety is concerned, so if you're single, check out what I've got to say here. I also cover workplace violence, and I haven't forgotten about college students either.

In **Part 3, "Home Sweet Home,"** I'll teach you how to keep your castle safe and secure when you're both home and away. What about safety on the telephone and the Internet? I'm going to give you the full scoop about all the latest means of communication. I'll finish this section by discussing the silent crime of domestic violence, and I'll teach you how to protect yourself from the crime that goes on behind closed doors.

In **Part 4, "Safe Drivers Wanted,"** I'll give you valuable information about protecting your vehicle and keeping it from driving off without you. This section covers all aspects of protecting yourself and your ride without having to spend a bunch of money in the process. Do you know what to do if you become stranded? If not, I've got everything you need to know right here. If you take the bus, a taxi, or the subway, you need to know the dangers involved so you can avoid them—all aboard the safety express!

In **Part 5, "Face to Face with the Enemy,"** I'll show you how to defend yourself when you're up against an enemy bent on hurting you. I even get personal here when I tell you about my own system of self-defense. If you're ever confronted by a criminal, you need to know what to do. This section tells you just that. Are you considering purchasing a product to help you defend yourself? If so, then you'll love this section. I give an overview of all the popular items on the market, but I don't think highly of all of them.

In **Part 6, "Defense for Special Situations,"** I cover some really great stuff. If you have children, you need to know how to protect them and how to teach them to protect themselves when you're not around. Have you ever been home alone? If you have, you need to know the rules for staying safe. Senior citizens definitely don't want to miss what I have to say here. And just because you're in a wheelchair doesn't mean you can't defend yourself, so let's get started training.

Did Someone Say Help?

In addition to the main text, you'll see many sidebars and icons cleverly planted throughout the book. These sidebars give you extra information as follows:

Street Talk

These are definitions of some common and not-so-common self-defense terms.

Bad Guys Beware!

These simple self-defense tips can keep you safe.

Stay on Your Toes

These are interesting facts and anecdotes to help complement the text. They work great for impressing your friends!

Safety Alert!

These warnings and cautions can lead to danger if ignored.

Life Savers

These real-life scenarios can teach you how to deal with tricky situations.

Acknowledgments

I would like to thank God for giving me this wonderful opportunity. A BIG thanks is owed to my wife, Corrie, and my son, Stanton, for their patience, support, and understanding during this project. A special thanks is owed to my mother-in-law, Martha Hedge, for being there when I needed her and to David Coats for the countless hours he spent doing all the tedious stuff that is so time-consuming. Great job, David! And what can be said about Amy Bryant? You are awesome, Amy! You do your job well and are a credit to your profession. Thank you to Mike Bailey for your friendship, understanding, and support. You are a good friend. Thank you to Dan Nelson for the great illustrations, and thank you to Regina Ortiz, Brad Jackson, Marlene Pack, and Scott Spangler for your help with the photos. Your help was greatly appreciated.

Special thanks are owed to Chris Ortiz, Michael Gamble, Lynton Turkington, Steve Price, and Randy Williamson. You stopped by to check on me frequently, you always asked me what I needed, and you watched my back for this entire project. A day did not go by that at least one of you didn't step up to the plate for me. What can I say? Thanks for caring.

I also would like to publicly congratulate the nine individuals who have persevered to the very end to earn their Black Belts in the Harris Self-Defense System. They are Jim Bussey, Bill Clee, Chris Clee, Dick Dandalides, Brandon Foster, Sean Henchey, Dan Matise, Floyd Powell, and Shane Villars. It wasn't easy, guys, but you did it and I'm proud of you. Training you has been an absolute pleasure.

Special Thanks to the Technical Reviewer

The Complete Idiot's Guide to Self-Defense was reviewed by an expert who checked the technical accuracy of what you'll learn here to help us ensure that this book gives you everything you need to know about self-defense. Special thanks are extended to Floyd Powell.

Floyd Powell is a certified Black Belt and a former police officer in the Dallas area. He has trained hundreds in self-defense and personal safety. He has given personal safety lectures to corporations, churches, schools, and women's groups. Floyd has spent months in foreign countries training Special Forces Soldiers and Law Enforcement personnel in hand-to-hand combat and the use of law enforcement weapons.

Trademarks

All terms mentioned in this book that are known to be or are suspected of being trademarks or service marks have been appropriately capitalized. Alpha Books and Macmillan USA, Inc. cannot attest to the accuracy of this information. Use of a term in this book should not be regarded as affecting the validity of any trademark or service mark.

Part 1

The Scoop on Safety

When was the last time you said, "Be careful"? We say it all the time to our family, our friends, even total strangers. The trick is knowing how to be careful. That's what this book addresses—practical ways for people of all ages and all physical abilities (or lack thereof) to live safely and without unreasonable fear.

Crime and violence have become part of our culture—even our entertainment. Self-defense and martial arts schools are popping up everywhere. The average couch potato, however, isn't interested in becoming another Walker, Texas Ranger; he just wants to be safe. Whatever your interests and abilities, this section will help you find the balance that fits you.

Maybe you already instinctively know some of what you need to confidently defend yourself. Learn how to use your instincts, when to swallow your pride, and how to be aware of danger by following the six Golden Rules. Can you recognize a criminal? Learn how a criminal thinks and how to avoid going by appearance. (Ever notice on the news that the men or women who have committed violent crimes often look too nice to be so bad?)

It doesn't matter whether you're a soccer mom, a college student, or a businessperson who travels internationally; you can defend yourself. You can learn to avoid danger, and if you do get caught in a deadly situation, you can deal with it—even if it becomes life-threatening. There really are safe ways to legally protect yourself and your family. It's time to get started!

Chapter 1

What's All the Fuss About?

In This Chapter

➤ Types of violent crime

➤ Types of property crime

➤ Guns

➤ Getting assistance from the police

Do you get depressed watching the evening news? Have you ever felt discouraged after reading the newspaper? Americans now rank violent crime as one of their greatest concerns, and it's no wonder. Crime in the United States has increased 550 percent since 1960 alone, with a 300-percent increase in violent crime. It is now estimated that the average American is more likely to be the victim of a violent crime than of an automobile accident.

This chapter takes a look at crime and violence. I'll give you some facts about crime that will let you decide for yourself how to look at this problem. Don't worry, I'm not going to scare or intimidate you. Instead, I'll carefully walk you through this information step by step, and I'll answer a bunch of helpful questions along the way. I'm going to teach you about all the different types of crimes out there and how often they occur. I'm also going to define some commonly used (but often misunderstood) terminology. To accomplish this, I've weeded through hundreds of pages of tedious and sometimes hard-to-interpret graphs, charts, and statistics, and I've pulled out only the ones I felt were relative to your concerns. I also have taken the time to arrange and word them in a way that will be easy for you to understand. Learning how to defend yourself is a great thing, and reading this book is a fun way to do it. So let's have at it!

Types of Violent Crime

Because we are going to be discussing crime and violence throughout this book, it's important for you to have a strong understanding of the terminology. I'll start by familiarizing you with what I consider to be the "Big Seven" crimes in the United States that are relative to self-defense: homicide, rape, robbery, aggravated assault, burglary, larceny-theft, and motor vehicle theft. These seven categories can be further broken down into two groups: violent crime, which includes homicide, rape, robbery, and aggravated assault, and property crime, which includes burglary, larceny-theft, and motor vehicle theft.

Street Talk

Self-defense is the defense of one-self or of one's rights, beliefs, actions, and so on. Self-defense is 80 percent mental and only 20 percent physical, and it is our right, our responsibility, and our privilege.

Author disclaimer: The majority of the statistics used for this book have been taken from the FBI Uniform Crime Report. Unless otherwise stated, these statistics are based on crimes dating back to 1994. Keep in mind that the numbers I use for statistical purposes always are approximate. I also would like to point out that I do not put a great deal of faith in these numbers for the simple reason that crime is extremely difficult to report accurately, even for the FBI. To compound the problem, there is no accurate way to know how many crimes are committed each day that don't get reported. Although these numbers provide us with a general idea of what's going on, try to keep their shortcomings in mind.

Homicide

The United States has the distinct honor of having the highest homicide rate in the world. The homicide count for 1994 in the United States totaled more than 23,300, which translates to a rate of nearly 64 homicides per day. For those of you who are under the impression that self-defense is just for women, the numbers also show that nearly 80 percent of homicide victims are male. In addition, 88 percent of all victims are over the age of 18.

On average, seven out of every ten homicides in America are committed with a firearm. To top it off, one out of every two homicides are random acts of violence. (In other words, the criminal and the victim are total strangers.)

Rape

For our purposes, a practical definition of rape is engaging in sexual acts with a person who has not consented. According to a U.S. Senate Report, one in five women will be raped during her lifetime.

There are four types of rape:

➤ **Domestic rape:** Rape committed by a spouse or significant other, usually in the home.

➤ **Date rape:** Rape committed by an individual you are dating.

➤ **Acquaintance rape:** Rape committed by a friend or an acquaintance (but not someone you are dating).

➤ **Stranger rape:** Rape committed by a total stranger in a random act of violence.

By taking the hardest step, which is confronting this issue head-on, you are strengthening your position. The way to confront an issue such as rape is to educate yourself on the subject, discuss it with others, and take steps to prevent it. Reading helpful material, taking a self-defense course, and watching a rape-prevention video all are excellent ways to confront this issue in a healthy manner.

See Chapter 10, "Staying Safe While Single," for more information.

Bad Guys Beware!

If another person ever makes a threat on your life, call the police department immediately and file a death-threat report. One of the advantages of making this report is that it helps prove your case if you ever have to defend yourself against this person legally.

Robbery

According to Webster's, robbery is "the felonious taking of personal property that is in the possession or immediate presence of another by the use of violence or intimidation."

In 1994, law enforcement recorded nearly 620,000 robberies. Fifty-five percent of these crimes were committed on our streets and highways. A firearm was used in 42 percent of all robberies, and strong-arm tactics were used in 39 percent. How much money does all of this equate to? Stolen property added up to a loss of about $496 million. Banks that were robbed took the hardest hit, averaging a loss of around $3,550 for every offense.

Life Savers

If someone is trying to rape you, remember that your first priority is to get away. Don't be afraid to do anything necessary to accomplish this. Your safety and escape are of the utmost importance. Act quickly and decisively to throw the attacker off guard while you escape. Never, under any circumstances, go with him to a second location.

Stay on Your Toes

Robbing a convenience store will net you an average of $387.

Aggravated Assault

Aggravated assault is defined as a physical and violent attack on another person. If someone intentionally hits you with a 9-iron from their golf bag, for example, that's considered to be aggravated assault. There are an estimated 1.12 million cases of aggravated assault in the United States each year. In fact, during 1994, aggravated assault made up almost 60 percent of all violent crimes committed. How were they committed? Thirty-two percent were acted out with blunt objects or weapons of a similar nature, 26 percent were committed without weapons, and 24 percent were carried out with firearms.

Bad Guys Beware!

If what a criminal wants from you can be replaced with money, quietly hand it over with no questions asked. If what the criminal wants cannot be replaced with money (such as telling you to get into a car), it's time to take a stand and fight back if necessary.

Types of Property Crime

Property crimes are a little easier to discuss because they don't involve personal injury. Houses that are broken into, vehicles that are stolen, and purses that are snatched all fall into the property crime category. The good news is that property crimes are very preventable, provided you learn what precautions to take in advance. (This is covered later in more detail.)

Burglary

Imagine coming home from a hard day's work, opening the front door of your apartment, and finding that it's been robbed while you were away. This is burglary. Webster's dictionary defines burglary as "the act of breaking into houses, shops, etc. to steal, especially at night." I would have to dispute Webster's definition, however, because over half of all burglaries occur during the daylight hours.

Let's start with some statistics about burglary. In 1994, more than 2.7 million burglaries were reported, and approximately 66 percent of them involved a personal residence. Two out of every three of these crimes involved a form of forcible entry (in other words, they didn't use the spare key under the doormat). Finally, burglars stole an estimated $3.6 billion worth of property in 1994.

Burglary.

Larceny-Theft

Larceny is the taking of personal property without consent and with the intention of permanently depriving the owner of it.

A whopping 56 percent of the entire crime index in 1994 comprised cases of larceny-theft. This probably is due to the fact that there were an estimated 7.9 million offenses in just one year, during which time victims lost more than $4 billion in stolen property. The average incident averaged a loss of around $505.

Safety Alert!

If you come home to find that you've been robbed, or if you even suspect that something's wrong, do not go inside. Instead, go to a neighbor's house and call the police. There's a good chance that someone could still be inside your home, and the last thing you want to do is startle a burglar.

Nearly 37 percent of these reported larcenies were made up of stolen motor vehicle parts, accessories, and contents. Makes you want to start locking up your vehicle, doesn't it?

Larceny-theft.

Robbery.

I don't know about you, but most people have a hard time remembering the differences between robbery, burglary, and larceny-theft. Because it can get a little confusing, let's review a few examples that should help you keep them straight. If someone breaks into your home or office when no one's there, it's burglary. If a criminal breaks into your car and steals your purse, it's considered larceny-theft. If a criminal rips you off while you're present, it's robbery. Get the picture?

Stay on Your Toes

Ninety percent of the time, criminals use some form of deception to help lure their target. Therefore, one of the best ways to prevent becoming a victim is to learn to recognize these deceptions in advance.

Every Few Seconds

So what do all these statistics mean anyway? Here is what it all boils down to:

➤ One homicide is committed every 25 seconds.

➤ One forcible rape is committed every 6 seconds.

➤ One robbery is committed every 60 seconds.

➤ One aggravated assault is committed every 35 seconds.

➤ One burglary is committed every 10 seconds.

➤ One larceny-theft is committed every 4 seconds.

➤ One motor vehicle theft is committed every 22 seconds.

Guns

On average, there are 40,000 deaths each year in our country due to gunshot wounds. Three-fourths of all gunshot victims are under the age of 30. In fact, the Department of Justice estimates that 125,000 kids take a gun to school daily. There are approximately 265 million people living in the United States, and there are nearly 220 million firearms.

Analysts now believe that, within the next five years, automobile accidents no longer will be the number one cause of injury and fatality in America. Instead, they predict that gunshot vic-

Bad Guys Beware!

To get good at defending yourself, it's necessary to learn about crime prevention as well as crime survival. Crime prevention is learning what you can do to prevent being targeted by a criminal. Crime survival is knowing what to do when you're face-to-face with the creep. The key to a well-rounded safety plan is to learn how to maintain a healthy balance between the two.

Bad Guys Beware!

If you plan to buy a second-hand firearm, you need to be careful. You don't want to purchase a gun that's been used to commit a crime. Ask the person from whom you're buying the gun if he minds that you want to call the police and have the gun's serial number checked out. If the seller panics or says he does mind, report him to the police.

Street Talk

A **misdemeanor** is considered to be a minor offense such as the breaking of a municipal ordinance. The penalty usually is a fine or a short stay in jail. A **felony,** however, is a major crime such as murder, rape, or arson, and the penalty usually is severe. For felonies, prison sentences usually are at least one year.

tims will become the new leaders in death. In addition to costing us many innocent lives, guns also cost this country nearly $20 billion each year in doctor's bills and other miscellaneous expenses. Based on gun manufacturers' annual productivity projections, it is estimated that 4 million guns are manufactured each year. That's a lot of guns.

Types of Guns

Several different types of guns are manufactured all over the world. Although each type of gun is made with a very specific purpose in mind, they all have the capability to kill. If you decide to purchase a gun for any reason, keep in mind that it is designed to fire a projectile thousands of feet per second at a particular target. Treat it carefully and with respect. Sporting guns have taken lives, target competition guns have taken lives, hunting guns have taken lives, and collectable antique guns have taken lives.

The following is a list of the four most popular firearms in the United States, their effective ranges, and a common use of each:

➤ Handguns—close-range weapons
  Common use: Americans' #1 choice for personal protection

➤ Shotguns—close-range weapons
  Common use: Hunting small game and sport shooting

➤ Sub-machine guns—mid-range weapons
  Common use: Military operations (It's illegal for civilians to own one.)

➤ Rifles—long-range weapons
  Common use: Medium to big game hunting and marksmanship competitions

Getting Assistance from the Police

Contrary to popular belief, the police probably not will arrive on the scene until after a crime has been committed. Like it or not, the police are not legally obligated to provide you with personal protection, and they have not broken the law if they fail to show up quickly (or at all). Check out the following excerpt from *American Jurisprudence* (57 Am Jur 2d 441):

> *In the absence of special circumstances, there is no duty resting on a municipality or other governmental body to provide police protection to any particular person and the government may not be held liable for its failure to do so...*

If you call the police, it's probably because you're already in a bad situation. By the time they get to where you are, the criminal more than likely will be long gone. This means you need to know how to take care of yourself until the police arrive. This is why self-defense is so important. Your family's immediate personal safety ultimately is your responsibility.

Life Savers

If you ever find yourself needing to call 911 for police assistance, make sure to stay on the line until the dispatcher has all the necessary information. After you get the dispatcher on the phone, tell him the situation at hand as specifically as possible. Of course, if you're truly in a life-threatening situation, chances are you won't have time to hang around and give out your personal information. Know that by merely leaving the phone off the hook, the police can trace the call and send someone out to you.

Long on Crime, Short on Police

Let me just throw out a couple of things: In many of America's major cities, only one cop is available for every ten violent crimes committed. In addition, no arrests are made in nearly 53 percent of all violent crimes. Therefore, if we are going to survive crime and violence, we must take preventative measures and prepare ourselves. I've covered a lot of negative information in this chapter, and you might be experiencing a little fear as a result. To be honest, that's not so bad. After all, fear motivates people to take the subject of self-defense seriously. The good news is that the majority of criminals are predictable, avoidable, and already accustomed to losing. By taking your time to carefully read through this material and by mixing it with some action, you'll be well on your way to living a safe, crime-free life. So what are you waiting for? Throw that victim mindset away and trade it in for a survival mindset. Read on!

The Least You Need To Know

➤ Crime can be broken down into two categories: violent crimes and property crimes.

➤ The best way to prevent violent crimes is to prepare yourself in advance.

➤ It is extremely difficult to produce accurate statistics relating to crime and violence because we can only go by criminal acts reported to the police.

➤ Guns should be handled carefully and responsibly because all guns can take lives.

➤ A police officer's duty is to help protect you. Because most Americans don't have a 24-hour escort, however, your safety often is your responsibility alone.

Self–Defense and the Martial Arts

Every time I tell people that I am a self-defense expert, the first thing they ask is "Are you a Black Belt?" The truth is, when most people hear the term self-defense, they think of a person wearing a clean, white uniform with a black belt and making a bunch of karate noises.

In this chapter, I'm going to teach you the differences and similarities between self-defense and the martial arts. I'll walk you through the martial arts, and I'll educate you about what's relevant to self-defense and what's not. I'll also teach you about the various types of martial arts in general by giving you a summary of each category. By knowing what's out there, you'll be able to decide which method of instruction might work best for you should you decide to take classes.

An Overview

In Chapter 1, "What's All the Fuss About?," you learned that self-defense is the defense of oneself or of one's rights, beliefs, or actions. The word "martial" means suitable for war and comes from the word "mars," which was the name of Rome's ancient god of war. Comparing the definitions shows us that the two terms have a great deal in common. Think about it. If you are in a situation in which you have to defend yourself, your actions, or your beliefs, how are you going to do it? This is where martial arts step into the picture. Because the two have a great deal in common, I am going to spend the rest of this chapter familiarizing you with the martial arts in general. I won't spend too much time discussing self-defense, however, because I've devoted the other 27 chapters to the subject.

Finding Your Balance

Chapter 1 discussed the difference between crime prevention and crime survival. You learned that, to really stay safe, you need to acquire a good balance between the two. I always have put a greater emphasis on the prevention part because my philosophy is that the best defense is to not be there. This does not, however, lessen the importance of learning good crime survival techniques. When it comes to knowing how to fight back, it's better to know it and never need it than to need it and not know it. A good self-defense expert will equip you with a full-coverage insurance policy and hope you only need liability.

Stay on Your Toes

The better you become at defending yourself physically, the less likely you are to ever need to defend yourself. As you get better, your confidence increases. Most criminals can spot confident people and will go out of their way to avoid them.

The Importance of a Punch

Although the majority of this book is dedicated to teaching you preventative medicine, don't get the idea that knowing how to throw a punch isn't important. Throughout this book, I place a great deal of emphasis on running from the attacker whenever possible. This doesn't mean I'm naïve enough to believe that there never will be a time when you just can't run. The main reason I spend such a small amount of time teaching you how to fight back is because there's not a great deal you need to know. One hard kick, one focused handstrike, one strong block, or one quick eye gouge usually can get you out of the worst of situations if performed correctly. Granted, you're not going to be a Black Belt by the end of this book, nor will you be winning any trophies for style and technique, but you will know enough to physically escape an attacker safely in most cases.

The Bottom Line

In a self-defense course, the goal is to teach the student how to avoid being in a crime situation in the first place. The rest of the time is spent showing the student what to do when he or she is face-to-face with a bad guy. In martial arts, the main emphasis usually is placed on teaching the student how to become an expert fighter, and very little if any time is spent on crime prevention.

Is there a difference between the hands-on techniques taught by a self-defense expert and the ones taught by a martial arts instructor? That's a great question. The answer is yes! You're thinking that a punch is a punch is a punch, right? Wrong! In martial arts, not only are there numerous ways to throw a punch, there are also dozens of targets on the human body at which to throw a punch.

Safety Alert!

If a criminal approaches you, don't stay and fight unless it's your only option. Although knowing how to fight back is very important, knowing when not to fight back is even more important. Fighting back when you don't need to is not only dangerous, it's illegal.

It's rare, however, that someone teaching you self-defense will go into that much detail and for good reason. A martial arts instructor knows that he is going to be your teacher for months, maybe even years, and he probably has made it a goal to make the material become second nature to you. Self-defense courses are designed to be much briefer in nature, and the instructor knows he might only teach you for a few hours or weeks at the most. As a result, he would rather teach you how to throw one punch really well and then move on.

The Origin of Martial Arts

The first thing we must do is confront the myths regarding where the martial arts actually originated. (I have heard more rumors on this topic than there are taxis in New York.) Every hard core practitioner likes to think that his style is the original martial art. The truth is, the martial arts derive from the efforts of many different countries and cultures.

Sharing the Credit

The martial arts stem from the cultures of Asia, Greece, India, Egypt, and others. Although each country had its own reasons for developing its unique fighting system, they all share one thing in common—pain. Each system, as different as they are from one another, has the capability to inflict some serious damage to an opponent.

Stay on Your Toes

Archeologists have discovered martial arts illustrations and hieroglyphics on the walls of Egyptian tombs. Dating back thousands of years, some of these illustrations even include fighters wearing hand protectors similar to the ones modern-day prizefighters wear.

Where the Styles Come From

The following are some of the different styles of martial arts and where it is commonly believed they originated. This list is not comprehensive and does not include all the countries or styles out there because there are just too many to name. This list, however, should give you a pretty good idea of what the general breakdown is:

> *Japan/Okinawa*—Aikido, Jiu-jitsu, Judo, Karate, Kendo
>
> *China*—Kung Fu, Tai Chi Chuan
>
> *Korea*—Hapkido, Tae Kwon Do, Tang Soo Do
>
> *Philippines*—Arnis/Escrima (stick fighting)
>
> *USA*—Kickboxing
>
> *Indonesia*—Silat (known for evasive tactics)
>
> *Thailand*—Muay Thai (kickboxing without rules)
>
> *Greece*—Wrestling, Boxing, Pankration
>
> *Rome*—Greco-Roman Wrestling (they did this naked, by the way)
>
> *India*—Kalaridpayattu (good luck at pronouncing this one)
>
> *Africa*—Capoeira (later adopted by Brazil)

The Big Five

You might be wondering why there are so many styles of martial arts. Aren't they all pretty much the same? Actually, each style is quite unique. To illustrate this, I'm going to take you on a little journey through five of the main categories available today (so fasten your black belt). Some of the main subjects on which the marital arts focus are sport, tradition, philosophy, spirituality, self-defense, and weaponry, to name a few. I'll provide you with a simple explanation of each category, an example of a style from that category, a positive attribute, and a negative attribute. Before we go into each one individually, however, here's a list of the five main categories of marital arts:

➤ Hard

➤ Soft

➤ Kicking and punching

➤ Grappling and throwing

➤ Weapons

Hard

The hard styles really make you work. They are known for the awesome amount of power they can generate, and they usually teach a good balance between blocking, kicking, and striking. Classes usually are very formal, and the instructor probably teaches class in the exact manner he or she was taught. This is a good thing because it prevents the system from getting watered down over the years. Martial arts devotees belonging to the hard school love to break stuff like boards and bricks with their bare hands and feet. This also is the group responsible for making the kiai famous.

Street Talk

Kiai (key-eye) means "energy harmony" and is the "yell of the spirit." The Japanese arts made it famous, and it's sometimes referred to as the "karate yell." This is the loud, intimidating noise martial artists make when they are punching, kicking, or blocking.

Throwing a hard-style punch.

Example: Shotokan Karate, which originated in Japan. It was founded by Gichin Funakoshi, who is considered to be the "Father of Modern Karate." Funakoshi was largely responsible for introducing karate to the United States in the mid-1900s.

Positive: This is great for equipping students with discipline and a serious respect for authority.

Negative: It's extremely hard on your joints and tendons, and there's a high burn-out rate because it takes a long time to advance in rank.

Soft

Soft styles are famous for teaching students how to avoid contact with their opponent. (If you think this sounds easy, you ought to try it sometime.) Soft styles place heavy emphasis on spirituality and meditation. They focus on self-discipline and respect as well. If you want to learn to move like the wind and to achieve the balance of a monkey, the soft styles are for you.

Avoiding a kick using a soft-style evasion technique.

Example: Kung Fu, which means "special skill" or "human struggle." Kung Fu originated in China and has laid the foundation for many other styles over the years. David Carradine brought a great deal of popularity to this style in the 1970s with his hit TV series *Kung Fu.*

Positive: This is great for improving balance, coordination, quickness, and leg strength.

Negative: It places a very strong emphasis on eastern spirituality and mysticism. This can be a distraction if your beliefs regarding spiritual issues are different from theirs.

Kicking and Punching

The kicking and punching styles are by far the most popular in the United States. In fact, the kicking and punching style of Tae Kwon Do is so popular that it's an Olympic event. These are the styles known for their flashy moves, fast hands, high aerial kicks, and really cool uniforms. (These also are the schools that have the corner on the kid's market.)

Many of the kicking and punching styles have gotten heavily into the tournament scene over the last several years. As a result, some of the styles have strayed from their origins and are now spending the majority of the class time preparing students for upcoming competitions. These schools usually spend a lot of time having students spar with one another. The majority of these schools are more beneficial for the sport aspect of marital arts than for actual self-defense training, which is great if that's what you're looking for.

Bad Guys Beware!

Before enrolling in a martial arts school, take some time to sit down with the instructor and find out what he believes regarding spiritual-related issues. Then decide if you're okay with his beliefs. Although this might not sound like a big deal, remember that whatever your instructor believes or stands for eventually will work its way into the training, whether directly or indirectly.

Kicking and punching style—throwing a high kick.

Example: Tae Kwon Do. Originating in Korea, its name means "way of the hand and foot." Tae Kwon Do is best known for tournament skills, high kicks, and having the best children's classes around.

Positive: It has extremely fun classes and is great for building self-confidence.

Negative: It has the potential to give students a false sense of their ability to protect themselves in a real situation because it is more for sport, health and fitness, and confidence than it is for self-defense.

Grappling and Throwing

If you've ever been "choked-out," you know just how effective this stuff really is. Being choked-out means someone has successfully cut off your air supply by wrapping their arms, hands, or legs, around your neck and throat area. (It's difficult to fight back when you can't breathe or when your leg is wrapped around the back of your head.)

The grappling and throwing schools' claim to fame is joint manipulation, choke holds, and being able to throw someone three times your size across the room. This stuff is not for everyone. It requires serious, hard-core training and, when you finish a class, you feel it for a few days.

Controlling with a grappling technique.

Example: Jiu-jitsu, which means "the soft, pliable, or gentle way." (Trust me, this name couldn't be further from the actuality of this martial art.) There's nothing gentle or soft about Jiu-jitsu. This Japanese style of fighting has become extremely popular over the last few years.

Positive: If anyone ever puts their hands on you or gets within an arm's reach, you own them.

Negative: It's not very practical against more that one attacker, and your opponent needs to be within an arm's reach before your techniques become effective. Jiu-jitsu teaches very few punching and kicking techniques.

Weapons

Have you ever heard the saying "Don't take a knife to a gunfight?" This rule doesn't apply to these members of the combat profession. Weapons participants are all about the mastery of weapons and usually can be found practicing with weapons such as knives, swords, a bo (a six-foot wooden staff), a bow and arrow, throwing stars, nunchakus, or any other implements of destruction they can get their hands on. These fighters take their training very seriously and usually become proficient with several weapons.

I've found that a good number of weapons practitioners are somewhat fanatical about their trade and will drive miles out of their way to learn from a good teacher. Most of these people aren't just interested in the ability aspects of weapons training, though. They usually are very interested in the spiritual benefits they feel are associated with obtaining a high level of mastery and proficiency with their particular weapon.

> **Life Savers**
>
> If you ever find yourself in a situation in which someone has you in a pretty good hold, don't try to free yourself by struggling. Instead, concentrate on the weapons you still have free and use one of them offensively to make the attacker let go. Your feet, knees, hands, elbows, head, and mouth are all weapons, and it is nearly impossible for someone to restrain all 10 of them. Focus on what is free.

A weapons practitioner throwing an overhand knife attack.

Safety Alert!

Carrying any type of martial arts weapon on your person or in your vehicle is a serious crime in most states. In some cases, the police will treat the situation as if you are carrying a firearm. If you're training with a weapon, either leave it at the school where you train or transport it to and from class locked in your trunk.

Street Talk

Dojo is the Japanese name for a martial arts school.

Example: Kendo, which means "way of the sword" and originated in Japan. These people like to train in a very realistic environment, imitating the ancient samurai warriors. (Watching them spar is really intense.)

Positive: This is great for releasing and dealing with stress, anger, and other bottled-up energy.

Negative: It provides you with skills that aren't very practical for self-defense purposes. (It's very unlikely that you'll have your sword handy if you're attacked.)

You now should be qualified to watch a class and determine which of the five categories it belongs to. You also should have a pretty good idea which one interests you most in case you ever decide to take a few classes.

Choosing the Right School

After you've made the decision to do some serious training, you have to decide which dojo is best for you. Approach your search for a martial arts school with the same seriousness you would have if you were shopping for a new car. Before you begin your search, ask yourself how much you can afford, how often you want to take classes, and what your goals in taking the classes are.

What Are Your Goals?

To help you decide which martial arts style is for you, go through the following list and check the goals that interest you the most:

❑ To get into shape and improve your health

❑ To build confidence

❑ To learn to defend yourself

❑ To improve your character

❑ To compete in tournaments

❑ To make new friends

❑ To earn a Black Belt

❑ To increase self-discipline

❑ To have fun

Staying Within Your Budget

Now that you know your goals and what you're looking for, you need to figure out how much you can afford. I don't care how excited you get about the new school you finally found, if it costs more money that you can comfortably afford, you won't be there long. The fact is, when money gets tight, extracurricular activities always are the first things to go, so stay within your budget. A good school will cost anywhere from $60 to $100 per month. For this amount of money, you should be able to attend a minimum of four classes per week. Sometimes, though, for a little extra money, a school will let you go month to month instead of signing a contract. This is a good idea if you're concerned that you won't stick with it.

Bad Guys Beware!

Most martial arts schools have an extremely high turnover rate, which has caused them to require students to sign contracts. These contracts range from three- to twelve-month terms and are taken very seriously by the school owner.

Fitting Martial Arts into Your Schedule

Regardless of how good a school is, it won't do you any good if you can't find time to attend. Martial arts training is just like anything else. The more you put into it, the more you'll get out of it. This is why you should carefully consider how much time you'll be able to spend training and practicing.

Compare the school's class schedule with your free-time calendar. You need to make sure the school's schedule offers a minimum of three classes per week that you can attend, whether you choose to or not. This means you'll get flexibility in your schedule. Four or five available classes per week should be the goal, but you can settle for three.

What to Look for When Choosing a School

To help prevent you from being taken advantage of by a martial arts school, I've put together the following list of questions to help you know what to look for when choosing the school that's best for you:

➤ **What is the ratio between students and instructors?**

A one to fifteen ratio is good.

➤ **Who does the majority of the teaching, the chief instructor or one of his assistants?**

The chief instructor should teach at least 50 percent of classes.

➤ **Do children and adults train together?**

Not a good idea. Children are confused or adults are bored.

➤ **What are the instructor's credentials?**

Needs to prove his or her ability to teach you.

➤ **How long has the school been in operation?**

The longer the better.

➤ **Does the class schedule work well with yours?**

If not, don't join because you won't go.

➤ **How far will you have to travel?**

More than 20 minutes each way is not recommended.

➤ **Can you try a few classes before you commit?**

A minimum of three trial classes is recommended.

➤ **Do you have to sign a contract or can you pay month by month?**

Go month to month whenever possible, especially with a new school.

If you really want to see how good the instructor is or how effective the style is, ask if you can observe an advanced class. If you're not impressed watching the school's Black Belts train and spar together, the school isn't for you.

Martial arts and self-defense both have a great deal to offer if you know what you want and what to look for. They both come down to learning how to take care of yourself, which is a great way to invest your time and money. The martial arts aren't for everyone, but if you feel like giving it a try, remember that it's a lot of hard work with great benefits if you stick it out. How many fun activities are there that work toward improving your character and physical health at the same time? The benefits of the right self-defense training are priceless. A good self-defense course can last you a lifetime and can save your life. The best scenario is if you can learn self-defense in combination with martial arts. This way, you get the best of both worlds.

The Least You Need to Know

➤ Although self-defense and martial arts have some similarities, they are not identical.

➤ The martial arts do not come from any one country or culture. Instead, they are the result of thousands of years of evolution and hard work from all over the world.

➤ Just because someone is training in the martial arts doesn't mean they're learning how to defend themselves from an attacker.

➤ Before you start hunting for the right school, you should decide which category of marital arts is best suited for you.

Chapter 3

The Golden Rules of Survival

In This Chapter

➤ Confidence is important

➤ Fear not

➤ It's okay to be offensive

➤ Swallow your pride

➤ Follow your instincts

➤ Awareness always wins

➤ Putting it all together

Pretend for a moment that you are a criminal. You're low on cash, so you decide to go to the park and choose someone to rob at gunpoint. When you arrive at the park, you notice five different potential targets. Which one of the five do you choose? What are you looking for in a victim? Does the fact that one seems to be more confident than the others make a difference? What about the person who seems aware? What are the criteria you would use to choose one of the five people in the park?

Confidence is the single most important aspect of self-defense. I can teach you about every physical aspect of self-defense from carjackings to burglaries, but if you don't know how to think like a survivor, it will be difficult to convince a criminal that he or she is making a bad decision in choosing you. Confidence is so crucial to self-defense that it tops my list of the six deterrents of crime:

#1 Confidence

#2 Intuition

#3 Awareness

#4 People nearby

#5 Proper lighting

#6 Abrupt sound

As I previously mentioned in this book, self-defense is about 80 percent mental and only about 20 percent physical. This chapter concentrates on the mental side of self-defense.

Before you can learn how to protect yourself, you first must cultivate something called the "survivor mentality." Attitude is everything, especially when it comes to a subject as important as your safety. I'm going to walk you through the six golden rules of survival. Most of this information can be put to use right away. It will benefit you not just in the field of safety but in many other aspects of your life. So let's get to it!

Golden Rule #1: Confidence Is Important

Webster's dictionary provides three definitions for confidence, all of which are important enough to list:

➤ Firm belief, trust, reliance

➤ The fact of being or feeling certain; assurance

➤ Belief in one's own abilities

These definitions tell us what the word "confidence" means, but they don't tell us how it relates to a potential crime situation. Confidence is a state of mind that shouts, "Leave me alone!" It is the steam in your stride that lets the world know that you know where you're going. Confidence is the tone in your voice that lets others know you've got everything under control.

Distinguishing Confidence from Arrogance

It's very important that you don't mistake confidence for arrogance. Arrogance is nothing more than insecurity in disguise, and most people can spot the difference between the two. An arrogant man is the one who brags about what he can do. A confident man *shows* others what he can do. Arrogance is bragging about your abilities. Confidence is an attitude that comes from being prepared.

So What Does Confidence Have to Do with Safety?

Prison inmates have been the subjects of many crime-related studies over the years in an attempt to learn how they choose their victims. In nearly every study, the results came back the same. The majority of convicts interviewed claim they always made it a rule to choose someone who looked unprepared, unaware, insecure, and easily intimidated. Furthermore, the prisoners maintained that they could accurately size someone up in all four of these categories with one simple look-over. Like bad cologne, everyone knows when you're wearing confidence.

A Safety Safari

We can learn an awful lot about crime by studying the animal kingdom. Take the lion, for example. As king of the jungle, the lion has a variety of choices when it comes to dining. Nonetheless, when the lion is chasing down a herd of tasty gazelle, he always goes for the little guy in the back of the pack. That's right. The lion always goes for the crippled, sick, injured, slow, unfortunate one dragging behind. The lion knows he can thump the big male buck and triple the amount of groceries he brings home. So why doesn't he? Because it's not worth getting his nose scratched up over. The strong gazelle might ultimately lose in a fight with a lion, but the stronger gazelle will make the lion earn the victory.

Stay on Your Toes

Protecting yourself from being targeted by a bad guy has little to do with how big and tough you are. It has a lot to do with how big and tough your body language is, however.

Criminals aren't that much different from lions in the sense that they don't like getting their nose scratched over grocery money. When a criminal is choosing his prey, he sees a confident person as a prepared person who won't give in without a fight. This is the last thing for which a criminal is looking, especially when he knows that, if he waits a few more minutes, an easier prey will most likely present itself. In addition, the perpetrator knows that confident people are more difficult to intimidate and are more likely to press charges and testify later.

Golden Rule #2: Fear Not

Just as confidence is your greatest strength in the area of safety, fear is your greatest weakness. Criminals can smell fear as well as a German Shepherd can! Criminals love fear because it's the secret to how they control their victims. The main reason criminals rely on weapons is to create enough fear and intimidation to get us to cooperate and comply with their demands.

Which of these two women do you think a criminal is more likely to target?

Fear and Your Health

Not only should you learn to deal with your fears for safety reasons, they also are bad for your overall health. The following are some common manifestations of fear:

➤ Ulcers

➤ Depression

➤ Headaches

➤ Anxiety

➤ Paranoia

➤ Anger

➤ Addictions

Confronting Your Fears

So how can you get rid of fear? One way is to confront it. Find an area of your life in which you're struggling with fear and confront it boldfaced, eye-to-eye, up close and personal.

You can do this in a number of ways. Sometimes it helps to talk to a friend or a family member or to speak to a professional counselor. You also might try writing your fears down. Whatever you do, don't deny that you have fears. Let's face it. Just because you ignore your fears doesn't mean they're not there. Freedom from fear isn't easy, but it can be achieved.

Education: Fear's Enemy

After you've confronted your fear, the best way to destroy it is to educate yourself about what it is you're afraid of. Let's say you're afraid that your child will be abducted. This is a very reasonable fear to have as a concerned parent; nonetheless, it still needs to be addressed. Therefore, you should read Chapter 24, "Children: The World's Most Valuable Resource," which talks about keeping your children safe. In doing so, you educate yourself about the subject, you teach your child what he or she needs to know to stay safe, you trade in some myths for some facts, and you should notice your fear subsiding. That's all there is to it.

Golden Rule #3: It's Okay to Be Offensive

Do you know how many people have put themselves in dangerous, life-threatening situations just because they didn't want to offend someone? Most likely, you've been in a situation in which you had to choose between doing something really stupid or offending someone. That's why this section is here. Criminals love polite people because a criminal is less likely to be challenged, questioned, or refused by someone who is trying to be nice. To put it simply, good manners on your part make a criminal's job much easier.

Look at the following example of just how easy it is to get reeled in:

Scene: An apartment complex parking lot. A woman is bringing groceries inside.

Stranger: Excuse me, Miss. Can I help you carry your groceries?

Woman: No, thank you. I've got it.

Stranger: Are you sure? I don't mind.

Woman: No, really; they're not heavy.

Stranger: Oh, come on. Let me give you a hand. (He puts his hands on the bag of groceries and starts to pull it toward him.)

Woman: Well, all right then. (Very uncomfortable but not wanting to offend the stranger, she complies.)

After the woman agrees to let the stranger help her with the groceries, she walks upstairs to her apartment with the stranger following close behind. As she unlocks her apartment door, he pushes her inside and locks the door behind him.

Unfortunately, this scenario actually happened to a woman I know who barely escaped with her life. She wasn't comfortable taking help from the stranger, but she accepted it anyway. Why did she give in? Because she didn't want to offend the man. In doing so, she broke one of the six golden rules of survival—it's okay to be offensive. By choosing not to offend in an uncomfortable situation, you're placing yourself in possible danger.

The Root of Offense

Most people don't want to offend a stranger for one of the following reasons:

➤ They feel sorry for the person.

➤ They don't want to feel guilty later.

➤ They don't want the person to dislike them.

Bad Guys Beware!

One big reason people don't like to offend others is because of the need for approval. It's human nature to desire the approval of another, even if that person is a stranger. Think about it, though. When your safety is in jeopardy, does it really matter whether a stranger approves of you? If you can learn to look out for yourself, even at the expense of others, you will lessen your chances of becoming a victim.

Life Savers

You walk out to the parking lot after working late one night and spot three teenagers standing near your brand new car and drinking beer. One of them is sitting on the hood of your car, which makes you angry. You could puff up with pride and shout at the teenagers to get off your car, but this might get you into a dangerous situation. On the other hand, you could swallow your pride, return to your office, and call the police. You decide.

➤ They don't want to hurt the person's feelings.

➤ They don't want the person to think they're mean.

➤ They don't want the person to stop being nice to others.

Golden Rule #4: Swallow Your Pride

Webster's defines pride as "an unduly high opinion of oneself; exaggerated self-esteem; conceit." What Webster's doesn't mention is that pride can cause you to put yourself and your loved ones in uncomfortable and sometimes dangerous situations. Pride can only get you into trouble when it comes to your safety. When it comes to danger, your pride rarely dictates the safest way out. Remember, the real hero does the right thing, not the macho thing.

A Sign of Strength

Most people have been taught that swallowing their pride is a sign of weakness. Nothing could be further from the truth. Actually, swallowing your pride is a sign of strength and maturity. It means you're secure enough with who you are not to care about what someone else thinks of you.

For those of you who are married and have children, one of your main responsibilities in life is to look after the safety of your family. This means you need to be *responding* instead of *reacting*. The next time you and your family are cruising down the highway and a rude driver cuts you off, decide to keep your cool, hold your tongue, and dispense with the sign language.

Golden Rule #5: Follow Your Instincts

Intuition, gut feeling, sixth sense—it doesn't matter what you call it because it all adds up to the same thing. You have been blessed with an internal alarm system, so listen to it. Ignoring it can get you into a lot of trouble, and paying attention to it can save your life. It's that simple.

A Prime Example

I recently was interviewed on a nationally syndicated radio program that reaches a few million listeners. During the program, a woman in her mid-20s called in to share her crime story and to ask for some advice. The woman had been sexually assaulted a few months earlier by her ex-boyfriend. Her reason for calling was to ask whether she could have done something to prevent it from happening. She said she was walking out the door of her upstairs apartment when she saw her ex-boyfriend walking up the steps. They had broken up a few weeks prior and no longer were talking to each other, so his visit was very unexpected. He asked if he could come in and discuss something important with her. Reluctantly, she said yes and the rest is history.

Bad Guys Beware!

If a stranger who makes you nervous ever approaches you, avoid engaging in conversation. The instant you start exchanging dialogue, you begin to make yourself vulnerable. The fewer words you exchange, the better.

First of all, in no way should this woman feel that what happened was her fault or that she deserved to be raped. I did ask the woman some important questions, however, in an effort to help others who might find themselves in her position. The first question I asked was what her instincts were saying when she saw her ex-boyfriend approaching her. She responded that, when she saw him, she immediately became frightened and her stomach tightened. She then confessed that she let him into her apartment in spite of this because she didn't want to hurt his feelings.

There is no way to know how things would have turned out if this woman had run into her house and locked the door behind her. I do know, however, that following your instincts is the smartest thing you can do in a situation like this. Maybe her ex-boyfriend would have forced the door open or come back another day, and maybe he wouldn't have. The point is that listening to your instincts and not worrying about being offensive can get you out of immediate danger.

Why do we so often ignore our instincts? The following are some of the main reasons:

➤ We don't want to offend. (We've been over this one.)

➤ We are in a hurry.

➤ We don't want to seem paranoid.

➤ We don't think anything bad could happen to us.

Golden Rule #6: Awareness Always Wins

Awareness is the last rule on my list, but don't let its rank convince you that it's not important. Awareness isn't something you need just for safety; it should be a way of

Safety Alert!

Being paranoid about crime and violence issues is a bad idea not only for safety reasons, it also can greatly affect your health and your social life. Paranoia is a serious disorder for many Americans. In addition to causing problems such as anxiety and stress, it can cause friends and family members to avoid you.

life. Learning to be on your guard and to be vigilant can help you do a better job when working, playing defense on the basketball court, shopping for bargains at the mall, driving to the grocery store, and almost anything else you can think of.

There are several reasons why being aware can keep you safe. One reason is because it greatly increases your reaction time. In a life-or-death situation, one second can make a big difference. Experts agree that the decisions you make within the first three seconds of being approached by a criminal will greatly affect the outcome.

Awareness is hearing a noise behind you and taking a quick look. It's spotting someone standing by your car in the parking lot and stopping for a moment to see what they're doing. It's keeping an eye on the door to the public restroom while your child is inside.

Now that you know what awareness is, let me tell you what it is not. Awareness is not paranoia! Being paranoid isn't going to do anything for you but cause you to be a more likely target and help you lose all your friends. Walking around paranoid (fidgety, nervous, anxious, fearful, moving quickly, holding possessions to your chest, looking around constantly, and so on) is like wearing a big red bull's eye on your back that says "Please rob me." Be prepared, be confident, be aware, but don't be paranoid.

Communicating with Body Language

Nothing communicates confidence and preparedness more than your body language. Your eyes, your posture, the speed at which you walk, it all speaks volumes about you to a bad guy. Awareness is not only an advanced mental state; it's also an action and an attitude. If you have the right body language, you'll be able get everything you need to across without saying a word.

The following are a few things you can do to heighten your awareness:

➤ Walk with good posture. Your head should be up, and your shoulders should be square.

➤ Look around continuously with your peripheral vision, but avoid making direct eye contact with strangers.

➤ Walk at a comfortable pace and don't look rushed.

➤ Before exiting a building, quickly survey the outside area.

➤ Don't look like you're lost.

➤ Don't look like a tourist.

Incorrect body language.

Correct body language.

Putting It All Together

And now, here are a few finishing touches. I want to make sure you know how to create a plan and how to keep a positive, survivor attitude. Once you've done this, you can begin looking forward to a safer tomorrow.

Your personal safety requires a good balance of being confident, confronting your fears, not being afraid to offend, swallowing your pride, being aware, and following your instincts. These attributes go hand in hand. Imagine confidence without awareness or always following your instincts without first confronting your fears. Putting action to all six of these golden rules of survival and making them a way of life keeps us safe at night.

Planning Ahead

As previously mentioned, the decisions you make within the first three seconds of being approached by a criminal will greatly affect the outcome. This is a fact that can either work to your advantage or be your biggest downfall. Do you remember the old saying, "If you fail to plan, then plan to fail"? This saying can very easily be related to personal safety. One of the keys to staying safe is knowing the answer to the question before the question is asked. Believe me, making a decision with a gun pointed at your head and with someone ordering you to get into a car is not an easy process.

Creating a plan in case of crime is no less important than creating a plan in case of a fire. Crime and violence planning is no different from general safety planning, and it is just as important.

A good safety plan consists of knowing what you will do in certain situations. For example, if someone breaks into your home while you're sleeping, know exactly what you're going to do in advance. Don't wait until you hear a noise in the middle of the night to consider your options.

Destroying Denial

For most people, the reason they don't plan for crime is denial. These are the people who walk quickly through the parking lot with their head down while thinking, "It will never happen to me." Well, more than anything, I hope these people are right. The truth is, by not creating a plan, you greatly increase the likelihood of it happening to you. Do yourself a favor: avoid living in denial, create a plan, and reduce your chances of being picked on.

The main thing I want you to remember is to keep a positive attitude and to get rid of the victim mentality. You can't do anything about the direction of the wind, but you can adjust your sails. Take pride in the fact that you've done your homework and know that, if crime ever does knock on your door, you're ready. Don't forget, having a good attitude means not being an alarmist and scaring all your friends. It means being prepared for whatever life throws your way.

The Least You Need To Know

➤ Confidence is an extremely effective deterrent to crime.

➤ Don't ever worry about offending a stranger if you feel uncomfortable.

➤ A bad guy can learn everything he needs to know about you just by looking at you.

➤ Being a survivor begins with thinking and speaking like one.

THE
"CRIMINAL MIND"

Knowing the Enemy's Mindset

Who are these bad guys lurking around the corner, behind the masks, and behind bars? Where do they come from and what exactly do they want? If you are going to be successful at defeating the enemy, you first must take the time to study and learn the enemy. Learning how these people think is a very important step toward being able to create a solid plan and, ultimately, defeat them down the road.

In this chapter, I am going to walk you through a step-by-step analysis of who these creeps are, what they want, and everything in between. The majority of information available on this subject is very technical, academic, and tough to understand. (If you've ever had to search through those thick, criminal psychology books located on the law floor of a university library, you know what I'm talking about.) I've taken the liberty, however, of translating this technical information into simple English. In this chapter, I'll give you the scoop on the lawbreaker's lifestyle in a way that's simple to understand, so prepare yourself for a journey through the mind of a criminal.

Who Are They?

As you probably know, there's a wide range of criminals plaguing our streets and neighborhoods today. They range from corporate executives to the homeless and the mentally ill, and to list them all would be impossible. To give you a good idea of who they are without confusing you and to help make the information easier to reference in the future, I have broken them down into five main groups: money, discipline, deprivation, social, and illness. Keep in mind that these groups cover the majority of today's criminals but definitely not all of them. Most criminals will fit best into one primary category but can easily cross over into several other secondary categories. I also will provide you with several scenarios for each group to help simplify the information even further.

Bad Guys Beware!

Have you ever been approached by a beggar on the street asking you for money? What about the guys at intersections who tap on your window to ask you if you want to buy a rose? Although these people usually are harmless, you still need to exercise caution when dealing with them. My recommendation is to avoid eye contact and not engage in conversation regardless of whether you make a donation. As for the ones who approach your vehicle, roll your windows up, lock your doors, and then answer them through the glass. I know this might seem rude, but when it comes to your safety, you must set some difficult guidelines.

Money Criminals

The first category of criminals we are going to discuss is the money group. These bad guys break the law because of lack of money (or a strong desire for more money). They can be greedy, needy, or broke, but it all ads up to the same thing—crime.

Scenario #1: A man who has a wife and three children is laid off from his job. After several weeks of job hunting, he can't seem to find work and his family's needs are increasing. He has no money, the cupboards are bare, and he becomes desperate. In an attempt to put food on the table, he shoplifts food from a grocery store and gets caught. The store presses charges and the man is convicted.

Scenario #2: Three teenagers are driving around late one night and are frustrated because they don't have the money to party. They decide to pull over at a convenience store and take what they need. All they want is enough money to have a good time, but instead, the clerk refuses to cooperate and is hurt badly. The teenagers get caught and now have prison to look forward to.

Scenario #3: A business executive working for a large corporation is earning a salary of $100,000 per year. Motivated by greed, she decides to begin embezzling money from the company, little by little. Within one year, she has managed to steal tens of thousands of dollars from her employer and no one suspects a thing, so she thinks. Her secret is discovered during the company's annual audit. Both her career and freedom are on the line.

Discipline Criminals

Next let's discuss the discipline criminals. I call them this because they each share a discipline problem. Doing what they feel like doing at the expense of others is typical of discipline criminals.

Scenario #1: A driver accelerates his vehicle to 100 mph in a 35-mph speed zone. He does this because a passenger told him to slow down before he gets a speeding ticket. All of a sudden, the car is wrapped around a tree because the rebellious driver didn't like being told what to do.

Rebellious criminals are people who despise authority and hate being told what to do. These types come from all types of backgrounds ranging from the ghetto to Beverly Hills. Motivating them to commit a crime usually is pretty simple. Most of the time, all it requires is someone pointing a finger in his or her face and telling him or her what he or she can't or shouldn't do. This usually is all the fuel required to get a rebellious criminal's jets going, and it can result in a potentially dangerous situation.

Stay on your Toes

Lack of discipline is a problem most Americans deal with in several areas in their life. Getting carried away at the dinner table, saying too much, not exercising, and having one drink too many all are discipline-related problems. Remember that discipline is a muscle, and it must be exercised regularly if it's going to work for you instead of against you. To achieve this, begin working on small areas of your life and eventually work your way up to the bigger ones.

Don't think you can recognize a rebellious criminal by his or her outfit, by the way. These days, a scary guy on a Harley might be an attorney on his way to court to defend a guy in a suit for rebelling against authority.

Scenario #2: Several gang members are bored and decide they need more excitement for the evening. To liven things up a little, they decide to drive through a rival gang's

Bad Guys Beware!

If you're a parent, encourage your children to do fun and creative things that cause them to use their mind. Avoid letting your child park him- or herself in front of the TV when he or she gets bored. It is now estimated that a child will view 70,000 murders on television before he or she reaches the age of 18.

turf while firing their weapons. Tragically, a young girl gets shot on her way out of a movie theater with her friends. The boredom of a few gang members has resulted in the devastation of a family.

Scenario #3: After leaving a party intoxicated, a woman behaves irresponsibly by deciding to drive herself home. Only minutes later, she hits a minivan carrying a family of five, head on.

Scenario #4: A parent leaves a loaded firearm in the top drawer of the night stand while children are in the house. One of the children finds the gun and pulls the trigger.

It's true that these last two scenarios don't involve people who intentionally hurt anyone. Nonetheless, they are accountable for their behavior, especially when it's reckless or irresponsible.

Deprivation Criminals

The third group we are going to discuss is deprivation criminals. Of the five groups of criminals mentioned in this chapter, this group tends to get the greatest amount of sympathy from society. Although their actions receive no favoritism from the law, it's hard not to feel just a little bit sorry for them every once in a while.

Scenario #1: A man in his mid-20s is trying to support his family while earning minimum wage. He can't seem to find a job that will pay him more because he is uneducated and lacks basic skills. Out of frustration, he decides to deal drugs on the side because it pays well. Within a matter of weeks, he becomes addicted to the same drugs he's selling and loses both his job and his family.

When I use the word "uneducated," I mean it in the sense of having little or no formal education. As you probably know, finding a decent paying job can be difficult even for a college graduate these days. Can you imagine trying to find work with a seventh-grade education? Although I agree that raising a family on $6 per hour is close to an impossible task, this doesn't give people the right to begin taking what they need from others. Dealing drugs, stealing cars, and armed robbery are just a few of the career moves of choice for a frustrated, uneducated person who has lost all hope of living the American dream.

Scenario #2: A teenage girl desperately wants attention from her busy parents. They both work full-time jobs and are hardly ever home. She begins shoplifting to get their attention, but it doesn't work. She then begins to hang around the wrong crowd and skips school with the hope that they will take notice, but they don't. She eventually begins taking drugs and committing crimes regularly. When they do finally take notice, they no longer recognize their daughter.

Many criminals suffered from neglect as children. You'd be amazed at the number of career criminals who began breaking the law at an early age in a mad attempt to earn their parents' approval. Our prisons are filled with men and women who have never heard the words "I love you" and, therefore, have never loved themselves.

Scenario #3: A boy is raised in a home where his father steals from others for a living. He brags to his son whenever he makes a big score, and he teaches his son how to deceive others without getting caught. Over the years, the boy matures into a man and makes a career out of stealing from others as well. He never works an honest day's work in his life. He is a product of his environment.

Many people believe that we mimic the lifestyles of those we see around us. Some criminals are raised in an environment where crime is the family trade. Can you imagine having a professional thief for a father or a career shoplifter for a mother? That's some mentor.

Social Criminals

Next let's discuss the social group, which probably makes up the majority of today's criminal society.

Scenario #1: A woman wearing nice clothes and expensive jewelry is enjoying a day of shopping when all of a sudden she is robbed at gunpoint. The robber is angry with her because he believes she is financially well off. He asks her if she thinks she is better than everyone else, and he becomes violent because, over the years, he has become jealous and envious.

Safety Alert!

If someone who strikes you as un-educated ever threatens your safety, be extremely careful with the words you use. These individuals tend to be very sensitive about their lack of education, and it only takes one misunderstood remark to offend them to the point of anger. Answer them politely and with respect and gladly give them what they ask for (as long as it doesn't put you in greater danger).

Street Talk

Webster's defines **social** as "a group of human beings living together in a situation in which their dealings with one another affect their common welfare."

Jealousy and envy are something we all struggle with from time to time in one form or another. When keeping up with the Joneses turns into hating the Joneses, however, the real problems begin. Criminals motivated by jealousy or envy usually perceive the world as being broken down into two classes: the haves and the have-nots. If you are a have-not, you're probably safe from these criminals. If you are a have, you're the enemy. These criminals usually have very little themselves and are likely to

Safety Alert!

Medical science has proven that unresolved anger and bitterness can lead to serious, life-threatening health problems. When you don't forgive, you injure yourself mentally, physically, and spiritually. When you do forgive, you let go of the "right" to hurt someone who has hurt you.

blame their situation on the rich (or anyone else that seems to have a leg up in life). They try to justify their lawbreaking deeds by claiming society owes them a living. They are convinced that the haves are a bunch of crooks and that life is unfair.

Scenario #2: A man is fired from his job after 10 years of loyal service. He feels that his supervisor is responsible for his termination and decides to take revenge on both his supervisor and his co-workers. He walks into work with a firearm and begins shooting people.

Have you ever seen the Western *Outlaw Josey Whales*? It's about a cowboy (played by Clint Eastwood) who spends his entire life getting revenge on a bunch of unfortunate souls. This movie does a great job of teaching us just how much damage you can do if your heart is consumed with vengeance. The root of revenge in a criminal's heart can stem from a variety of different things. It can come from losing a loved one, being fired from a job, being divorced by a spouse, being cut off by another driver, being turned down for a promotion, and so on. In these cases, the criminal feels that there's a "reason" behind the victimization.

Scenario #3: A teenage girl joins a gang in the city in which she lives and begins committing crimes within a matter of days. All she wants is to be a part of a family and to be loved, but now she is involved in a dangerous situation. As a loyal follower, she pulls the trigger on an innocent person to earn the approval of her new family. As a result, she is convicted of murder and sent to prison.

Many social criminals end up as members of gangs or mobs. Loyalty is the key to the code by which these criminals live and, if necessary, die. Gangs appeal to young kids who have never been accepted by society or who don't feel like they belong. In the gang, the young person gains acceptance and feels as if he or she is part of a family. When people achieve this level of acceptance, they will do anything to hold on to it. It is not uncommon for gang members to commit murder, and they remain loyal even while in prison. This is one of the hardest groups to rehabilitate because, to do so, you must first undo years of brainwashing.

Scenario #4: A young computer programmer is consumed with anger and bitterness and resents that others aren't as miserable as he is. He creates a computer virus and emails it to hundreds of people. It destroys hard drives and thousands of pages of invaluable information. His goal is to make others miserable, too, but what he has really done is made matters worse by breaking the law. Anger and bitterness only lead to trouble.

Stay on Your Toes

A popular gang motto is "Blood in, blood out." This simply means once a gang member, always a gang member. If a loved one is in a gang, don't try to deal with the problem yourself. There are professional agencies that specialize in this delicate situation.

Illness Criminals

Illness criminals make up the last of the criminal groups discussed in this chapter. These criminals suffer from some form of debilitation such as drug addiction or mental illness.

Scenario #1: A woman is addicted to drugs and hides it from people around her. At first, her habit is mild and unnoticeable, but over time, it begins to become unmanageable. She is fired from her job for excessive absence and sells all her valuables one by one to help support her habit. She begins to borrow money from her friends and family to buy drugs until there's no one left to borrow from. Eventually, she begins to steal from people around her and must lie to avoid getting caught.

Most Americans suffer from an addiction of some kind such as caffeine, sugar, or cigarettes. The addicts I am referring to here are hooked on something that eventually will drive them to take another individual's wallet (and sometimes life) just to get their next fix. Addicts tend to destroy their relationships with friends and family members because they have lied, borrowed, and stolen from them until they're no longer welcome.

Scenario #2: A man who suffers from extreme mental illness believes his dog has ordered him to take the lives of others. Months later, after the police finally catch him, he explains that he was only following orders from his dog.

Some people are unfortunate enough to suffer from mental illness, which can make their actions unpredictable. More and more efforts are being made to help the mentally ill, but not every mentally ill individual has been fortunate enough to benefit from these efforts. These criminals are the hardest to explain because their actions usually lack any kind of rational thought.

Gangs

You might be wondering whether gangs are prevalent enough for you to worry about. In 1980, approximately 180 cities encountered problems with gangs. From 1980 to 1995, the number of cities experiencing gang problems jumped to 800, and nearly 60 percent of U.S. cities exceeding 25,000 residents have reported gang-related incidents. This is an awful lot of growth in just 15 years, don't you think?

It is believed that more than 16,000 gangs exist in the United State, totaling more than 500,000 members. It's hard to give an accurate number for their total member-ship because some gang members are very young (elementary and middle school age) and don't have criminal records yet. The average age of a gang member is between 15 and 29 years old. This helps us understand why 75 percent of all gunshot victims are under the age of 30.

What Makes It So Enticing?

Let's look at some of the reasons gangs appeal to children and adolescents:

➤ Gangs act as a family and a provider. This is attractive when home life is troubled.

➤ Gangs encourage and reward faithful members.

➤ Gang leaders become heroes and mentors to kids.

➤ Gangs are filled with kids with similar problems, making members easy to relate to.

➤ Gangs provide kids with money and excitement.

I hope this makes it a little easier to understand why our youth are so attracted to the gang life. What would you do if you were raised in a large city without a father, if your mother worked constantly in an effort to pay the bills, and if you had no money, no role models, and no self-esteem? Wouldn't you be just a little tempted to listen to the lies of someone your own age who is wearing a gold Rolex and carrying a bunch of cash?

Street Talk

Have you ever heard the term MO? It stands for *modus operandi* and refers to a criminal's pattern of behavior. Criminals tend to get into a habit or a niche and begin doing things the same way over a period of time. This becomes their MO, and it is used by law enforcement to help track them down.

Making Sense of It All

So what exactly do these criminals want? Why don't they care about the welfare of others? This section addresses these important questions. Knowing what motivates criminals is an important step toward staying out of their way.

What Do They Want?

Now that you understand who these criminals are, I'll tell you what they're after. By reviewing the five cate-gories of criminals previously discussed, we can target what their agenda is with decent accuracy. (Their deeds are self-serving, to say the least.)

The following is a list of some common motivations for crime. Some of these probably motivate your hon-est pursuits as well.

➤ Acceptance

➤ Approval

➤ Drugs

➤ Excitement

➤ Love

➤ Money

➤ Necessity

➤ Respect

➤ Revenge

➤ Satisfaction

Why Don't They Care?

The reason criminals don't care is because the majority of them are recidivists (repeat offenders). They are career criminals who spend their life in and out of jail. Recidivists are responsible for the majority of the crimes committed.

According to Webster's dictionary, recidivism means "to fall back or to have a habitual or chronic relapse, especially into crime or antisocial behavior."

The more we do something, the more desensitized we become to it. It's proven that after someone has killed once it becomes more likely they will kill again because it gets easier for them.

Stay on Your Toes

Recidivists make up only 10 percent of the criminal population but are responsible for committing approximately 75 percent of all crimes in the United States.

Here are some shocking statistics Sanford Strong gives us on recidivists in his book *Strong on Defense*:

➤ Once a recidivist is released from prison, he or she commits an average of 187 crimes per year.

➤ Less than 1 percent of our population is responsible for destroying the peace in our country.

➤ 96 percent of prison inmates have prior convictions for serious and violent crimes before ending up in prison.

➤ 45 percent of prisoners have three or more prior convictions.

➤ 70 percent of prisoners who are released return to crime within the first twelve months.

➤ Out of all the recidivists who are caught breaking the law, only 49 percent of them are sent back to prison, while the other 51 percent are given yet another chance.

How Do We Recognize Them?

The first thing you need to know is that criminals come in all shapes and sizes. They can be short, fat, tall, or skinny. They can be male or female, and their age can vary from a child to a little old lady with a cane. Don't let their attire fool you; they could be wearing a black leather jacket, a three-piece Armani suit, or a pair of swimming trunks.

Don't Go by Appearance

It's important for you to know that what makes someone a criminal isn't what's on the surface. You need to go by what's on the inside. In some instances, Hollywood has done the American public an injustice by stereotyping bad guys. This has caused us to let our guard down around strangers who are dressed well, who seem to be really nice, or who come across as being well educated.

Bad Guys Beware

It is extremely difficult to determine whether someone is about to rip you off when going solely by appearance. If you really want some forewarning, be aware of your surroundings, watch people's behavior, listen to the language they use, and pay attention to their actions.

The following list contains some things to watch out for other than appearance:

➤ Does the person look out of place?

➤ Does the person look nervous or fidgety?

➤ Do you notice the person staring at you or at others?

➤ Is the person properly dressed for the weather (or is he or she wearing a coat in 90°F temperatures)?

➤ Is the person being overly nice?

➤ Does the person make you nervous or uncomfortable?

➤ Does the person act like he or she is on drugs or alcohol?

Going only by appearance, could you accurately guess which one of these people is the convicted criminal?

➤ Is the person being pushy or persistent?

➤ Do you notice the person discreetly using gestures to communicate with someone a good distance away?

If you feel that a particular stranger fits into one of these categories, don't panic. Instead, just keep a watchful eye on the person and keep a safe distance. It could be nothing, but you should pay attention just in case, be alert, and stay aware. If your instincts are screaming at you to get away from the person immediately, do so. Remember, listening to your instincts is very important.

Now that you're an *Idiot's Guide* expert on criminal psychology and bad guy behavior, try having a little fun with it. Next time you're watching the evening news and it features a story about someone who's been arrested, try guessing which category the person best fits into. Then try guessing which of the 10 motives best fits the person's profile. You'll have it down in no time.

The Least You Need to Know

➤ To stay safe from crime, you first should take the time to study the bad guys and learn the way they think.

➤ Crime is not motivated by money alone; it also is driven by social, character, and health–related issues.

➤ Don't trust stereotypes and don't judge people by their appearance.

➤ Regardless of the circumstances, always trust your instincts and act on them.

Chapter 5

I CAN'T DO ANYTHING UNTIL HE DOES WHAT TO ME?!

Defending Yourself and the Law

In This Chapter

➤ The need for boundaries

➤ Protecting yourself legally

➤ Life-threatening scenarios

➤ Special circumstances

While leaving work late one evening, three teenagers surround you in the parking lot. They begin pushing you back and forth, and one of them verbally threatens your life. You are carrying a small handgun in your purse, but are you legally justified to use it in this situation?

Knowing what the law has to say about defending yourself is extremely important. After all, who wants to go to jail or, even worse, prison? The truth of the matter is that, every day in the United States, people are sent to prison because they crossed the line when defending themselves. You might think you have every right to defend yourself any way you see fit if someone is attacking you. Unfortunately, this isn't the case.

The law is very specific about what you can and cannot do, and you are expected to know your responsibilities. Going too far and then pleading ignorance won't keep you out of trouble, so it's a good idea to know the facts in advance. It only takes one mistake to alter the rest of your life—and it can happen in the blink of an eye.

In this chapter, I'm going to teach you what the law has to say about self-defense as it relates to your right to protect yourself. I'll discuss a number of practical scenarios such as being physically attacked, having a gun pointed at you, having a verbal threat made on your life, and waking up in the middle of the night to the sounds of a stranger in your home. I'll also discuss your rights when defending someone else.

The Need for Boundaries

Remember that self-defense is your right, your responsibility, and your privilege. Standing still and closing your eyes while someone attacks you or a loved one is definitely not what's expected of you. You are, however, expected to know the law and obey it accordingly. This includes life-or-death situations.

Safety Alert!

If you use any type of force toward another person without knowing the law, you could very easily end up on trial for assault or attempted murder. Knowing the law isn't always enough, though. You must learn it, obey it, and always maintain proper motives.

Every state has its own laws that clearly define when someone can physically defend him- or herself against an attacker. These laws set the guidelines for when it's legal to use nonlethal force and when it's legal to use lethal force (or, in other words, take someone's life). The government has put these laws into place regarding this issue not to limit or restrain the victim and definitely not to protect the rights of the attacker. Instead, these laws were created to prevent people from abusing the system. By abusing the system, I mean people hurting or killing others without cause or legal justification and getting away with it by claiming it was done in self-defense.

There always will be people who are tempted to manipulate the system to their advantage. As a result, self-defense laws are strongly enforced. Try not to resent these laws; instead, you should embrace them.

You can use the following information to gain an unfair advantage over people who seek to cause you harm. Not only is knowledge power, applied knowledge can mean the difference between freedom and life in prison.

Nondeadly Force

Nondeadly force is when a victim uses only the force necessary to protect him- or herself and does not attempt to take the attacker's life. Nondeadly force can be used to repel either a deadly or nondeadly attack. Let's say you pull your car into a parking space at a crowded mall, only to learn you have greatly offended a man who claims you stole his spot. As a result, the man begins swinging punches at you. In this situation, you are permitted to use nondeadly force to physically defend yourself—and nothing more. It would be very difficult to legally prove your life was in danger in this situation. Remember that, to prevent bodily injury, you are legally permitted to use nondeadly force only.

The following are some examples of nondeadly force:

➤ Punching an attacker

➤ Kicking an attacker

➤ Biting an attacker

➤ Blocking oncoming strikes from an attacker

➤ Restraining an attacker

Using this type of force makes it less likely that you will go to jail. Unfortunately, it increases your chances of being sued by the attacker down the road.

Deadly Force

Deadly force, on the other hand, is using enough force to take an attacker's life. Shooting someone with a firearm is just one example of deadly force. Keep in mind that this level of force can be used only to fend off an attacker using deadly force toward you. It cannot be used to repel an attacker who is not using deadly force. Defending yourself legally in a self-defense situation requires that you only use the amount of force required to successfully repel the attack. This means your goal should be only to prevent an impending injury.

Using deadly force just to prevent bodily injury can earn you a lengthy prison sentence. You'd better be sure you're in danger of losing your life before escalating the amount of force you use to this level.

Stay on Your Toes

It is vitally important to know the difference between the threat of bodily injury and the threat of great bodily harm. The threat of bodily injury means you could get hurt if immediate action isn't taken, and it justifies the use of nondeadly force. The threat of great bodily harm means you could lose your life if immediate action isn't taken, and it justifies the use of deadly force.

The following are some scenarios that could justify using deadly force:

➤ An attacker points a gun at you in an attempt to shoot you.

➤ An attacker tries to cut you with a knife.

➤ An attacker is violently choking you to prevent you from breathing.

➤ Several attackers are punching and kicking you.

➤ An attacker begins swinging an object at your head.

Safety Alert!

Remember, never touch a crime scene weapon! The police will have cause to suspect you if your fingerprints are found on the weapon. Not only that, you don't want to smudge or remove the owner's prints. How would you like it if the only prints on a murder weapon belonged to you? Leave it where it is and call the police.

The Importance of Character

In cases involving one person's word against another's, character is looked at very carefully. This especially holds true with cases involving the use of deadly force in a self-defense situation. The defense will place the person's character under a microscope and will look at it from every possible angle. The prosecution might speak to friends, family members, co-workers, past employers, people you used to date, ex-business partners, and your third grade teacher, just to name a few.

These types of character assessment can work toward your advantage or disadvantage, depending on what kind of person you are. After this information is gathered, it will be weighed carefully and can have a huge impact on the outcome of the case. Criminals don't like character evaluations and law-abiding citizens usually do. This is why character can be an effective measuring tool if used properly.

The following are a few character-related issues that will be studied closely by the defense:

➤ Your overall reputation

➤ Other people's opinions of you

➤ Your driving record

➤ Your criminal record

➤ Your credit report

➤ Your tax history

➤ Any police matters such as domestic violence complaints or child support or alimony debts

➤ Your employment history

➤ Any threatening remarks you might have made to others

➤ Your state of mind during the attack

Protecting Yourself Legally

The rules I'm about to outline are crucial to maintaining your freedom and should be used as a guideline if you are ever attacked. These rules should act as your legal checklist to be followed at all times. According to the law, there's a very thin line that stands between self-defense and murder, and it's your responsibility to understand the difference.

Stay on Your Toes

Much of the information available on this subject is written in heavy legal terms and is very difficult for laymen to interpret. This is why I recommend a book titled *Safe not Sorry* by Tanya K. Metaksa. It is partly because of her research on this subject that I can give you this information in a way that is so easy to understand.

Fault

After a crime has been committed, the police first try to determine whose fault it was. Your goal should be to prevent any doubt in the law's eyes as to who was responsible. If any doubt exists as to whether you played a role, however, get ready to take a ride downtown. Even though you are innocent until proven guilty, it still makes for a huge hassle, a long night, and possibly a lot of money. If a burglar is lying on your living room floor with several gunshot wounds in his back, there is reason for doubt. If there is only one gunshot wound and it is in the burglar's chest, there is less cause for doubt.

If you ever are in a situation in which you use lethal force to defend yourself and kill someone as a result, the following things can really complicate your case and can begin to cast doubt on your innocence:

➤ You and the attacker knew each other before the incident took place.

➤ You don't have a good explanation for why you were at the location where the incident took place.

➤ You were in a location you knew was dangerous.

➤ You consented to fight.

➤ You provoked the attacker (such as by making threats).

Necessity

Determining whether your life actually was at stake is extremely subjective to each individual's opinions, fears, and emotions, and it can be argued for months with no resolve. The bad news for the victim is that she has to prove to the courts beyond the shadow of a doubt that her life was in jeopardy. If the defendant can't prove this point, she stands a good chance of being convicted.

Telling the judge how scared you were or that you just knew the attacker was going to take your life is not enough to prove necessity. Fear alone is never enough to justify legitimate grounds and could result in the jury deciding that you're just paranoid. You have to be able to convince the jury that your life was in danger and that they would have taken the same course of action if they were in your shoes. Not being able to prove this point has tripped up both the innocent and the guilty. Knowing your life is in danger is one thing, but being able to prove it is another.

Street Talk

Webster's dictionary defines **necessity** as "logical or moral conditions making certain actions inevitable or obligatory."

Physical Threats

Being threatened verbally and being threatened physically are not the same thing. Just because someone tells you he is going to kill you does not give you the right to use force. Even if your attacker has a gun or a knife, you still might not have the right to use force.

Being verbally threatened can be a frightening experience, but it does not give you the legal right to use force.

An occasion might arise in which you legally have only a split second window of opportunity to use force as a means to defend yourself. Here is an example:

➤ **Too early:** An attacker is holding a knife by his side while threatening you.

➤ **On Time:** The attacker raises the knife in preparation to cut you.

➤ **Too Late:** The attacker misses you with the knife, drops it, and runs.

Excessive Force

It is only lawful for you to equal or match the level of force being used against you. If you exceed it, you've gone too far. This means that, if someone pushes you, it's illegal to retaliate by punching him in the nose.

Stay on Your Toes

Police officers are bound by the same set of laws as regular citizens when it comes to force. This is referred to as force continuum. Here's how it works: If a police officer attempts to restrain someone who chooses not to peaceably comply, the officer must first use his hands. If this doesn't work, he can use mace and then wield his nightstick. Only when these efforts to restrain fail can he draw his gun.

Excessive force has many gray areas that have proven very difficult to define in the past. For example, what if two unarmed attackers jump one person? The victim is at an obvious disadvantage and shouldn't be limited to only using his hands, right? What if a tiny woman is attacked by a 250-pound man using only his bare hands? What if a martial arts expert attacks an average-size man? For these reasons, excessive force cases are dealt with individually without strict adherence to the black and white of the law.

Knowing When to Quit

Not knowing when to let up is one of the quickest ways to end up behind bars. Firing six bullets into the chest of an attacker is pretty difficult to justify and more than likely will be considered murder. When the attacker no longer is a threat, you must immediately cease action. The law does not give a great deal of latitude on this matter. However difficult, this is no time to let your anger take over, to lose your self-control, or to get revenge. It doesn't matter how justifiable your initial action was. If you don't know when to quit, you more than likely will be punished for it.

Safety Alert!

The moment an attacker attempts to flee, you no longer are permitted to use force. If you choose to use force after your attacker makes an effort to get away from you, you are considered the attacker. By chasing a bad guy, you put yourself in danger of going to jail or losing your life, and you promptly remove the incident from the category of self-defense.

An exception to this rule is a situation in which the attacker hits the ground but still poses a threat to your life. Reaching for a gun or getting back up while making additional threats on your life are just a couple scenarios that could justify further action on your part. Just keep in mind that today's actions more than likely will have to be justified tomorrow.

Chasing a Criminal

There is never a time when pursuit can be considered self-defense. If the criminal begins to flee, thank God that you survived and call the police. Pursuing a criminal can only bring you trouble. If you catch the criminal, one of two things will probably happen. Either you will hurt the criminal and break the law in the process, or you'll end up getting hurt yourself. It's a no-win situation, so resist the urge to chase.

This is an example of how quickly you can go from exercising your right to defend yourself to breaking the law.

The Opportunity to Retreat

According to the law, attempting to retreat is your duty. Before you can use lethal power to protect yourself, you first must be in a situation in which you have no chance of escape. This means that, if you are afforded an opportunity to retreat during an attack, you must take it. (Even if the law didn't require this, I wouldn't recommend hanging around a crime scene.) There are two exceptions to this rule:

1. The first exception is when fleeing or making an attempt to flee could put you at an even greater risk than staying put.

2. The second exception to this rule is if the incident takes place in your home. Although in some situations it would be wiser to run out of your residence, the law says you don't have to. Keep in mind that the assailant's intent will be looked at very closely in cases involving home intrusions.

Street Talk

No–bill means that, because the reason for you defending yourself is self-evident, no arrests need to be made and no charges need to be brought against you.

Motive

This is a biggie. The law takes the subject of motive very seriously. Taking another human being's life is a very heavy matter, and it will affect you for the rest of your life. Your motives for using lethal force toward an attacker must be self-preservation. Killing someone because he was in the process of robbing you may not fly, but killing a robber when he's about to pull the trigger of a gun may. These laws were created to help us protect ourselves against anyone who attempts to do us serious, life-threatening, great bodily harm.

Simplify to Survive

How in the world can anyone remember all these rules in a split-second, life-or-death situation? Because of the importance of knowing this information and the intense circumstances in which it might need to be recalled, I've created a way to make things easier to remember. The following cheat sheet should help you recall the main principles of what you need to know without having to memorize this chapter. Read over this list a few times until you feel confident that you know what the legal guidelines are for using lethal force.

➤ Make sure your life depends on it.

➤ Don't use force unless your life is physically threatened.

➤ Never take any action that isn't absolutely necessary.

➤ When you're out of danger, stop using force.

➤ Never chase your attacker.

➤ Run away whenever possible.

➤ Your primary motive for homicide should be to stay alive or to prevent great bodily damage.

Safety Alert!

If you attempt to disarm an attacker pointing a gun at you, make sure there are no bystanders. If the gun accidentally goes off (and there's a good chance it will), you can be held legally responsible if someone catches a stray bullet. As if the legal problems of being considered reckless wouldn't be enough, you also would have to deal with the guilt of feeling responsible for someone being shot.

Bad Guys Beware!

If someone challenges you to fight, leave the scene immediately. It is not enough to just ignore the person challenging you and hope that he or she goes away. You must physically leave before you're really out of danger. If you can't leave, call the police and let them deal with the person.

Life-Threatening Scenarios

Now that we've gone over what the law says about using deadly force, let's apply what we know to some practical scenarios.

Held at Gunpoint

To use excessive force, the gun must be pointed at you (or on its way to being pointed at you). Not only that, you must be certain that the robber is about to fire it in your direction. If you knock the gun out of the robber's hand, if the robber drops the gun, or if the robber flees the scene, you may lose your legal right to use deadly force.

Attacked by Muggers

If three people jump you and they are not using weapons, you still might be justified in using deadly force. This is because they have an unfair advantage (because there are three of them and one of you). You still must run if possible, however, and must maintain proper motives. If your muggers break out weapons, you then are justified to use deadly force under the conditions outlined in the preceding scenario.

Punched from Behind

If someone sucker punches you from behind, your best bet is to call the police and file assault charges. If you hit the individual in retaliation and the two of you begin fighting, you both could be arrested for disorderly conduct. You are not, however, justified to use any force in return unless the person continues to hit you—and then you can only match his or her level of force. The best thing to do in a situation such as this is to walk away, call the police, or both.

Challenged to Fight

If someone challenges you to a fight and you accept, you will be in violation of the first aspect of law that I addressed in this chapter—who is at fault. By agreeing to fight, you are accepting partial responsibility for the outcome. This holds true even if the other person attempts to stab you. It becomes almost impossible to prove a case of self-defense if one individual agrees to fight another.

Being Aggressively Pushed

Although being pushed hard is no fun, very little physical damage can come from it (unless, of course, you happen to be standing on the edge of a cliff). What usually hurts the most in this situation is pride. Most juries won't view a push as a life-threatening situation.

Someone Threatens to Kill You

Verbal threats do not justify force on your part of any kind. Someone who says he's going to take your life or do you bodily harm should be taken extremely seriously, but you still are not legally permitted to react physically. If someone you know makes a threat toward your life, I strongly recommend that you file a complaint with the police department. This complaint will act as evidence and can help strengthen your defense if you ever have to use lethal power to defend yourself against this person.

Stay on Your Toes

In some states, you are not required to flee from your place of business if attacked. Some state laws even let a victim stay with his or her vehicle. Depending on where you live, your home, your place of business, and/or your automobile might be considered legal exceptions to your obligation to flee.

You Discover an Intruder in Your Home

Just because an intruder enters your home does not mean it's legal to use deadly force. The same rules apply inside your home that apply outside your home. You have to be certain that your life is in danger before you use lethal power. The only thing unique about this scenario is that you may not be required by law to flee from your home if the opportunity presents itself. In this situation, the assailant's intent will be looked at very closely and will hold a lot of weight in determining fault. Note that the law varies from state to state regarding your rights in this situation.

Special Circumstances

Some situations fall outside of what I've described in this chapter. Some examples are provided here to give you an idea of what lawmakers mean when they use the term "special circumstances."

Another Person Is Attacked in Your Presence

Before defending another person, you first must honestly and reasonably believe it is necessary to protect him from harm. If you do assist, the same rules of defending yourself apply. If the person is only in danger of bodily harm, you can only use non-deadly force to stop the attacker. The threat of great bodily harm must be present before deadly force can be used.

Spousal Abuse

If your spouse is beating you, you are held accountable to the same laws as everyone else and are given no special privileges. Even if your spouse has a record of 10 prior domestic violence offenses against you, you can only use deadly force at the moment your life is in danger. Getting back at him while he's sleeping will only get you time in prison. This subject is discussed further in Chapter 16, "When Home Is no Longer Safe," which deals with violence in the home.

Sexual Assault

In most states, sexual assault is considered to be great bodily harm, and deadly force can be used to prevent it. The same rules still apply here, however. It's a good idea to do a little research into whether your state considers sexual assault to be a legal justification for using deadly force. Every state is different, and it's each individual's responsibility to know where his or her state stands on these issues.

Street Talk

When it comes to police officers, **excessive force** means that the officer can only use the amount of force necessary to take a person into custody or to defend himself, herself, or another person from bodily injury. When the officer uses more force than what is absolutely necessary, it becomes excessive.

A Police Officer Uses Excessive Force Without Cause

If a police officer tries to restrain you, the law says you must peaceably cooperate. The requirement that a person must peaceably yield to an officer's authority, however, is subject to three exceptions:

1. If you aren't aware that the person trying to restrain you is a police officer.

2. If the officer is not performing a lawful duty. (An example of an officer not performing a lawful duty would be if he entered your home without a warrant, without your permission, or without just cause.)

3. The officer is using excessive force without cause. (This means a police officer cannot begin hitting you with his nightstick just because you say something rude.)

Resisting arrest and assaulting an officer are very serious offenses that can get you into a lot of trouble, so be absolutely certain you're in the right before getting difficult. Here's a good rule of thumb: When in doubt, don't!

By now, you should have a general idea of what your rights are in terms of defending yourself, using nondeadly force, and using deadly force. Keep in mind that this information was not written in legal terms; therefore, it does not spell out the exact letter of the law. Entire books have been written on this subject that still don't cover all the legalities involved. Also keep in mind that each state views these issues differently. If you want to be better equipped, you need to do some additional research for the state in which you live.

The Least You Need To Know

➤ The type of force you can use in self-defense is determined by whether the level of threat is great bodily injury or bodily harm.

➤ Avoid using deadly force unless you or someone else is in a life-or-death situation.

➤ Being afraid for your life or having your life verbally threatened may not be enough to justify the use of deadly force.

➤ Always question your motives before using any level of force.

Part 2
Staying Safe While Out and About

In the movies, it's a thriller if someone is being stalked or if an obsessive con man is after the heroine. We sit on the edge of our seats when the good-looking jogger runs in the dark, and we can see the thug waiting in the bushes. When we leave the theater, however, it's no longer entertainment—it's our lives. Learn how to avoid those thrilling moments and leave such action for the movies. You can safely shop, jog, go to the beach, or have a night on the town.

Do you have a vacation or an international trip coming up? Learn how to make it uneventful and eliminate a tragic ending. Maybe you're single and like it that way. You can safely date someone new without running an FBI background check. Are your kids ready to go to college? Prepare them for the dangers of campus life without taking away the fun. Danger even shows up in the workplace, but you can learn to recognize it and avoid it. Paranoia is not the answer—knowledge is. Ready?

Dangerous Places

A man travels for business to a large city he's never visited before. After a long day of seminars in his hotel, he decides to venture out on his own in hopes of finding a place to enjoy a nice dinner. After walking several blocks from the hotel without seeing anything that looks good, two men step out from around a corner and pull him into the alley. They rob him at gunpoint, taking his wallet and his jewelry and leaving him with a few bruises. Little did this man know, when he passed the corner, he entered a high-crime neighborhood known for this sort of thing. If he had asked someone at the hotel in advance, he would have been advised where to go and to avoid the neighborhood where he was robbed.

It's no secret that one of the easiest ways to avoid being a victim of crime is to stay away from places where crime is most likely to occur. But where is crime most likely to occur? Thanks to studies done by agencies such as the FBI and the National Institute of Justice, I can equip you with the right information, and you can stay out of trouble.

In this chapter, you'll learn what the word "dangerous" really means. I'll tell you about places that could be hazardous to your health and why. As far as cities go, I'll cover everything from staying out of dark alleys to knowing which money machine is safer to use at night. I'll also give you the lowdown about what forms of entertainment might cost you more than just the price of admission. By the time you finish this chapter, you'll be an expert on keeping danger at bay.

The Definition of Dangerous

What exactly is dangerous, anyway? This relative term means a lot of different things to a lot of different people. Jogging alone late at night, traveling to a developing country, and getting lost in a dangerous part of a city all can be dangerous when it comes to self-defense. In this section, I'll discuss the different levels of danger that relate to your personal safety, and I'll cover the difference between night and day.

Levels of Danger

Some people view danger as being a part of life and don't give it much thought; other people are so afraid of getting into a dangerous situation that they worry every time they leave home to run an errand. The more dangerous something is, the more likely you are to get hurt or injured. Because getting hurt or injured is what you are trying to avoid, you must know how to identify these places and know what sort of danger they represent. For the purposes of this book, I have identified three different levels of danger to help you measure or gauge the amount of potential damage. You can use these threat levels to help identify potential risks. The following are the three threat levels and an explanation of what they mean:

➤ **Threat Level White:** This means you should be careful, aware, and alert. It indicates a potential for harm or injury if you don't exercise common sense and take the proper precautions.

➤ **Threat Level Red:** This threat level is for situations that could result in serious injury (or worse) if you're not careful.

➤ **Threat Level Black:** This level indicates life-threatening levels of danger.

The Difference Between Night and Day

You've probably been hearing your entire life that you must be more careful at night than during the day. It's true that the majority of all crime and violence take place at night. In some cases, however, crime is more likely to take place during the day. Back in Chapter 1, "What's All the Fuss About?," I told you that more than half of resident robberies occur during the daytime. So don't get into the habit of being less careful during the day; instead, get into the habit of being more careful at night.

The following is a list of reasons why most criminals prefer to work at night:

➤ The darkness provides excellent cover, making it more difficult to be seen and easier to get away.

➤ There are fewer people around.

➤ The police are much busier at night than during the day, which increases their response time.

➤ Darkness naturally increases fear, making it easier for bad guys to scare and intimidate people.

Dangerous Outdoor Locations

Being aware of dangerous locations (and the risk they put you in) is a very important step toward staying out of harm's way. Remember, the best defense is to not be there!

The purpose of discussing these locations is not to suggest that you shouldn't visit them. Instead, this list is intended to provide helpful information and to assist you in making decisions that relate to your overall safety. A good safety plan always requires a little bit of inconvenience, but how far you take it is totally up to you.

In addition to assigning each location a threat-level rating, I've also indicated at which times the location is most dangerous.

Alleys

Threat level: Black
Most dangerous: Night and day

Alleys need to be avoided. In an alley, you have very few ways to escape, and you're generally out of the sight and earshot of others. Even if people can hear you, there's no guarantee they'll be willing to run into an alley after you. Alleys have been known to host robberies, rapes, gang violence, and drug distribution because of the excellent cover they provide. The bottom line? Criminals love to hang out in alleys!

Safety Alert!

If you are ever forced into an alley, it is crucial that you position your-self with your back against a wall. This prevents someone from getting behind you and reduces your chances of being pushed backward and falling. If you struggle with someone who has a gun, this also makes it less likely that a stray bullet will hit an innocent bystander.

Outdoor Pay Telephones

Threat level: White
Most dangerous: Night and day

Bad guys like to target people using pay phones because the users generally are concentrating on their conversation and are unaware of their surroundings. People using pay phones also have a habit of setting their purses, bags, or briefcases down beside them, which makes it even more tempting for the crook to reach out and touch someone. Purse snatching and other quick robberies are common at outdoor pay tele-phones, so pay attention.

When using a public pay phone, don't face the phone. Instead, turn your back to the phone and face your surroundings. By doing this, you greatly reduce your chances of being targeted for a robbery. In addition, never set your personal items down; instead, place them behind your back and against the phone. If this isn't possible, keep them in your hand.

Large Cities

Threat level: Black
Most dangerous: Night and day

You need to be careful when traveling to a large city, especially if you don't know the area very well. You can be in a very nice part of town, walk one block further, and all of a sudden you're in gang central. Bad guys in the city tend to look for people to rob who look out of place, so try to pretend like you know where you're going. Learn which parts of town to avoid in advance and stay away from gang areas. Auto thefts, muggings, and robberies are common in some of our nation's larger cities.

Don't go to an unfamiliar place in the city without first taking the time to do your homework.

Parking Lots

Threat level: Red
Most dangerous: Night

Stay out of parking lots that are dark or vacant. If choosing a safe spot in a parking lot means walking an extra 50 yards, do it. (The exercise is good for you.) Rape, murder, robbery, and abduction all have taken place in parking lots.

Parking Garages

Threat level: Red
Most dangerous: Night and day

It doesn't matter how you look at it, parking garages are flat out unsafe. (There's a reason why Hollywood frequently features parking garages as crime scenes.) The following is a list of reasons why criminals love parking garages so much:

➤ Cars provide excellent cover for hiding.

➤ Because of the garage's design and echoing, it's very difficult to determine where cries for help are coming from.

➤ The bad guy has easy access to a getaway vehicle (his or yours).

➤ When filled with cars, parking garages are like being in one huge labyrinth, making it easy for the criminal to get away on foot.

If used correctly, a vehicle can be a great defensive weapon.

Life Savers

If you notice you're being followed in a parking garage, run to your car and lay on the horn for about 30 seconds to draw attention to yourself. This should cause your follower to flee. If you are grabbed in a parking garage, scream "Fire!" instead of "Help!" (You're more likely to motivate people to help you if they don't think you're with an attacker.) If you can, break free for a split second, sprint to the nearest vehicle, and begin running around it while screaming. It is virtually impossible to catch someone running around a vehicle, especially someone running for his or her life. The vehicle also can act as a protective shield if the attacker has a firearm.

Highway Rest Areas

Threat level: White
Most dangerous: Night

Highway rest areas have been known to host some pretty crazy crimes on occasion. They are fairly safe during the day but can pose somewhat of a threat at night, especially between midnight and dawn. The good news is that they're usually looked after by the highway patrol.

Parks and Wooded Areas

Threat level: Red
Most dangerous: Night

Parks can be fun during the day, but stay away from them at night. In general, putting yourself in a secluded, unpopulated area at night is never a smart move.

Automatic Teller Machines

Threat level: Red
Most dangerous: Night

Robbers love money machines. They hide around the corner while you pull out some cash, and then they point a weapon in your face and demand that you hand it over. There are two ways to make sure this doesn't happen to you. First, never use bank lobby

ATMs at night. They provide the robber with both the perfect cover to come in and trap you and plenty of time to have you empty your account. Second, never use outdoor ATMs. It's too easy for the person who just stole your money to get away. Try to use only drive-up ATMs or the ones located in convenience stores. Spend the extra buck in fees and make an investment in your safety.

Dangerous Indoor Locations

Indoor locations are popular with criminals for a couple of reasons. First, bad guys generally need a good place to wait for the right target without looking conspicuous. Second, indoor areas provide excellent camouflage for hiding.

Apartment Laundry Rooms

Threat level: Red
Most dangerous: Night

Everyone has to do laundry. If you live in an apartment complex, consider doing it during the day. Because they are quiet and isolated, apartment laundry rooms have been known to be crime magnets at night. If you must wash your clothes at night, get into the habit of taking someone with you. This advice also applies to public laundromats that traditionally are empty in the evening.

Bad Guys Beware!

Never count your money while standing at an ATM. By doing this, you could attract the attention of a crook. What good does it do to count your money at the machine anyway? If it shorts you on cash, you still have to visit the bank during normal business hours to get it straightened out. In addition, when using the keypad, be sure to use your body to block the view from behind you so no one can see you enter your pin number. Finally, if a robber approaches you, leave your card in the machine. It will be gobbled up because of a built-in safety feature.

Truck Stops

Threat level: Red
Most dangerous: Night

I'm not telling you that truck drivers are dangerous, just truck stops. Most truckers are hard-working, honest people. Truck stops, on the other hand, are full of all sorts of suspicious activities. Robberies are not uncommon because criminals know that most people who stop at truck stops are traveling by highway and probably are far from home. People who are traveling often carry cash and are less likely to come back to press charges if the robber is caught. Be sure to lock your vehicle while you're inside because a lot of automobiles are stolen from truck stops.

Life Savers

If you are alone in an enclosed area such as an apartment laundry room and you are attacked, here are a few tricks that can help you get out safely. The first thing you can do is activate the fire alarm if you can find it. Second, don't be afraid to throw an object through a window to get the attention of passersby. The sound of breaking glass can be heard from a far distance and more than likely will cause someone to investigate. Next, use large objects such as chairs, washing machines, or trash cans to your advantage. By keeping these objects between you and your attacker, they become obstacles for him or her to overcome and can buy you some valuable time to scream for help or get out. Finally, turn off the lights and make a break for it, especially if you're in familiar territory. It will surprise the attacker, and it will take his or her eyes a few moments to adjust, which is all the time you need to get out of Dodge.

Public Restrooms

Threat level: White
Most dangerous: Night and day

Adults usually don't have a lot of problems in public restrooms, but kids are another story. Perverts and kidnappers are attracted to bathrooms because it gives them time to pick and choose their victims. The good news is that this is a very simple hazard to avoid. As parents, make it a habit to either accompany your child to the restroom or simply wait by the door.

Stairwells and Elevators

Threat level: Red
Most dangerous: Night

Being in a stairwell or an elevator with an attacker is as close to being trapped as you can get. Be sure to study your surroundings prior to getting onto an elevator. Try to avoid stairwells altogether unless it's daytime and you're only going up one flight of stairs. It's hard to hear cries for help in elevators and stairwells, making them even more desirable for criminals.

Safety in the City

America has gone through many changes over the past 50 years, some for the better, and some for the worse. The increase in crime definitely falls into the worse category. The United States now has the highest crime rate in the world.

The 12 Most Dangerous Cities

This section contains a list of the 12 most dangerous U.S. cities, starting with the most dangerous and ending with the twelfth most dangerous city. If you're going to travel to a rough city or are living in one, it's good to know how it's ranked so you can prepare yourself mentally and can turn up your internal awareness monitor accordingly.

The 12 most dangerous cities in the United States (keep in mind that population is a factor in this list) are

#1   Miami, Florida

#2   New York, New York

#3   Tallahassee, Florida

#4   Baton Rouge, Louisiana

#5   Jacksonville, Florida

#6   Dallas, Texas

#7   Los Angeles, California

#8   Gainesville, Florida

#9   West Palm Beach/Boca Raton, Florida

#10   New Orleans, Louisiana

#11   Fayetteville, North Carolina

#12   St. Petersburg/Clearwater, Florida

Source: *Places Rated Almanac*, 1997, based on FBI and city crime statistics

Bad Guys Beware!

When on an elevator, stand by the control panel. The floor destination buttons, the emergency stop and start buttons, the alarm, and the phone all are located on this panel. If you notice someone who makes you feel uncomfortable, don't get on!

Stay on Your Toes

Did you notice that six of the top twelve most dangerous cities are located in the state of Florida? One reason for this is the large number of senior citizens living there. Over the years, Florida has become our country's retirement capital, and criminals have taken full advantage of this fact because senior citizens are less likely to fight back. In Chapter 25, "Good-Old-Fashioned Safety for Seniors," I'll discuss what senior citizens can do to defend themselves against crime.

The 12 Safest Cities

Thinking about relocating? Wondering where to vacation? You might want to consider one of the following cities:

#1 Johnstown, Pennsylvania

#2 Wheeling, West Virginia

#3 Parkersburg, West Virginia & Marietta, Ohio

#4 Williamsport, Pennsylvania

#5 Altoona, Pennsylvania

#6 Scranton/Wilkes-Barre, Pennsylvania

#7 Sharon, Pennsylvania

#8 Danville, Virginia

#9 Lancaster, Pennsylvania

#10 Danbury, Connecticut

#11 Utica/Rome, New York

#12 Wausau, Wisconsin

Source: *Places Rated Almanac*, 1997, based on FBI and city crime statistics

Fun but Dangerous Places

The next time you're planning some excitement and entertainment for the weekend, you might want to keep the following information in mind. This section contains a short list of places that attract a variety of personalities, cultures, and attitudes that don't always end up mixing well (especially when some have had a few drinks too many). Again, I'm not suggesting that you avoid these places altogether. I'm just warning you about their dangers so you can be better prepared.

Bad Guys Beware!

If you are going to do the club scene, go with a friend, have a designated driver, and leave at least 30 minutes before closing time. That's when trouble is most likely to occur.

Night Clubs and Bars

Threat level: Red
Most dangerous: Night

The biggest problem with these places is that many people who go to clubs do so to drink, sometimes heavily and irresponsibly. Take the fact that men usually go to night clubs to meet women, mix this with some liquor and loud music, and then shake it up until about 2 A.M.

Rock Concerts

Threat level: Red
Most dangerous: Night and day

Rock concerts are known for public inebriation, violence, and sometimes rioting. Unless you absolutely have to go, do yourself a favor and stay home with the CD. If you do attend a concert, go with a group and sit near an exit.

Pool Halls

Threat level: Red
Most dangerous: Night

Billiards have been around for a long time and have become especially popular in the United States, especially with the 16- to 30-year-old age group. Pool halls have been known to host their fair share of violence because betting is very common and alcohol usually is served. If you're going to visit a pool hall, choose one that's frequented by more adults than teens. If things get heated, let that be your cue to leave.

Carnivals and Fairs

Threat level: White
Most dangerous: Night and day

Don't get me wrong, fairs and carnivals are fun. Unfortunately, they also can be unsafe because they attract a variety of people and are often a hangout for gangs. If you're going to go to the fair, go with a group of people and don't let your children go off alone. If you plan ahead and think smart, you shouldn't have any problems.

Some of the potential problems you need to watch out for at fairs include pickpockets and fights. A lot of problems also arise at these events because of inebriation.

Public Sporting Events

Threat level: Red
Most dangerous: Night and day

Sports fans sometimes can get out of hand, especially around playoff time. Public intoxication only escalates the problem. Two fans sitting side-by-side and rooting for opposite teams is not always a safe environment. With one perceived bad call by the referee, things can get out of hand.

Stay on Your Toes

One of the most dangerous sporting events to attend is an international soccer match. These games have hosted some of the world's most intense rioting, resulting in people losing their lives.

To avoid trouble, try not to argue with fans you don't know. If possible, always sit on the side of the field or court that is rooting for the same team you are. If you find yourself sitting next to someone who is obnoxious or overly angry, don't take matters into your own hands. Instead, notify security and let them deal with it.

You now have learned one of the most important lessons in self-defense—how to not be in a dangerous location. Remember, you still can frequent these places as often as you'd like, but keep in mind the dangers they represent and use common sense.

The Least You Need to Know

➤ Most places are more dangerous at night than during the day. The later it gets, the more dangerous they become.

➤ Before traveling to a strange location for the first time, do your homework and learn what areas to avoid.

➤ If you are going to enjoy a night on the town, plan your evening wisely and take a friend whenever possible.

➤ Anytime your instincts tell you it's time to leave, trust them.

➤ Be extra careful in any environment in which people are going to be drinking alcohol.

Chapter 7

Stalkers, Impersonators, and Other Weirdoes

In This Chapter

➤ An overview of stalkers

➤ Con men: career liars

➤ Scams and impersonators

➤ Closing the blinds on peeping Toms

Have you ever looked in your rearview mirror and suspected you were being followed? Have you ever been propositioned by a salesman who made you feel very uncomfortable, but you weren't sure why? Have you ever had a feeling that someone was looking at you through the window? And what about those ex's that won't seem to leave you alone?

This chapter takes a good hard look at the outcasts of the criminal world. I'm going to answer questions such as what makes a stalker stalk, an impersonator impersonate, and a peeping Tom peep. By the time I get finished, you're going to know how to identify these goons and, more importantly, how to avoid being victimized by them.

An Overview of Stalkers

The first category we're going to discuss is stalkers. According to John Douglas and Mark Olshaker in their book *Obsession*, a stalker is someone who engages "in a course of conduct that would place a reasonable person in fear of his or her safety, and that the stalker intended and did, in fact, place the victim in such fear."

Stalkers can range from shy, passive, and hardly noticeable teenagers to crazed serial killers on the FBI's most wanted list. Twenty years ago, stalkers were viewed by the general public as a problem that only affected celebrities. Movies such as *The Bodyguard* showed us just how much torment one puny stalker can create in the life of the famous. It wasn't too long ago that one of Madonna's personal bodyguards shot and killed a stalker who forced himself onto her property screaming threats and obscenities. You're also probably familiar with John Hinkley Jr., the man who shot President Reagan to impress Jodie Foster.

The truth of the matter is, stalking isn't just for celebrities anymore. Stalking is a problem that can affect anyone from the cashier at the grocery story to a soccer mom. It seems everyone is fair game. Saying hello to the wrong person might be all it takes to become the object of a stalker's obsession. Don't think women are the only ones being stalked either. Actors like Brad Pitt have had this problem as well. In fact, it is not uncommon for men to have to obtain restraining orders against women who just won't leave them alone.

A Few Facts

According to the National Victim Center in Arlington, Virginia, nearly 80 percent of all stalking crimes involve a man stalking a woman. There are believed to be more than 200,000 Americans being stalked at any given time, and one out of every twenty women will be targeted by a stalker at some point in her life.

Stay on Your Toes

Two-thirds of all stalkers are ex-husbands or ex-boyfriends.

The Characteristics of a Stalker

Stalkers generally share some common characteristics. These characteristics are worth knowing so you can be on the lookout. Keep in mind, however, that this list is very general and is only meant to serve as a rough guide. Stalkers tend to be

➤ 20 to 40 years old on average.

➤ Usually very intelligent.

➤ Introverts or withdrawn socially.

➤ Not sexually active.

➤ Lacking in healthy relationships with members of the opposite sex.

➤ Television fanatics.

➤ Usually very lonely.

➤ Extremely persistent.

➤ Made jealous easily.

Keep in mind that, just because someone fits one of these characteristics, it does not mean he or she is a potential stalker. (For example, a lot of people spend a great deal of time watching television.) It's when someone fits several of these categories that you might have something to worry about. The book *Obsession*, written by John Douglas and Mark Olshaker, provided most of the information used to compile this list.

Stalkers can be divided into two main categories. The first group is love obsession stalkers. These people target total strangers for no apparent reason. Two-thirds of convicted stalkers, however, fall into the second category of simple obsession stalkers. Simple obsession stalkers usually target someone they already know. The person usually has rejected the stalker in some way, generally by not returning his or her affections. Sometimes these are just perceived slights, of which the victim isn't even aware.

Obsession and Retribution

For the most part, stalking is a crime of obsession and retribution, and the culprit usually suffers from some degree of mental illness.

Obsessive behavior is a very difficult illness to treat, and it usually works its way through every aspect of the person's life. Retribution is an insatiable desire to pay someone back for causing pain. Love, rage, and anger usually drive the stalkers who want payback.

Stalkers are people who have trouble accepting the word *no*. Unfortunately, people who are truly obsessed can't shake their desires on their own no matter how hard they try. If you think someone you know is stalking you, it's very important for you to understand that there's nothing you can say to deter these people. Professional help is mandatory.

Street Talk

Webster's dictionary defines **obsession** as "the act of an evil spirit in possessing or ruling a person. The fact or state of being obsessed with an idea, desire, emotion, etc. Such a persistent idea, desire, emotion, etc., especially one that cannot be gotten rid of by reasoning."

What to Do if You're Being Stalked

Before I teach you how to deal with a stalker, I want to show you how to recognize a stalker. Learning to recognize a potential stalker can save you from a lot of future pain. The following are some early warning signs to keep an eye out for:

➤ You have a secret admirer.

➤ Your phone is always ringing but messages aren't left.

➤ You receive strange emails.

➤ You receive strange letters and notes.

➤ You see this person at the same places you frequent, and it seems too coincidental.

➤ You receive a lot of hang-ups or prank calls.

➤ You get the feeling you're being followed from time to time.

➤ You're always receiving (sometimes anonymous) gifts, flowers, or candy.

➤ The person starts showing up at places uninvited and doesn't take the hint that he or she is not welcome.

Safety Alert!

If you ever notice someone following you in a car, do not drive home. Instead, drive to the nearest police station. Not only will this help protect you, it will send a very strong message to the person following you. The last thing you want this person to know is where you live.

If you find yourself locked in the sights of a stalker, whether it's an ex-boyfriend or a total stranger, there are some things you can do. First, take the matter very seriously. Then take immediate action. Whatever you do, don't take well-meaning advice that the situation is harmless or flattering. Let the police make that judgment.

Remember that stalkers can switch from being shy, timid, and quiet introverts to being kidnappers and cold-blooded killers with little or no notice. Being stalked is a very serious problem that needs to be treated as such. Regardless of what people around you think, stalking is not okay. Contrary to popular belief, these are not schoolboys experiencing their first case of puppy love. Stalking is a sick crime, it is illegal, it puts your life in potential danger, and it needs to be dealt with properly and swiftly.

Taking Action

The following is a checklist of important things you need to do if you believe you are being stalked:

1. Learn what the stalking laws are in your state so you know your rights and your legal course of action.

A stalker hiding behind a car.

A stalker hiding behind a bush.

2. If you choose to confront the person, do so only once and make sure you have a witness.

3. If you are breaking up with the person, it is crucial that you make your rejection final! (Avoid saying things like "I don't think we should see each other for a while.")

4. Every time there's an incident or a threat, no matter how trivial, call the police and file a complaint. (I know this can be a hassle, but it's well worth your time in the end.)

5. Keep a detailed journal of everything that goes on, from threats made to complaints filed. Also keep any letters, phone messages, and so on.

6. If the stalker is someone you know, you might want to discuss the situation with someone he or she trusts or respects. If you do this, make sure to give only facts and avoid slander and gossip. Also make sure to take a witness.

7. Get a restraining order against the person and legally enforce your rights every time it is violated.

8. If a co-worker is stalking you, tell your supervisor. If your supervisor refuses to take immediate action, work your way up the chain of command until you find someone who will.

9. Until the issue is resolved, try to spend very little time alone, especially when out and about. Being with a friend is the best deterrent money can't buy.

10. If the stalker threatens you in response to turning him in to the police, report it.

11. Carry some form of personal protection, such as mace, and learn how to use it proficiently (see Chapter 22, "Weapons and Gadgets: What Really Works?").

12. Change your habits. Vary the time you leave for work, the route you drive home, how you get to the gym, and so on.

13. Consider changing your phone number to an unlisted one.

14. Don't make decisions out of fear or intimidation. This is one of the worst things you can do because it's difficult to make wise decisions under these circumstances.

15. Surround yourself with family and friends and be completely honest with them about what's going on. This is no time to be keeping secrets, and it's definitely not something you want to go through alone.

Bad Guys Beware!

Being stalked is a situation that involves predator and prey. If you are going to be victorious in this situation, you must change your mindset so you become the predator. Remember that you cannot think like a victim. Become the predator and don't give up until your stalker goes away or goes to jail. You are a survivor, not a victim!

Con Men: Career Liars

A man knocks on your front door after a devastating storm to inform you that your roof shows signs of tremendous storm damage. The man is driving a work truck with door magnets that reveal the name of his roofing company, and his shirt, hat, and business cards all bear the same company name. He says he is running a one-time special of $500 to repair your roof, and he can complete the job in just one day. You hire the man and, when he's finished, you pay him. Later you learn that he performed no work. When you call the number on his business card, you find that it's been disconnected. You call information but there is no listing for the man's business. You have just been conned!

The following are some precautions you can take to prevent being conned in the preceding situation:

➤ Before agreeing to any work, call the phone number on the business card to verify the legitimacy of the business.

➤ Call the Better Business Bureau and find out whether any complaints have been filed.

➤ Ask for a list of references to call.

➤ Have the person's work inspected before paying the invoice.

Stay on Your Toes

The Better Business Bureau is an organization that was set up to provide the general public with important information about large and small businesses. The Better Business Bureau's free service will tell you if any complaints have been filed against the company you are researching. You also can use this service to file complaints yourself, which can help prevent others from being taken advantage of.

Con men and impersonators usually are after your money, valuables, property, or anything they can turn into cash. Your trust is the con's weapon of choice. They are deceptive by nature and are very good at getting what they want. Their stories are believable, and they come in all shapes and sizes. The following sections are intended to help you identify cons and to teach you how they operate.

Props

Cons and props go together like ham and eggs. If you can learn to identify popular con props in advance, you can avoid being scammed altogether.

The following are some con props to keep an eye out for:

➤ Vehicle door magnets signifying a business can help a con gain access to your home or business. They make you less suspicious of the vehicle circling your neighborhood.

➤ Crutches, walking canes, arm casts, neck braces, and wheelchairs can play on your sympathy or persuade you to assist them.

➤ Bouquets of flowers or balloons can help cons gain access to your home or business.

➤ Clipboards make them look more professional.

➤ Strollers or baby carriages make them look less suspicious because parents are less likely to be perceived as being a threat.

Safety Alert!

Be extremely careful of men who ask for your assistance in loading a vehicle. Wearing a cast, a neck brace, or a similar prop that creates sympathy and then requesting help is a trick criminals have used to lure victims close to their vehicle. The criminal then forces the victim inside the vehicle and drives off.

Bad Guys Beware!

Get into the habit of checking people's stories. Don't just take someone's word because the person looks innocent or is wearing the right uniform. Remember, it only takes a second to look past the surface.

Popular Cons

The following scenarios will show you just how deceptive professional thieves can be:

Scenario #1: A man dressed as an exterminator walks into an office and asks everyone to leave for 10 minutes while he sprays for bugs. He then casually goes through purses, drawers, and briefcases. This thief's total investment consisted of a $10 insecticide canister, a hard hat, and an inexpensive jumpsuit. It takes him less than one minute to dress up and even less time to take it off and throw it away. One quick phone call to verify his story would have crushed him like a roach.

Scenario #2: A woman in the mall is holding a clipboard and standing in the middle of the floor. She says she is doing a survey about "favorite shops in the mall." If you answer a few simple questions, she'll send you a free $25 gift certificate that can be used at any store in the mall. Within three minutes, she has obtained your address, phone number, and possibly even your social security and driver's license numbers. She might even have gotten you to tell her how much money you make in a year. For the price of a clipboard, she now knows everything she needs to know about your life.

This con might be looking for the perfect house to rob. Professionals like to know how much money a potential target earns in a year and during what hours the house is most likely to be empty. By knowing your banking information, social security number, or driver's license number, a professional can wipe out your bank account. There are endless possibilities to what a professional con can do with this information. Asking for her credentials would have resulted in her walking right out the door.

Scenario #3: A woman wearing a jogging suit pushes a baby stroller through your neighborhood while a man walks his dog up and down your street. They both look like they belong, but they actually are casing your neighborhood with the intention of burglarizing it. Take the time to investigate new faces in the neighborhood with a few polite questions. You'll be glad you did.

Scams and Impersonators

Although this section is not comprehensive, it does provide enough information about scams and tricks to give you a feel for how the game is played. By using these boilerplates as training tools, you should be able to recognize trouble in advance and avoid it.

Impersonating a Police Officer

If an officer approaches you on foot and asks you to do something that makes you uncomfortable, ask him or her to call another officer over. If someone is impersonating a police officer, he or she most likely will be working alone and will not be able to call for another officer (or want to for that matter). A real police officer can have another officer on the scene in a matter of minutes. If someone really is an officer of the law, he or she should have no problem with this request. If the person is not, this request will make it readily apparent.

Stay on Your Toes

People trust police officers, but a phony police uniform can be rented for about $40 and can be purchased for about $100. A nice, shiny badge only costs about $50, and a removable siren for your dashboard costs about $60.

If an unmarked police car tries to pull you over, slow down, turn on your hazards, and drive to the nearest populated area before pulling over. Any good officer of the law will understand your concerns.

Classified Ads

Criminals like to use classified ads to scam the innocent. One way they do this is by calling about items listed for sale. This gives them entry into your home, at which point they'll preview your merchandise.

Another tactic criminals use is placing an ad. One reason bad guys like to sell stuff in the classifieds is because it gets you to come to them. They can sell you phony stuff such as diamond rings and Rolex watches. By the time you discover that the merchandise you bought is fake, they've disappeared. Be wary of items you see in the newspaper that are for sale way below market value.

Another favorite trick is to advertise a car for sale. When you come to look at it alone, the person test drives the car with you in the passenger seat. Now you're in a car with a total stranger, and he or she didn't even lift a finger to get you there. And what about the guy who takes your car out for a test drive and never returns?

The following are some precautions you can take to reduce your chances of getting scammed while using the classifieds:

➤ If you place an ad in the paper to sell something, avoid giving out your home telephone number. (Give out a pager number, a cell phone number, or a work number instead.)

➤ Meet the stranger at a location you know well and are comfortable with and have a friend go with you.

➤ If a stranger must come to your home to look at an item, make sure a friend is there with you.

Safety Alert!

If you're going to let a stranger test drive your car alone, ask to see his or her driver's license first and write down the license number and address. Don't take a test ride with a stranger unless you have a friend in the car with you.

Models Wanted

A smooth-talking photographer approaches you and tells you how perfect you are for his latest project. You're confident the person is really a photographer because he's wearing a camera around his neck. The next thing you know, the "photographer" is snapping photos faster than you can say scam.

Here's how you'll get burned. The photographer will ask you for $50 cash to pay for the developing costs, or you might be asked to go to a van, an RV, or a studio to take some more professional shots with better lighting and equipment. You also might be asked for your personal information so the negatives can be mailed to you or so you can be contacted about doing some modeling. The photographer no doubt will assure you that your negatives will be passed on to someone even more important than he is. Kids should be especially wary of photographers because, unfortunately, this is a popular scam used by sex offenders.

If you get approached by a photographer, simply ask for the person's information and say you will call the following day. If everything checks out, you're fine. If the person won't give you any information, be grateful that your interaction is over.

Closing the Blinds on Peeping Toms

Peeping Toms are people who sneak around to the back of your house and peak through the window, hoping to catch a glimpse of someone undressing. Some voyeurs even have taken it so far as to purchase a high-power telescope and set it up in their home with it aimed at a particular target.

Sometimes a peeping Tom is just a curious teenager going too far. The police usually are pretty lenient about these offenders the first time it happens and just inform a parent. If a teenager makes voyeurism a habit, however, professional counseling might be necessary.

Street Talk

Webster's dictionary defines a **voyeur** as "a person who is sexually gratified by viewing, especially furtively and habitually, persons who are disrobing, engaged in sexual activity, etc.; a peeping Tom."

Staying Out of Sight

Here's my advice for people who want to steer clear of voyeurs:

➤ Keep your windows covered when you're uncovered.

➤ Keep mini-blinds shut and curtains drawn, especially at night.

➤ Invest in a robe.

➤ If you're suspicious of a potential peeper, report it to the police.

➤ If you live in a house, invest in outdoor lighting, particularly the type that turns on automatically when it senses movement.

➤ If your dog begins barking for no apparent reason, investigate.

I hope you feel less vulnerable now. It's amazing how learning a few things about a particular type of criminal can help you understand more about the entire group. Remember that applied knowledge is power.

Bad Guys Beware!

Give your house the final peeping Tom test: determine whether you can see through your curtains or mini-blinds when looking from the outside in. Turn all the lights on in your home when it's dark outside and close all your curtains and mini-blinds. Walk around the exterior of your home. If you can see in, so can others.

The Least You Need To Know

➤ Stalking usually is the result of obsession.

➤ Don't be convinced that someone is telling the truth just because they're using a convincing prop.

➤ Get into the habit of maintaining a healthy level of suspicion about people who approach you.

➤ Keeping voyeurs out of the picture is as easy as keeping windows covered.

Playing It Safe When Out of the House

You decide to go to a new club your friends told you about. You have a pretty good idea where it's located, so instead of calling for directions, you decide to try to find it on your own. Before you know it, you're lost in a bad part of town. It's 10 P.M. and you're alone. To make matters worse, a car full of teens is following you closely and honking their horn at you.

This disaster could have been prevented if you had planned ahead by calling the club in advance and getting clear directions. Having a friend with you wouldn't have hurt either.

Everybody likes to get out of the house once in a while to have fun. In this chapter, I'm going to be the fun police. You're going to learn how to stay safe while enjoying yourself outside of the house.

Recreation and relaxation are important, but you still need to exercise common sense. The bad guys don't care if it's your day off. All they care about is getting what they want, when they want it. This is why it's so important to find a healthy balance between having fun and staying safe.

The Buddy System

When it comes to going out and having fun, there isn't much that's more beneficial to your safety than having a friend or two accompany you. You've probably heard the expression that there's safety in numbers. This makes sense because criminals don't usually target people who are with someone. Instead, criminals prefer targets that are alone because handling one person is much less difficult than handling several.

Street Talk

According to *Webster's*, a **buddy** is "a close friend; companion; comrade; especially, a comrade in arms. Either of two persons paired off in a partnership arrangement for mutual help and protection, as in combat or in children's camp activities."

The buddy system isn't just for fun outings. Let's say it's 11 P.M. on Friday night, and you're baking cookies for a picnic in the morning. You discover that you've run out of sugar. You call your buddy. Your buddy goes to the store with you so you don't have to go alone and, in doing so, helps keep you safe. Your buddy doesn't mind being inconvenienced because he knows you would do it for him. You don't need to ask your buddy to accompany you every time you leave the house—just when you're going out late at night or when you're going somewhere that's not very safe.

Choosing Your Buddy

It's important to use wisdom when choosing a buddy because it could prove to be one of the most crucial decisions you ever make. The following are a few guidelines to help you choose the right buddy. You should choose

➤ Someone who's dependable.

➤ Someone who takes safety just as seriously as you do.

➤ Someone whose schedule is flexible (or similar to yours).

➤ Someone you can trust. (You don't want a buddy who'd leave you stranded in a dangerous situation.)

➤ Someone who is fun to be with.

Outdoor Exercise

The first category of fun and recreation that I'm going to discuss is outdoor exercise. This information can be used for just about anything you do outdoors.

Stay on Your Toes

According to *Street Sense For Women,* written by Louis R. Mizell Jr., every year more than 7,000 American women are the victims of crime while jogging.

Jogging and Taking Walks

As you know, jogging and walking are both very popular activities. They're healthy, they're fun, they relieve stress, and they drop the excess pounds. Not only that, they're activities you can do outdoors. After being cooped up all day, physical exercise can work miracles on both your mind and your body.

So is there anything you can do to continue jogging and walking without being afraid and without putting yourself in such a vulnerable environment? The answer is yes, but it's going to take a little extra effort on your part.

Setting Boundaries

Setting new boundaries for your safety is going to feel like an inconvenience at first. You'll be freer in the end, however, just because you're safe. Going out for a walk with the knowledge that you've taken wise precautions and that you're prepared for whatever comes your way is liberating. With it comes a peace of mind from not living in fear.

Let's take a look at how to keep safe in the great outdoors in terms of who, what, where, when, and how. I'll use jogging as an example.

Who You Jog With: Jog with a partner. No other single choice you can make will play a greater role in keeping you safe.

When You Jog: Choosing when to exercise is very important. As discussed in Chapter 6, "Dangerous Places," crime is much more likely to occur at night. Because of this, you should try to get into the habit of jogging during the hours of daylight. By doing this, you will greatly decrease your chances of running into trouble.

Where You Jog: Avoid secluded, isolated, or unpopulated areas. Stay away from areas with crime problems as well. Don't jog in areas that aren't well lit and stay out of wooded areas (unless you're doing it during the day and unless you're with a friend).

What You Jog With: First, don't wear headphones when you jog. Headphones put you at a serious disadvantage in terms of being able to notice trouble in advance, and

Bad Guys Beware!

When jogging, avoid parked cars, dumpsters, and wooded areas. These make for excellent hiding if someone wants to surprise you.

this reduces your response time. Criminals look for headphones. Second, consider bringing a dog along. Larger breeds are known for being awesome crime deterrents because of their appearance and reputations. They also make great running partners. Keep in mind, however, that one disadvantage of having a dog is that walking it will lead you to be outdoors at night more often. It also is a good idea to carry a fanny pack with you. They're comfortable, lightweight, and can hold some important safety items such as mace. When it comes to mace, though, it's important that you learn how to use it properly. (This will be discussed in a later chapter.) If you don't know how to use mace properly, it can be taken away from you by an attacker and then used on you.

It's also a good idea to carry a form of identification and some change in case you need to make an emergency phone call. (You can carry a cell phone if you prefer, or a prepaid phone card.) Fanny packs also keep the bad guys guessing as to whether you're carrying a weapon.

How You Jog: Remember what I told you about body language in Chapter 3, "The Golden Rules of Survival"? Keep your head up, your shoulders back, and your eyes forward. Don't look down at the ground or continually look at people around you. Be perceived as alert, aware, prepared, and most of all, confident.

Stay on Your Toes

Great Danes, German Shepherds, Rottweilers, Boxers, and Doberman pinschers all make great running partners (and bodyguards).

Beaches and Boardwalks

During the day, beaches don't really pose a big threat as far as violent crimes, but you do need to take some precautions regarding theft of personal belongings. Boardwalks, on the other hand, can present a whole package of problems if you're not careful and if you don't know what to look for. Sometimes it takes more than sunscreen to keep from getting burned!

Beaches

What's easier than pilfering through a family's belongings while they frolic in the ocean? Even if you happen to spot someone going through your stuff while you're out swimming, it's hard to get back to shore in time to put a stop to the thievery.

With that in mind, the following are a few key tips to keep in mind while spending a day on the beach:

➤ Sit next to people who seem trustworthy (preferably a family). Introduce yourself and, before you head into the water, ask them to keep an eye on your stuff.

➤ Instead of taking your good camera, bring a disposable one. It takes great pictures in the sunlight and, if it gets stolen, it's no biggie.

➤ Leave your camcorder at home. Not only do thieves love camcorders, sun and heat are bad for them.

➤ Purchase a small, waterproof container to carry your cash and keys while you're in the water. These containers can be worn around your waste, wrist, or neck.

➤ As with the camera, bring an inexpensive radio along.

Other Beach Hazards

In addition to theft, other problems can arise at the beach. Robbery, child abduction, and assault have been known to take place from time to time. These incidents not only are rare, however, they are easy to avoid if you're careful and know what to watch for (suspicious-looking people who seem out of place—wearing the wrong attire and so on).

Avoid hanging out on public beaches by yourself at night. They're not nearly as safe after the sun goes down. The same rule applies to beaches that applies everywhere else: The later it gets, the more dangerous the beach becomes.

Bad Guys Beware!

Keep a watchful eye on your children while at the beach. Not only does this make it less likely that they'll be abducted, it also reduces their chances of drowning. It's never a good idea for small children to swim unsupervised, but this is especially true in the ocean due to the force of the waves, currents, and tides.

Boardwalks

Boardwalks have been known to host all sorts of gang activity and a large number of violent crimes to boot. At night, boardwalks can become havens for drug use and distribution as well as alcohol-related gatherings for local teens. If you must go to the boardwalk, go with a group and keep your wits about you. Think twice before letting your children enjoy the boardwalk unsupervised.

A Night On the Town

Heading downtown for the evening? Going to that new nightclub everyone's been talking about? Maybe you're just going to a movie. You guessed it. Before you go out, there are some things you need to know about safety.

It's All in the Planning

The first thing you should do is carefully plan your evening. You need to know exactly where you're going and how to get there. Driving downtown at night is no time to get lost, and it can happen with one wrong turn. (Remember what happened to you at the beginning of this chapter, when you went to the club without directions?) In some cities, you can go from safe to unsafe territory in only a few blocks. If you're going somewhere for the first time, call ahead, get clear directions, and resist the temptation to take shortcuts.

Safety Alert!

If you get lost while driving, head back in the direction from which you came. The worst thing you can do is to continue driving in the same direction. Retracing your steps is the only way you can be sure you know where you're going.

Go with a Group

It's a very good idea to go out with friends. It's not enough just to meet your friends there, however; you need to travel with at least one of them, even if you have to go out of your way to pick someone up. Having a friend in the car with you reduces your chances of being targeted by a criminal. If you get lost or stranded, it's much safer than being alone. If you have one drink too many, your friend can drive you home.

Parking

Choose your parking space wisely. Remember that wherever you park now is where you have to walk back to later. Therefore, avoid parking in areas that aren't well lit. I recommend that you shell out the cash for a lot looked after by an attendant. This also protects your car because attendants usually are pretty good about keeping an eye on things.

Nightclubs and Bars

Americans always have enjoyed these evening hot spots and probably always will. If you're going to visit these places, though, it's important to keep in mind the cons of night life.

The first thing you need to remember is that alcohol and liquor have a tendency to make people inebriated. Everyone reacts differently to alcohol, so you never know what to expect from people around you. One thing drunk people have in common is that they tend to do and say things they would never do or say sober. Because of this, you need to be on your guard, especially if you're going to be drinking, too. Safety and alcohol have never made a good team, just ask the cops.

If you're going to drink alcohol outside of your home, the following are a few tips to help keep you safe while doing it:

➤ Don't drink if you're doing the driving.

➤ Make sure the person doing the driving isn't drinking.

➤ Never under any circumstances accept a ride home from a stranger! Call a friend or take a cab, even if you're out of money and have to charge it to your credit card.

➤ Leave establishments at least 30 minutes before closing time.

➤ Never drink in public alone!

➤ Don't leave without the person you came with. This is a good idea not only for your safety but for theirs as well.

Keep in mind that if you're victimized and you've been drinking—no matter how little—your court case is greatly weakened. You could even lose validity to the point of having no case at all. Most courts take the stance that, if you were drinking alcohol during the time of an incident, you are partly to blame.

Keep Your Eyes on Your Mai Tai's

One last thing to remember when drinking in public is that you need to keep an eye on your drink so someone doesn't put something in it. This has become a popular date rape technique lately, but it can easily be prevented if you follow these simple rules:

➤ Don't accept a drink from someone you just met. If a stranger wants to buy you a drink, go to the bar with him or her and make sure the bartender hands it directly to you.

➤ If you are at a party with strangers, either pour your own drink or watch whoever is pouring it for you.

➤ Don't leave your drink unattended.

Shopping

You just enjoyed a nice day at the mall and found a lot of really good deals. To pay at the counter of the last store you visited, you set your bags down beside you to sign your credit card slip. After you paid, you reached down to get your bags and discovered that they were gone, every one of them. Hundreds of dollars worth of merchandise vanished in a matter of seconds. A few simple steps on your part, however, could have prevented it.

Slum It

To help prevent theft, be careful not to wear expensive-looking jewelry that draws a lot of attention. Jewelry gives the impression that you are someone of means and are quite possibly carrying cash, a gold card, or both. A woman wearing a Rolex watch or a lot of diamonds while out shopping might as well wear a bull's eye on her back. There's a time and a place for everything, and shopping is not the time or the place for expensive, flashy jewelry. Besides, if you plan to barter, it makes it harder to negotiate a better price if the salesperson thinks you're loaded.

Cash or Credit?

When it's time to pay, don't pull out all your cash and flip through it. Instead, discreetly take out enough cash for your purchase before it's your turn and keep it separate from the rest of your money. You might even want to distribute your cash in different pockets before you leave the house. I recommend leaving the cash in the bank and using a credit card when possible. (This is, of course, if you have the money to pay the bill when it arrives.) Or use a debit card—they are now accepted as widely as cash.

Bad Guys Beware!

It's a good idea to back into your parking space. By nosing your vehicle in, you can't get out in a hurry. By backing in, however, you're ready to go if you're being followed or are fleeing an attacker. You have to back up at least once every time you park, so it might as well be when you arrive. You can also position your car for a quick exit by pulling through one parking space to get to another.

Parking Lot Safety

I can't say this enough. When it comes to parking lots, you need to be aware of your surroundings. Try to choose your parking space with safety as your first concern and convenience as your second. Well-lit areas are very important. Check for lights if you're heading into a store during daylight but won't be coming out until dark.

Don't hesitate to ask a security guard or a police officer to walk you to your vehicle if it's dark, if you're parked far away, or if you just feel like being safe. Chances are he or she will be happy to assist you.

When approaching your vehicle, make it a habit to look inside the window before unlocking it. The chances are extremely small that anyone would be inside your vehicle, but it sends a good message about your level of awareness to any criminals in the parking lot who might be sizing you up. Carry your bags in a way that would allow you to drop them quickly in an emergency and try to keep one hand free. In addition, have your keys ready before you leave the store. You don't want to be digging through your purse for your keys with all your bags sitting on the ground next to you. If your arms are tangled up with bags and your keys aren't ready, you look vulnerable!

Pickpockets and Purse Snatchers

Shoppers are very susceptible to pickpockets and purse snatchers. More than 500,000 Americans are hit by these sharks every year simply because they don't know how the game works. If you know what to look for, though, these types should be pretty easy to avoid. The first thing you need to know is that these thieves generally work in groups of two or more. One thief usually does the distracting while the other does the lifting.

Stay on Your Toes

Restrooms are a favorite hangout for pickpockets and purse snatchers. People hang jackets on doors, put briefcases down, and set purses on counters in bathrooms. Whenever you're in a public restroom, pay extra attention to your belongings.

Here are four examples of popular distractions and diversions that pickpockets and purse snatchers like to use. If you get the hang of how these examples work, you should be able to spot the rest of their tricks because they all work on the same principles.

There's not much you can do to prevent the following from happening except learn to carry your purse or wallet in a way that makes it very difficult to take them. If you notice one of these scenarios taking place, immediately stop and check to make sure you haven't just been taken, and then report the pickpocket or purse-snatcher. By recognizing these distractions as possible crime aids, you can decrease their effectiveness and, hopefully, stay out of their way.

Baby Bounce: A small child is used to get your attention while someone cleans you out. The child might tug on your pants leg or fall in front of you. When you lean over to assist the child, the bad guy moves in. When the child pulls on your pants leg, you're distracted. Either way, they have you if you're not prepared. If this happens to you, immediately stop and feel for your valuables.

Ketchup Squirt: A thief pokes a pinhole in a ketchup package and squirts a little on your back. He then politely tells you about the ketchup on your back. If you set your purse down to wipe the ketchup off, you lose. If you let him wipe it off for you, your wallet, purse, watch, or ring disappears. If this ever happens to you, thank the person and check to make sure your valuables are still intact before moving on.

Here is an example of a pickpocket using a small child to distract you long enough to steal your wallet.

Elevators: A team working together will hop on the elevator with you and make it a tight fit, bumping into you from time to time. When they exit the elevator, they usually do so with your possessions. If you find yourself in this situation, guard your possessions carefully until you're out of the elevator.

Escalators: Someone drops coins on the escalator and begins to pick them up or gets their shoestring caught in one of the steps. This causes people to get backed up for a moment. When people begin bumping into one another, someone rips you off. That person signals a partner who then travels toward him on the adjacent escalator. As the two partners pass one another, your possessions are quickly handed off.

Bad Guys Beware!

If you're approaching an escalator and notice anything odd or unusual taking place, don't get on right away. The good news is that, for a distraction on an escalator to be effective for the criminal, it must take place in front of you.

Wallets

Pickpockets tend to find out where you're carrying your wallet before they take it. The following are a few ways they accomplish this:

➤ They ask for change for a $10 bill. When you check, they know.

➤ They watch you purchase something and pay attention to where you put your wallet after the purchase.

➤ They put up a sign that says "Please guard your valuables, pickpockets active in this area." When people see this sign, they instinctively reach for their wallet to make sure it's still there.

➤ A pickpocket with a wallet in his or her hand approaches a man and says "I just found this wallet, is it yours?" When the man reaches to feel his wallet, the pickpocket knows.

There is very little you can do to prevent a pickpocket from learning where you keep your wallet. Just being aware of their tricks, however, can help you be more aware.

Bags and Purses

There are several ways to carry your bag or purse, but only one way prevents crime. The best way to carry your bag is with the strap going over your shoulder and the bag hanging down the same side. You should rest your hand on the top of the bag. This makes a thief think twice about trying to steal your bag, but it enables you to release it if you need to.

Safety Alert!

Women have been dragged and seriously beaten because robbers couldn't get their purses free from their bodies. Don't let this happen. Carry your purse in a way that deters a thief from wanting to take it, but don't let the purse strap wrap around your body. If it's grabbed, it's best to just let it go!

Incorrect: You could be dragged or seriously injured.

Incorrect: This looks too inviting, and you could be dragged or seriously injured.

Correct: The purse doesn't look inviting to thieves, and it can be let go of quickly.

97

If you keep a good attitude, stay aware of your surroundings, and keep the information in this chapter in mind, you should enjoy many fun days and nights away from home and away from danger. Holding onto your valuables and staying safe while out and about is your right—settle for nothing less.

The Least You Need to Know

➤ When it comes to staying safe away from home, nothing protects you more than being with a buddy.

➤ Make wise decisions when jogging or walking, especially at night.

➤ If you're going to drink alcohol, be responsible about it.

➤ Shopping can be a fun, crime-free experience provided that you implement a few simple precautions into your shopping plan.

Chapter 9

Making All Trips Round Trips

In This Chapter

➤ Planning ahead

➤ Traveling by car

➤ Hotels and motels

➤ Airports and rental cars

➤ International travel

➤ Cruises

After years of saving and dreaming, you've finally made it to a small island in the middle of nowhere. Sunshine, sand, and relaxation are the only things you have planned for the next two weeks. Unfortunately, after returning to your hotel room your first night on the island, you find that all your valuables have been stolen. Your passport, traveler's checks, airline ticket, and jewelry are all gone. By taking just a few simple precautions, this catastrophe could have been prevented.

As far as American pastimes go, traveling ranks right up there with apple pie, hot dogs, and baseball. Although traveling can be loads of fun, it has the potential to put you at risk if you're not aware of the dangers.

In this chapter, I'm going to teach you the do's and don'ts of hitting the open road and flying the friendly skies. Some of the topics I'll discuss include hotels, airports, international travel, cruises, and rental cars, just to name a few. Whether you're traveling for business or pleasure, you need to be prepared for the worst, and this information could very well be the most important item you pack. So put your seat-back in the upright position and prepare for takeoff as we head out to Safety Land, U.S.A.

Planning Ahead

Traveling can be lots of fun provided you know what precautions to take. Americans spend a great deal of time and money traveling, and it's not always safe. Therefore, you need to learn to travel wisely.

Stay on Your Toes

The Internet is emerging as a reliable source of good travel options. The Internet is loaded with frequent specials for cruises, airfare, rental cars, and package vacation deals. You can even purchase everything online if you choose.

Before You Leave

You need to accomplish two very important things before going on a trip. First, make your home look occupied when you're gone. This can be easily accomplished with proper lighting, sensors, and so on. Nothing can ruin fond memories of your vacation quicker than coming back to a home that's been burglarized. This topic will be discussed in greater detail in Chapter 13, "Fortifying Your Castle."

Second, make sure you always plan the specifics of your trip in advance. Arriving in a strange city for the first time is no time to be looking for a hotel. The more details you work out in advance, the smoother your trip will go and the safer you'll be. I recommend that you use professional travel agencies whenever possible. They usually can get you better deals on everything from hotels to airfare, and they provide a step-by-step itinerary. It's definitely the only way to travel, and it will cost you less money and hassle in the end.

It's a good idea to make a copy of your itinerary and leave it with a friend or a family member. This itinerary should include names and numbers of places you'll be staying as well as corresponding dates. If for some reason you don't return home when you're supposed to, this will make it a whole lot easier to trace your steps. It also enables others to find you in case of an emergency back home.

Traveling by Car

If you're going to travel by vehicle, you need to make sure whatever you're driving is in tip-top mechanical shape. The last thing you want is to end up stranded on the side of the road in the middle of nowhere.

The following are a few safety pointers to keep in mind when you're doing the driving:

➤ Make sure you have your registration and proof of insurance.

➤ Don't speed! Depending on the state, if you get caught speeding in a state other than the one in which you're licensed, you may have to follow the police officer to the station and stay there until your fine is paid in full.

➤ Carry mace or another form of protection if you're going to be driving and making pit stops late at night.

➤ Pack necessities for an emergency such as a first-aid kit, a blanket, a flashlight, a gas can, and a can of tire sealant.

➤ Take an extra set of keys and either keep them on your person or hide them under the vehicle in a magnetic key case.

➤ Take either a cellular phone or a CB radio with you.

➤ Unpack everything from your vehicle when staying at a hotel or motel for the night.

➤ Be cautious of others when stopping at highway rest areas late at night. If you have to pull over to rest or nap, make sure you lock your doors.

Bad Guys Beware!

Don't let your vehicle's fuel tank get below one-quarter of a tank. If you make this a habit, it is very unlikely you will ever run out of gas.

Life Savers

When out on the open road, never pick up a hitchhiker or stop to help a stranded vehicle. Many people have been murdered, raped, kidnapped, or robbed while trying to be kind.

Hotels and Motels

These are the places we lay our weary heads at night as well as all of our belongings. Every possible crime you can imagine has been committed against travelers who only wanted a good night's rest.

Choosing a Hotel

When choosing a hotel, be sure to pick one that is in a safe neighborhood and that has a good reputation for taking safety seriously. If you're not sure of a hotel's reputation, call a reputable travel agency and ask for advice. (Chances are the agency will be glad to give you this information in the hope of earning your business in the future.) Ask the hotel's staff if security cameras are installed, if security personnel work around the clock, and if they use metal keys or key cards. (Key cards are much safer.) The answers to these questions will give you a good indication of how important safety is to the hotel.

Stay on Your Toes

Key cards are safer than metal keys because locks that use key cards are much more difficult to pick. In addition, metal keys are easy to duplicate, but most hotels reset a room's key card code every time a new guest checks in.

Hotel Safety

The best thing you can do to stay safe during your next hotel visit is to follow these simple precautions. This is a very comprehensive list, and if you follow it, you should have no problem checking out in the same condition you checked in.

➤ Do not give personal information to the person driving you to the airport. Sometimes these people work directly with crooked hotel employees, informing them of who's who.

➤ If you aren't comfortable with the ground transportation arranged by the hotel, arrange different transportation.

➤ Don't trust someone just because he or she is a hotel employee or is wearing a uniform. Hotel employees have committed their share of crimes against guests, and sometimes criminals pose as staff members.

➤ When checking in or out of the hotel, don't let your belongings out of sight. If you want the bellhop to carry your bags, make sure to walk with them.

➤ Try to get a room on a lower floor (floors two through five) but not on the ground floor. Statistically, these rooms are safest because ground floors usually have windows or balconies that can be entered, and really high floors are dangerous because of the amount of time it takes for help to arrive.

Furthermore, the higher floors are filled up last, so they may have fewer people around.

➤ Avoid being the victim of a push-in. This is what happens when a guest is opening the door to the room, and someone comes up from behind and pushes him- or herself into the room. This can be avoided simply by looking around before opening the door. If someone is nearby, wait until the person is gone before entering your room.

➤ Don't be embarrassed to ask a member of the hotel's staff or security to escort you to your room.

Bad Guys Beware!

The first time you enter your room, give it a good inspection. Prop the door open with a piece of luggage or a chair, turn the lights on, and check the shower, under the bed, behind the curtains, and in the closet. If you run into a problem, the door is open for a quick escape.

➤ Make sure all doors are double-locked whenever you're in the room. This includes balcony doors, regardless of what floor you're on. Also check the doors to adjoining rooms.

➤ Don't open your door for anyone you aren't expecting. If the person claims to be hotel staff, call the front desk to confirm the person's need to be there before opening the door. Have room service slip the receipt under the door; this tactic will catch an impostor off-guard.

➤ Don't invite other guests into your room and never tell anyone your room number. Meeting in the lobby is the safest way to socialize with guests you don't know very well.

Leaving valuables out in your hotel room can easily lead to theft.

➤ Don't leave valuables laying around your room. Airline tickets, passports, keys, jewelry, cash, cameras, purses, and wallets should be kept in a hotel safe or locked in your suitcase.

➤ Whenever you're not in your room, leave the Do Not Disturb sign on the door and the television on. Have maids clean your room when you're in it.

➤ Take a few minutes to identify the emergency fire exits on your floor. If you wait for a crisis before searching for these locations, you'll lose valuable time.

➤ If someone from the hotel calls your room and requests that you come down to discuss a matter of importance, call the front desk to verify the request. This is a popular tactic used by criminals to get you out of your room.

Street Talk

What's the difference between a **hotel** and a **motel**? In hotels, the doors of each room lead into a hallway inside the building. A motel room door exits directly outside.

To help secure your hotel or motel room at night when you're sleeping, place a chair against the door. If someone tries to enter, he or she will be startled by the noise, and you will be alerted in advance. There also are several hotel travel alarms on the market that detect a human's motion, movement of the door, or someone touching the doorknob.

Airports and Rental Cars

Before flying the friendly skies, there are a few things you should know about American airports and the dangers they can represent. For the most part, theft is the most common crime in airports. Violence usually is not an issue because people are always around. International airports are discussed later in this chapter.

Theft in the Terminal

Any time you set your bags down, you need to keep a watchful eye on them. This especially holds true for airport restrooms. Thieves love airport restrooms because a lot of valuables are left alone for seconds at a time. Also, don't be deceived by someone's appearance: Airport thieves usually dress like travelers and carry a piece of luggage as their prop.

When you set down a briefcase, purse, document bag, or laptop computer, don't set it beside you. This makes it too inviting to a criminal and too easy to steal. The best place to set your bag is on the floor between your legs or between the counter and your feet. A thief is unlikely to reach between or around your legs to swipe a bag, and it sends a message to everyone around that you're aware and prepared. (This technique also works great when you're out shopping.)

Correct: Placing the bag between your legs.

Correct: Placing the bag between the counter and your feet.

Incorrect: Placing the bag beside you.

The Laptop Scam

The targets of choice for airport thieves are laptop computers. They're valuable, they're easy to sell, and they're even easier to steal. Here's a typical scam: Two criminals wait for you to go through airport security. As soon as you place your laptop on the conveyer belt, one of the thieves steps in front of you and walks through the detector with a wad of keys. When the detector goes off, he is called back to figure out the problem. In the meantime, the criminal's partner is on the other side of the conveyer belt picking up your laptop and heading out the door to a waiting vehicle. After the laptop is dropped off, the crook goes in for another hit, maybe several. This is a popular technique for stealing purses and briefcases as well.

Stay on Your Toes

Airports have really tightened up security over the past few years. If any bag is left unattended in an airport, even if just for a second, security will likely pick it up. It then will be taken to a private room and searched for explosives.

Airport Safety Tips

The following are some handy tips to help keep you and your bags intact at the airport:

➤ Try to book nonstop flights to avoid layovers in strange airports. (Not only is this safer, your luggage also has a better chance of reaching your destination.)

➤ Whenever possible, have tickets mailed to you in advance or use ticketless travel. That way, you don't have to check in at the counter and can go directly to the gate. (The sooner you board the aircraft, the sooner you can put your guard down and relax.)

➤ The sooner you check your luggage, the less likely it is to get stolen.

➤ Never leave your luggage unattended, not even for a second.

➤ Go through security as soon as you can and stay at your gate. (Criminals do the majority of their work on the unsecured side of the airport because it's much easier to exit the airport in a hurry.)

➤ Keep a close eye on your personal belongings as they are checked through security.

➤ Place important documents such as your ticket, passport, or visa in a safe place. Don't walk around with them sticking out of your pocket. It's a good idea to keep these items secure on your person and not with your carry-on luggage.

➤ Lock your luggage and make sure it is properly tagged with your address. If you have a P.O. box or a business address, use that instead of your home address. (If a criminal steals your luggage, you don't want to make matters worse by letting him know where you live as well.)

Ground Transportation

Another thing you need to know about airport safety is how to choose safe ground transportation. It's not uncommon for a stranger to approach you and ask if he can drive you where you need to go. Don't accept rides from these people! Choose a cab or a shuttle service referred to you by airport security. The vehicle should be clearly marked the same as all the others waiting at the curb. A good rule of thumb is to leave with someone you choose instead of someone who chooses you.

Rental Cars

Driving around town in a rental car says a great deal about you to a criminal. The first thing it says is that you are from out of town. Being from out of town means you probably are carrying some spending money, and you probably don't know your way around very well. It also means that, if the criminal gets caught, it is very unlikely that you will fly all the way back for a 30-minute court case. How does the criminal know you flew into town? If you drove, you wouldn't need a rental car.

Bad Guys Beware!

When you're in flight, ask a flight attendant for the scoop on your destination as it relates to safety. Flight attendants and pilots usually travel to the same locations several times a year, and because they're trained to be very safe and cautious, they're usually full of valuable information.

Blending In

Because driving a rental car makes you a more desirable target, it's important that you don't look like you're driving one. Bumper stickers, labels, and logos that advertise the agency from which you rented your car double as bull's eye stickers that say "Come and get me." If you rent a vehicle with one of these stickers, ask the attendant either to remove it or to give you a vehicle that doesn't have one. After you tell the attendant why, getting the person to cooperate shouldn't be a problem. Another thing you need to be careful about is a rental car with a specially marked license plate. These plates used to be marked with a Y or a Z, but most companies have done away with this for your safety. In some states, laws have been implemented forbidding rental car companies to mark their vehicles.

Stay on Your Toes

Criminals can identify tourists by the luggage stacked in the back of the vehicle, the luggage strapped to the top of the vehicle, or someone in the car looking at a map.

International Travel

Traveling internationally opens a whole new can of worms when it comes to crime and violence. International travel should be taken much more seriously than domestic travel. With domestic travel you may get scammed or robbed, but with international travel the stakes are much higher—as are the risks.

Methods of Payment

It's best to consider how you're going to pay for things before you leave the country. It's also a good idea to write down all your credit card information such as card numbers, expiration dates, and phone numbers to call if you need to cancel a stolen card and have a new one sent to you. I recommend that you keep a copy of this information with someone you trust. If you get in a bind or your credit cards get stolen, you can call the person with whom you left the information and get the problem resolved quickly.

The best way to pay for everything is with traveler's checks because, if they're lost or stolen, you're not out anything. The issuing company usually will send you new ones within 24 hours. When using traveler's checks, however, be sure to do the following:

➤ Sign the checks as soon as you get them. Without your signature, a thief can easily use them, and you'll be out the money.

➤ Don't sign the second signature line until you are in the process of cashing the check. When you sign your name for the second time, the check becomes valid.

➤ Write down the check numbers and keep this information separate from the checks themselves.

➤ Make sure you keep the phone number for lost or stolen checks in a separate location (but one that is easily accessible).

➤ Don't carry all your traveler's checks or money with you at one time. Only take with you the amount you will need for the day.

Exchanging Currency

When it comes to exchanging currency, your best bet is to do it in advance. If the country to which you're traveling widely accepts U.S. currency, it's still a good idea to use the local form of money. If something costs 40,000 Yin, for example, it's much easier to count 40,000 Yin than to convert this amount to U.S. dollars in your head and possibly make a mistake. If you mess up on your math and pay too much, it is unlikely that the mistake will be brought to your attention. Also remember that the same rules apply as when you're at home in terms of using an ATM machine.

Police and Bribes

In some foreign countries, police officers live way below the poverty level. To help offset their financial burden, some rely heavily on bribes. There's nothing like an American tourist to help pay rent. You need to be prepared for this hassle because, if it happens to you, you'll likely be given two simple choices: pay up or go to jail.

For example, imagine getting pulled over by a police officer while in your rental car. He says you are driving drunk, and you say you aren't. He gives you the choice of going to jail overnight and paying a $1,000 fine or giving him $200 to let you go.

Safety Alert!

Steer clear of discussing your political and religious views when traveling in foreign countries. If someone ask you about these issues, be polite and then change the subject.

Because giving bribes to police officers is illegal, I recommend that you learn where the U.S. Embassy is located in the country you're visiting and memorize the phone number in case you end up in jail. Writing it down and keeping it on your person might not be a good idea because your possessions might be taken from you. It's also not a good idea to rely on the police to give you the phone number of the U.S. Embassy. If the country you're in has a U.S. military base, it's a good idea to know where it's located and how to reach it by phone as well.

Dangerous Countries

Some countries have a reputation of being downright brutal to American tourists. Before you decide to see the world, take the time to research the country or countries to which you will be traveling. I recommend that you avoid countries in political turmoil and with strict laws over human rights, such as Iran or Afghanistan.

Poor Countries

Some countries can be dangerous because of a lack of basic provisions and necessities such as Bangladesh, Ethiopia, and Vietnam, just to name a few. If you're going to travel to one of these places, keep in mind that the poor are very desperate and will do almost anything to survive. Make sure you don't walk the streets alone, especially after dark. Avoid wearing jewelry that looks expensive and don't show your money.

Bad Guys Beware!

When visiting a poor country, don't show the poor any disrespect because of their position, and always place whatever you give them in their hand. This way, other beggars aren't as likely to see you. If they do, you will be surrounded.

Be a Local or Just Look like One

The last thing you want to do when you're on vacation is look like you're from out of town. Your goal is to blend in and look like one of the locals if you want to increase your chances of having a crime-free vacation.

The following are a few precautions to help keep you from looking like a tourist:

➤ Don't wear a camera around your neck.

➤ Don't point at everything neat you see.

➤ Don't look at your map in public.

➤ Don't wear souvenir hats and T-shirts until you get home.

Stay on Your Toes

There are several reasons criminals love to target tourists. Criminals know that tourists usually carry cash, they don't know their way around town, they are less likely to press charges, and they probably won't come back later to testify.

Cruises

Cruises can be a lot of fun and are a great way to get some quality rest away from the real world. As far as safety is concerned, the main thing you need to watch out for is getting off the ship to check out the scenery when the boat stops at ports. You usually get some shore leave for every port at which you stop, and you should exercise the same precautions as you would anywhere else. The locals can spot *Love Boat* people with their eyes closed and know they are easy targets. If they rob you and get caught, chances are you're not going to stick around to make a fuss about it because you don't want to miss your boat.

To avoid a cruise disaster, avoid looking like a tourist, don't flash cash around, be aware of pickpockets, conceal your passport and boarding pass, and only take the amount of money you need for the day. Also be sure to get back to the ship at least one hour before it leaves. The captain always leaves on time and doesn't conduct a passenger role call, if you get my drift.

Take the same safety precautions in your cabin as you would if you were staying in a hotel: lock up your valuables, look around before unlocking your cabin door, don't invite strangers inside, and so on. Think of it as a hotel that floats; follow the same rules, and you'll be fine. Bon voyage!

The Least You Need to Know

➤ Choose hotels that are in safe locations and that take your safety seriously.

➤ If traveling overseas, create a detailed itinerary and leave a copy of it with a friend or loved one.

➤ When overseas, know where the U.S. Embassy is located and keep its phone number with you at all times.

➤ Avoid looking or acting like a tourist.

➤ When in airports, be suspicious of people who look like other travelers because these cons are slick.

Chapter 10

Staying Safe While Single

In This Chapter

➤ The first encounter

➤ Safe dating

➤ Before you get serious

➤ Getting out of trouble

One night at a party you meet a handsome, charming guy who seems too good to be true. You agree to go out on a date with him over the weekend. You spend hours preparing yourself and sprucing up your home before he arrives. After a great date, he drives you home and you invite him to come in but only for a moment. Once inside, Mr. Right becomes Mr. Aggressive, and he won't take "No" for an answer. Within minutes, he becomes violent and attempts to rape you. Thankfully, your roommate walks in just in time and he flees. But what if she hadn't? This disaster not only could have turned into a tragedy, it could have been prevented.

You never can tell when you'll encounter the person with whom you belong. Unfortunately, you never know when you might run into a real head case either. You need to know who or what you're dealing with before saying yes to marriage, before saying I love you, and even before going out on a date. Hooking up with the right person can bring a lifetime of happiness, but you have to know what to look for and what to avoid.

In this chapter, I'm going to teach women how to avoid dating disasters. You'll learn how to date safely and how to handle the first encounter without putting yourself at risk. I'll also teach you some ways to prevent date rape and how to defend yourself against it in an emergency. And what if a guy just won't go away? I'll help you get rid of him as well. I'll also walk you through the process of legally checking a person out before you get serious.

This chapter is geared toward women because, according to statistics, they usually are the victims of dating-related crimes. Some of my advice also can be helpful for men, however, who find themselves in similar situations.

The First Encounter

It's never too early to begin evaluating someone you're interested in. Taking a good look at a guy's character before he knows you're interested often is the best time to get honest answers. If your answer to five or more of the following questions is less than favorable, you've got someone on your hands that you don't want to begin dating:

➤ Is he controlling?

➤ Is he pushy?

➤ Is his personality consistent around everyone or does it change when other women are around? (In other words, does he treat you differently than other women or does he show attractive women favoritism?)

➤ Does he seem chauvinistic?

➤ Does he tell jokes that are degrading to women?

➤ Is he courteous to all women or just the ones he's trying to impress?

➤ Does he show concern for others?

Bad Guys Beware!

If a man stares, makes comments, acts childish, or changes his personality in another negative way when a woman is in the room, he's probably someone you want to steer clear of.

Be Careful What You Say

You don't want to give away too much information about yourself too quickly. Instead, take your time revealing personal information. The following are a few things to avoid telling a stranger about yourself, no matter how cute he is:

➤ Don't give out your home telephone number the first time you meet. A pager number is safe, as is a work number.

➤ Don't tell him specifics about where you live. It's okay to give him a general idea but nothing more.

➤ Don't let him know whether you live alone.

If you're interested, however, there's nothing wrong with asking a fair amount of questions yourself. The more you learn about him early on, the better choices you'll be able to make later. But by all means, don't let him drive you home after your first meeting!

Safe Dating

You met a guy and so far everything seems to check out fine. He seems to be trustworthy enough to go out on a date with. It's my job, however, to make sure you take a few precautions.

Before the Date

When you arrange a first date, make sure you meet in a public place instead of having your date come to your house. This keeps things neutral in the beginning, and it makes good sense to keep your address a secret from someone you don't know very well. I also recommend that you make the first date a lunch date or something else casual.

If you must have your date pick you up where you live, have someone with you when your date arrives. It's a good idea for the date to see that someone else knows where you're going and has gotten a good look at him. If you live alone, have a friend come over to accomplish this.

The next thing you need to consider is how you're going to dress. The first date might not be the best time to wear that sexy red dress you've been saving for Mr. Right. I recommend finding a good balance between something you look really nice in, something that won't be taken the wrong way by a jerk, and something in which you're comfortable. If this guy turns out to be a jerk and you need to start swinging punches or running, a pair of high heels and a constricting dress can make things difficult for you.

Safety Alert!

If you decide to run a singles ad in the paper, don't include your home telephone number, address, or full name. You never know whose interest your ad might spark, and giving out personal information can put you in serious danger. If you're going to run ads in the classifieds, I strongly suggest that you invest in a pager.

Street Talk

Webster's dictionary defines **flirting** as "paying amorous attention to someone without serious intentions or emotional commitment; to play at love; to trifle or toy with."

During the Date

During the date, you should be careful about what you communicate to your date and how much alcohol you consume.

What you communicate: Choose your words carefully. You don't want to say things that might lead your date on or give him the wrong impression about what to expect. Before finishing dinner, for example, you might already have come to the conclusion that you don't want to see this guy anymore because he just isn't your type. Because you used the wrong words, however, he now thinks you like him and want him to pursue you. You might not have said anything verbally to give him the wrong impression, but you might have communicated this with your body language. Be careful with the words you choose and the body language you use when on a first date. Don't say things such as, "The night is young." Also, don't do a lot of physical touching; touching is very personal and communicates affection.

Bad Guys Beware!

When considering where to meet for a first date, choose somewhere you know well and with which you are very comfortable. Be cautious around men who insist on a specific location to meet and who are very pushy about planning the evening. If he's a gentleman, he'll be happy to let you decide.

How much alcohol you consume: The last thing you need is to be tipsy while sitting across from a guy you hardly know who thinks you're interested in him. Be very wary of men who actively encourage you to drink. If your date keeps insisting that you have another drink or does things like refill your glass without your consent, leave. If you get the feeling your date is trying to get you drunk, he probably is.

After the Date

End a first date earlier than you would a third or fourth date. Make it a rule that, anytime you begin dating someone new, he has to earn your trust before you'll stay out late with him. When the first date is over, I don't recommend inviting the guy in unless someone else is home. This rule, of course, is not necessary if your date didn't pick you up where you live.

Before Getting Serious

Let's say you've been seeing a guy for a couple months, and you believe he could be the one. Before you get serious, you might want to do a little homework first. This means doing a thorough background check. There are two ways you can do this. The first way is to talk to people who know him best and ask them some important questions. The second way is to contact an agency or two that specializes in getting information.

The man you're dating might be as genuine and as harmless as they come. He also might be married to someone else in another state, have children he hasn't mentioned, be an ex-convict, or have complaints filed against him for stalking an ex-girlfriend. He might be financially irresponsible and owe back child support or taxes. All these things are important to know because they can greatly affect your future, especially if you're considering marriage. What should worry you is not that he's guilty of this stuff but that he's guilty and has kept it from you. If he didn't tell you about one of these things, what else hasn't he told you? The bottom line is that, if your mate has a history of dishonesty or violence, you need to know about it!

Getting Other Opinions

The easiest and cheapest way to find out what you need to know is by asking your boyfriend's friends and family members what they think about him. Don't beat around the bush as to why you're asking the questions. You'll find that, for the most part, people will answer you honestly if they understand your motives.

The following are some good, general questions to start with:

➤ How long have you known him?

➤ Would you recommend that I get involved with him?

➤ What do you see as his biggest fault?

➤ What do you see as his greatest strength?

➤ Do you think he is a responsible person?

➤ Do you trust him?

➤ How is he at managing anger?

➤ How does he resolve conflicts with others?

➤ Do you think he would ever hurt me physically or emotionally?

Safety Alert!

It's very important that you ask the guy you're dating if he minds you asking a few people for their opinion of him. If he gets upset and says no, you've got some thinking to do. If he says he doesn't mind, you can ask around with a clear conscience and probably will get more cooperation from the people you talk to because of his consent. If you don't ask him before talking to his friends and he's hiding big secrets, he could get extremely angry with you, and it could turn into a dangerous situation.

How to Legally Check Him Out

Getting legal information about a person is as easy as calling information and asking for the number of a few agencies. For the most part, the information with which you will be provided will either be free or cost you a minimal amount. Considering what you're getting, it's well worth the investment. The following are a couple of places to start:

1. *Driving and automobile records*   Contact the Department of Motor Vehicles to obtain information about traffic tickets, unpaid fines, reckless or drunken driving charges, date and place of birth, and place of employment.

2. *Divorce records*   Contact the county hall of records in the county where your boyfriend's divorce took place for information about children; property owned

and disbursement of assets; allegations of physical, mental, or child abuse; past restraining orders; girlfriends named in a divorce; and financial information including debt and amount of alimony or child support owed.

Stay on Your Toes

I highly recommend the book *When In Doubt Check Him Out* by Joseph J. Culligan. This book is an incredible source of information about the subject of legally checking out a person, and it can save you a great deal of time, effort, and money.

The following are some other places to contact for help. They should be listed in your local phone book.

Social Security Administration

Child Support Enforcement

County records

State records

Federal records

Bankruptcy records

Workers' compensation records

Corporations and UCC filings

National Cemetery System

Federal Prison Locator Service

Birth and death records

Another way to have your friend checked out is to hire a private investigator (PI). A PI is not nearly as inexpensive as doing it yourself, but he or she will do an extremely thorough job. If you want it done right and can afford it, a private eye is the best way to go.

Get the Facts

At a minimum, make sure you know the following information about your boyfriend:

➤ His first, middle, and last name

➤ His drivers license number

➤ His social security number

➤ His date of birth

➤ His place of birth

➤ His vehicle's license plate number

➤ His home address

Bad Guys Beware!

Before getting married, find out how much debt your fiancé is carrying. You also need to find out whether he is being sued or has bill collectors on his tail.

Getting Out of Trouble

You're sitting in a car late one night with your date. You've told him goodbye several times now, but he insists that you stay and talk to him just a little longer. You finally become frustrated and start to open the car door, but he pushes the automatic lock button and prevents you from exiting. The next thing you know, he is crawling all over you and tearing your clothes. Do you fight back, scream, passively resist, or hope he comes to his senses? Or what about that ex-boyfriend who won't quit calling you? Hang-up after hang-up, day after day, at work, at home, and at your friends', the phone just keeps ringing.

When He Won't Go Away

Stalking is a huge problem in the United States and a dangerous one at that. Two types of stalkers are out there: the ones who know their targets and the ones who don't. This chapter only discusses stalkers who know their targets. For more information about stalkers, refer to Chapter 7, "Stalkers, Impersonators, and Other Weirdoes."

Two thirds of all stalkers are ex-boyfriends or ex-husbands. The best way to deal with an ex who won't go away is to get the police involved as well as family and friends, both yours and his. Be direct and tell him there's no chance that the two of you will ever get back together. Make sure he understands that your decision is final and take a friend if you see him in person. If he continues to bother you, keep a journal of every contact he makes with you. If he threatens you, write it down and report it to the police.

Date Rape

Statistics show that a high percentage of rapes are committed by acquaintances. It is for this very reason that you cannot let your guard down just because you know someone. The mental anguish that a woman has to deal with after this horrible ordeal is more than any human should ever have to go through. The emotional and psychological wounds caused by date rape can take an extremely long time to heal.

119

Stay on Your Toes

Most people are under the impression that rape is a sex crime. Rape actually is an act of violence. Sex is nothing more than the vehicle used by the attacker to vent his anger, frustration, and feelings of deprivation.

It's very important that, if your date begins to get out of line, you must correct him quickly. You need to assert yourself and be very polite but firm from the moment he makes you uncomfortable. Don't be polite when it comes to saying "No" the second time because it won't get you anywhere. If your date begins to get intimate prematurely, don't say "I think you need to slow down." Instead say "No, No, No. What do you think you're doing?" Your "No" must be firm, direct, and spoken with authority. When you say it, look him in the eye. This is no time to be polite or to worry about hurting his feelings.

If your date puts his hand on your knee and you don't like it, you might say, as a first warning, "Please don't touch me there." As a second warning, say, "Take your hand off of me" as you help him remove it. It's important for your date to know that you don't play around when it comes to these issues. Being forceful also is a good idea because a potential rapist will know that you are the type of woman who will fight back and press charges.

The following are some warning signs that should make you suspicious of the person you're dating:

➤ He stares at any attractive woman who walks near him.

➤ He talks disrespectfully about women.

➤ He can't talk to you without putting his hands on you.

➤ He becomes very pushy.

➤ He is very controlling.

➤ He has an anger problem.

➤ He doesn't handle being told "No" very well.

➤ He stares at your body when he thinks you're not looking.

This woman is handling an uncomfortable situation correctly—directly and with authority.

This is not the proper way to handle this situation.

Physically Defending Yourself

There's been a great deal of controversy over the years regarding whether a woman should fight back or passively comply during a rape. Statistics show that a woman who is being raped by an acquaintance and fights back has a much greater chance of surviving and getting away. Statistics also show that there's only a slight increase in injuries suffered by the women who choose to fight back. If you choose to physically resist, do whatever it takes. Now is not the time to fight clean.

Bad Guys Beware!

By being aware and watching how a guy acts around other women, you can save yourself a great deal of grief. A guy who is interested in dating you usually is going to be on his best behavior when you're around. It's when he thinks you're not watching that he's more likely to let his guard down and let his true colors show. This is when you need to pay the closest attention by observing his actions.

Life Savers

If you are being attacked or restrained by a man using a knife, grab the blade of the knife with your hand and squeeze tightly. Yes, this technique will probably cut your hand, but it can save your life! After you've grabbed the blade of the knife, you gain a strength advantage because of the additional leverage the length of the blade provides. The longer the blade, the greater leverage you have. This might give you enough of an advantage to pry the knife out of your attacker's hand. Either way, it's better to receive a cut on your hand than on an area of your body that can cost you your life.

Safety Alert!

Before calling the police, don't change your clothes, take a shower, or touch any of the evidence. This is going to be very important in proving your case and getting a conviction. I know it sounds like an impossible task, especially after going through such a horrible ordeal, but it's vital. Lack of evidence can make a conviction difficult to get.

If you ever find yourself in a situation in which you have to defend yourself, the following are some things you can do:

➤ If he tries to kiss you, bite his lip or mouth area very hard and then run.

➤ Throw a good kick, knee, or punch to the groin area. (This is one of the most sensitive areas on a man's body.)

➤ Use your fingers to poke his eyes and then run.

➤ If you have fingernails, use them to scratch his nose, groin, or throat area.

➤ If you're going to kick him, throw your kick to the groin or knee area. (Any higher than the groin area increases the likelihood that you will lose your balance and fall.)

➤ If he grabs you from behind, aggressively throw the back of your head into his face.

➤ Scream as loudly and as much as you can.

➤ Never give up.

After an Attack

If you've been raped, there are a few things you can do to prevent matters from getting worse. The first thing you should do is call the police and report the crime. Rape is one of the lowest-reported violent crimes in the United States because most women are ashamed or embarrassed. Remember that rape is never your fault. If you don't report it, you are letting the person who attacked you to go unpunished to victimize someone else. Even if you choose not to press charges, you still should report the crime so your attacker can be arrested and the incident documented.

It's very important that you see a physician specializing in rape cases immediately following an attack. This is one doctor's visit that cannot wait until the next day. The police will be able to refer you after you have filed your report.

The most important thing for you to do is surround yourself with friends and family who love you and will support you. The worst thing you can do is bottle it all up and keep it a secret. Not telling anyone will only make matters worse. Letting others help you is one of the hardest things you'll have to do, but it is by far the most crucial.

You also might want to consider attending a support group for people who have been victimized by rape. These groups usually are filled with loving people who can help you understand and deal with your pain because they also have experienced it. A support group can help heal in months what might take years or even a lifetime to heal on your own.

The Least You Need to Know

➤ Study a guy's character closely before letting him know you're interested.

➤ When meeting someone for the first time, be careful not to give away too much personal information.

➤ On a first date, meet somewhere with which you're both familiar and comfortable.

➤ On a first date, don't consume too much alcohol and don't give your date false impressions.

➤ A large percentage of rapes are committed by acquaintances. Don't let your guard down just because you're with someone you know.

➤ If you ever find yourself in a situation in which you must physically defend yourself, do whatever it takes to survive.

Chapter 11

Staying Safe On the College Campus

In This Chapter

➤ And you thought college was safe

➤ Everyday stuff

➤ Night life

➤ Campus crimes

You go to a college party off campus one night with hopes of unwinding, meeting new people, and having a little fun. You don't know anything about the students hosting the party, but you've heard that a lot of people are going to be there. When you arrive, things seem to be just as you expected. A lot of new faces, loud music, lots of alcohol, and rooms packed with so many people you can't move. What you didn't count on was having to physically defend yourself from a creep who had too much to drink, who wants to dance with you, and who won't take no for an answer. Unfortunately, everyone around you knows him and thinks it's funny—but no one knows who you are, and worse, they seem to think you're being a prude. He likes the attention he's getting from his friends so he becomes aggressive and begins fondling you. Before you know it, you're in tears and have to run out of the party. This situation could have turned out a lot worse, but it could have been prevented as well.

The problems affecting colleges and universities are just as real and just as big as everywhere else. Campus violence has skyrocketed over the years, and crimes against property seem to be more and more typical.

In this chapter, I'm first going to educate you about just how big the campus problem is, and then I'm going to show you what you can do about it. I'm going to discuss how to properly check out a college before committing. You'll also learn how to stay safe while enjoying the college night life, and you'll get some advice about dating as well. I'll walk you through the everyday stuff such as living in the dormitory, walking around campus, and avoiding the bad crowd that always seems to be getting into trouble. I'll finish the chapter with an overview of the different types of crimes that are popular and how to avoid being victimized by them.

And You Thought College Was Safe

The safety record of a school should be just as high on your priority list as academics and reputation. College can be a pleasurable experience, but the same precautions must be taken here that are taken anywhere else. Don't think that, just because you're not looking for trouble, it won't find you. Being prepared for whatever comes your way is the key to survival—whether you're taking a walk on campus or shopping at your local grocery store. You can stay safe at school and have fun in the process, but you've got to do your homework first.

Street Talk

Colleges usually offer undergraduate studies such as two- and four-year degrees. If you want to work toward a master's degree or higher, you usually have to attend a **university.**

Why College Crime Is on the Rise

The following is a list of reasons why college crime is on the rise:

➤ The average student age is 18–22, which is a problem in itself due to the maturity level it represents.

➤ The majority of full-time students never have lived away from home before. This means it's the first time a lot of students have been free to do as they choose without much adult supervision.

➤ Alcohol is used frequently and in excess.

➤ Curfews are rarely imposed, and when they are, they're difficult to enforce.

➤ There is a high number of students walking alone at night.

➤ Students have few restrictions imposed on them.

➤ Many college campuses aren't heavily patrolled by security or the police.

➤ Safety is not a high priority for most students.

➤ There are an enormous amount of nighttime social activities. This frequently leads to rowdiness and misconduct.

➤ Dormitory security isn't taken seriously by most students.

Doing Your Other Homework

Before choosing a college, it's vitally important that you do some research. When looking at colleges, most people look at everything in detail except safety. Sure, they get an idea when they visit the campus about whether it feels safe, but the investigation usually stops there. Don't be fooled—looks can be deceiving!

According to J. J. Bittenbinder's book *Tough Target,* a family lost their daughter to a violent murder while she was living on campus. They specifically chose the school she was attending because it looked and felt safe, but they didn't know that 38 violent crimes had taken place there in just a three-year period of time. This is a prime example of why it is so important to do some deeper checking.

Stay on Your Toes

Thanks to some college safety support groups, you now have better access to campus crime histories. If you go to the admissions office of a college and request a copy of the crime report, the law states that they must provide it.

The following are some suggestions to help you check out a potential college thoroughly:

➤ Try to hang around long enough to walk the campus once at night. Is the campus well lit?

➤ Find out how many full-time security officers the college has on staff.

➤ Take a close look at the surrounding area. What is the prevailing attitude of locals toward the students? Are the surrounding neighborhoods relatively safe?

➤ Ask a few students for their opinions about these matters.

Everyday Stuff

Whether you live in a dormitory or off campus, you need to know about things such as parking lots, walking at night, and riding your bike. This section discusses what you need to know when you're minding your own business, when taking care of everyday affairs, and most importantly, when you least expect trouble.

The Dormitory

Before you start looking into colleges, here are some reasons why dormitories can be the safest place on campus:

➤ Most dorms are very well lit.

➤ Most dorms have sturdy entry doors and strong locks.

➤ Dormitories usually are occupied by many people at any given time.

➤ The rooms usually are close together and have individual locks on the doors.

➤ Almost everyone has a roommate.

➤ Most rooms have a window and, in many cases, a telephone.

Although all these things go a long way toward creating a safe environment, students still have to do their part. It's when students neglect their responsibilities in this area that things go down hill. It doesn't matter how safe an environment is to begin with, if people don't take their safety seriously, positive results cannot be expected. How effective is a lock if it's not used? How effective is a light if it's turned off? How effective is a hall monitor if he doesn't want to seem like a snitch?

Safety Alert!

Students have gone out of their way to keep dormitory doors unlocked, and other students have been victimized as a result. Taking a door that's supposed to be locked and propping it open with a pizza box might seem like a harmless way to sneak your friends in after hours, but it's actually a dangerous practice that can get someone seriously injured (or worse). Keep dormitory doors locked at all times. This means all doors, including side and rear access doors.

Securing Your Dorm

Most dorms already have policies implemented that relate to student safety, but this is not always enough. The following are some things you can do to make sure your dorm stays safe:

➤ Keep doors locked at all times.

➤ If you see someone you don't recognize entering the dorm, challenge the person by asking questions.

➤ Have a sign-in sheet for any guests who visit the dorm after normal hours. (This usually falls under the responsibility of the dorm resident advisor or monitor.)

➤ Make sure all windows remain locked.

➤ Don't hesitate to report someone who violates dorm policies.

If your college is in a high-crime area, it might be a good idea for students to go before the school board and make a request for a security camera to be installed in the entryway of your dorm. You also can request that an alarm be installed that sounds whenever a door is used that's not supposed to be such as an emergency exit door. College authorities might prove to be surprisingly resistant at first to these types of changes, so be prepared and don't give up easily. Your safety is worth the extra effort.

Living Off Campus

Imagine living in a large house off campus that you share with five other roommates. After a long day of classes, you return home to find that your house has been robbed. Everything you've ever owned of value was kept in your bedroom and now it's gone. With five roommates, people are always coming and going. It seemed like someone was always home, so it didn't seem necessary to lock the front door. Your street is filled with other college students and everyone knows everyone, so how could something like this happen? To make matters worse, your house was robbed in broad daylight.

Stay on Your Toes

If you're living off campus, you need to practice the same precautions you would if you lived anywhere else. Protecting your home is such a broad subject that I wrote an entire chapter on it. If you want to know how to stay safe while living off campus, see Chapter 13, "Fortifying Your Castle."

Getting Around Campus

Because many students don't have automobiles and because parking often is scarce for those who do, walking usually is the name of the college game. If you have to do a lot of walking, the best thing you can do is walk with a buddy. Having a friend with you probably is the best crime deterrent when on foot. Most criminals aren't very excited about messing with more than one person at a time because it makes it more likely that they'll get hurt or caught. If you can't walk with a friend, be sure to travel in well populated or high traffic areas. Stay away from short cuts and rabbit trails.

Safety Alert!

If you ever have to walk alone at night on campus, I strongly recommend that you carry mace with you. Learn how to use it properly and keep it in your hand ready to use. Otherwise, it will be useless to you. Mace can save your life and, if visible, is an excellent deterrent to crime.

If you're a bike rider, make sure to lock it up when you're not riding it. Unlocked bikes don't hang around too long, so secure it even when you're only going to be away for a moment. Take the same precautions you would when walking. Stay near high-traffic areas and avoid shortcuts. If taking a safer route means taking five minutes longer to get there, that's okay. Avoid riding past groups of suspicious people. Just go around them and stay out of arm's reach. The advantage of being on a bike is that you can outpace anyone on foot (assuming you're not in horrible shape).

Night Life

As you know, most crime occurs at night. This means that you should never be out walking alone, especially in questionable areas. If you're taking night classes and have to be out late, find the safest route possible and always take it, even if it's not the quickest. Get into the habit of calling someone and checking in when you arrive home every night. This way, if something happens and you don't call, you've got friends looking for you.

College campuses have been known to host their share of evening activities, and finding something to do on a Friday night usually isn't very difficult. Although most of these social events are harmless, the alcohol and drugs that might be present are a different story. Whether going to a party, a college pub, or out on a date, you need to be careful and keep your sense about you. There's nothing wrong with taking some time to unwind and having a little fun now and then, but you need to be aware of the risks involved.

Alcohol and Drugs

When it comes to college crimes such as violence and rape, drugs or alcohol often factor into the picture in one way or another. In 75 percent of all sexual assault and rape cases, for example, the attacker had been drinking alcohol. To make matters worse, more than 50 percent of the victims of these crimes also had been drinking. This means that, in many cases, both the attacker and the victim had been drinking.

These statistics prove the importance of moderation and of staying away from people who drink in excess. Alcohol makes people do things they wouldn't normally do, but the alcohol can't be blamed for a mistake. The blame falls on the person who chooses to use alcohol irresponsibly. When you get drunk, what you're really doing is surrendering control and giving up your right to make good decisions.

Keep in mind that drugs are illegal. This means it is against the law to use them or to have them in your possession. If you are with someone or are considering going out with a person who does drugs, you're asking for trouble. A person who has no respect or fear for the law in one area of his or her life is likely to have little regard for the law in other areas as well. In addition, drugs can make a person's behavior unpredictable. Protect yourself by avoiding people who use drugs.

Stay on Your Toes

Unfortunately, victims of rape who were under the influence of alcohol at the time often suffer a weakened court case as a result.

Parties and Bars

College parties are known for running into the wee hours of the morning and for having greater quantities of alcohol than the local convenience store. Regardless of whether you'll be attending a bar or a party for the evening, there are a few things you should practice to help keep you out of trouble:

➤ Go with a friend.

➤ Don't leave with a stranger. (Yes, those cool people you just met count as strangers.)

➤ Never drive if you've been drinking.

➤ Keep an eye out for your friend and make sure he or she is looking out for you.

➤ Don't be one of the last ones to leave.

➤ Don't drink to the point that you can no longer make wise decisions or can't physically defend yourself (if you're slurring or staggering, this is the case).

➤ Do not crash at the party location.

➤ Leave with the person you came with.

Students to Avoid

Most schools are filled with ordinary students who are attempting to find themselves and create a path for their future like everyone else. Some are shy; others are more outgoing. For the most part, everyone is just interested in earning their degree and getting on their way. Troublemakers do exist, however, who go to college with different, less admirable motives.

Bad Guys Beware!

Don't accept a drink from someone you hardly know unless you watched the person pour it. In addition, it's important that you always keep an eye on your drink and never leave it unattended. Putting drugs in a woman's drink is an increasingly common practice among college males.

131

The following are some traits common in a troublemaker:

➤ Skips classes

➤ Fails classes

➤ Drinks alcohol excessively or takes drugs

➤ Is rebellious toward authority

➤ Lies, cheats, or steals

➤ Has an anger problem

➤ Has a bad attitude

➤ Has a reputation for being rowdy

➤ Has little concern for others

Campus Crimes

Two of the most common crimes committed on college campuses are theft and date rape. Because these crimes are discussed in detail in other chapters, I am only going to briefly review them here. Each of the following sections contains a common scenario followed by some simple preventative medicine.

Safety Alert!

Theft is a crime of opportunity. Many victims of theft claim they only turned their head for a moment. Don't leave valuables unattended in a public place! Leaving your child in the car while you go inside to pay for your gas, leaving your car running in the driveway while you're waiting for it to warm up in the morning, and leaving your purse in the grocery cart while you shop for an item are all examples of terrible ideas. Guard your valuables and don't take chances.

Theft

While studying at the college library, you leave your backpack on the table where you're sitting while you look for a book nearby. You stay close to your table and peek around the corner to check on it from time to time. You might think, who would steal someone's backpack from a place with so many people watching? Inside the backpack you have your books, term papers, checkbook, student ID, dorm key, calling card, and enough cash to get you through the week. One minute later, you look around the corner to find that your backpack is gone. Sixty seconds was all the thief needed to ruin the rest of your week. Now you have to get a new dorm key, call the bank and cancel checks, get a new student ID, explain to your professors why you don't have your assignments ready to turn in, cancel your calling card, buy new books, and possibly borrow some money.

All of this could have been prevented by taking your backpack with you when you left the table. Theft is one of the easiest crimes on campus to guard against. If you don't, however, it can catch you off guard in a matter of seconds.

Date Rape

You agree to go on a date with a guy because he seems really nice and has been persistent about asking you out. You met him in one of your classes, but you don't know that much about him except his name, what he's majoring in, and where he's from. Saturday night he picks you up at your dorm and drives you to a party that some friends of his are throwing. You don't know anyone there. The date seems to be going fine, but you notice that he encourages you to drink more alcohol than you're comfortable with. You keep telling him you don't want anymore, but he is politely persistent as he continues to freshen your drink. When leaving, you notice that he's slurring a little and suspect he's had too much to drink, but you don't say anything about it as he opens your car door in preparation to drive you home. When you arrive, he asks you if he can come in, but you say no. He continues to press the issue but you don't give in. Finally, he reaches over and becomes physically aggressive with you. Within minutes, you have become the victim of date rape.

Stay on Your Toes

In J. J. Bittenbinder's book *Tough Target,* he says "A study sponsored by the Association of American Colleges Project indicates that members of closely knit, all-male groups such as fraternities and athletic teams are involved in a disproportionate number of rapes, especially those committed by a group. They can be encouraged to prove their sexual prowess to the other members of the group. This results in these guys participating in a group rape when they might never commit rape alone."

The following are several feelings that, if acted on, can prevent situations like this from happening:

➤ "I should have met him somewhere I was both comfortable and familiar with."

➤ "I should have noticed he was very persistent from the moment I met him, and I should have been extra cautious as a result."

➤ "I shouldn't have allowed him to take me home on the first date."

➤ "I shouldn't have allowed him to take me to a frat party on the first date."

➤ "I should have left early when I noticed his persistence in trying to get me to drink more alcohol than I was comfortable with."

➤ "I shouldn't have gotten in the vehicle with him after I suspected he had had too much to drink."

I hope I haven't given you the wrong idea about college life. College can be a lot of fun, and many people will tell you that some of their best memories are from their school days. My goal is to make sure it gets logged as one of your best memories, too. College is a time for learning, growing, maturing, friendships, and laughs. By taking this chapter to heart, you will be doing a lot to make sure that's exactly what you get. This can be a great time to develop habits relating to your safety that you can carry with you for the rest of your life.

The Least You Need to Know

➤ When deciding which college to attend, carefully check out the college's crime rate including the surrounding area.

➤ Dorms can only be as safe as you are responsible.

➤ When walking on campus, don't take shortcuts, stay on well-traveled paths, and never walk alone at night.

➤ Get into the habit of carrying mace with you.

➤ If you're living off campus, follow the same guidelines for safety as you would if you had your own home.

➤ Alcohol is involved in the majority of all crimes that take place on campus.

Chapter 12

Dealing with Violence in the Workplace

In This Chapter

➤ Defining workplace violence

➤ What can you do?

➤ What can your company do?

While at work one afternoon, a man overhears a co-worker yelling at someone on the telephone. He hears his co-worker say with anger, "I am so sick of this place. I feel like taking a gun and killing myself." The man decides not to do anything about the incident because he doesn't feel like it's any of his business. He figures the man is just frustrated and is blowing off some steam. A few hours later, the man overheard making the suicidal threat walks into his boss's office and opens fire with a shotgun. After killing his boss and wounding two other employees, he turns the gun on himself and takes his own life.

Is there anything you can do to protect yourself when an angry co-worker turns violent? The answer is yes, but you need to be prepared in advance.

In this chapter, I will define what workplace violence is and will teach you how to spot it in advance. You'll learn how to legally deal with someone who has threatened you or who makes you feel uncomfortable. I'll also discuss preventative measures that can be implemented to reduce the risk of a problem ever occurring.

Defining Workplace Violence

So what exactly is workplace violence? Workplace violence can range from damaging company property to murder. It's true that there are several different levels of workplace violence, but they all should be taken seriously.

How Bad Is the Problem?

Workplace violence now has edged out accidents and natural causes as the leading cause of death in the workplace. To make matters worse, a lot of companies in the United States have not yet implemented a plan to help deal with this growing problem.

The homicide rate in the workplace has more than doubled in the past 10 years, making it the fastest growing form of murder in America. If a person gets angry at work, he or she is two to three times more likely to become violent than if he or she were using alcohol or drugs. Now that's a scary statistic!

Who Is Responsible?

So who's responsible for all this violence? Shockingly enough, in the vast majority of all workplace-related homicides, the killer's profile is the same. These crimes are committed primarily by men who fit the following description:

➤ A loner

➤ A jealous lover or an angry spouse of an employee

➤ Someone with a history of sexual harassment

What Can You Do?

You are more likely to spot warning signs in advance if you become more aware of your surroundings. This is the key to avoiding trouble down the road.

Stay on Your Toes

It is now estimated that companies are losing more than $4 billion each year in lawsuits filed by victims of workplace violence and their families.

Spotting the Warning Signs

The following behavioral patterns are common among workplace offenders and can be early warning signs of violence. You might have a potential problem if you notice that a co-worker or employee does any of the following:

➤ Makes others aware that he or she has access to firearms

➤ Is easily angered

➤ Tends to question the motives of others

➤ Has never held a job for long

➤ Has poor work habits

➤ Is bitter or vengeful

➤ Has a tendency to be violent outside the workplace

➤ Has a problem with alcohol or drugs

➤ Is very insecure

➤ Is irresponsible

➤ Blames others for his or her problems

➤ Is extremely defensive

➤ Has very few friends and is socially isolated

Let's face it. All of us deal with a few of these traits every once in a while. It's when a person shows several of these warning signs at once that you need to look at the situation more closely and consider taking action.

Being Aware

As discussed in Chapter 3, "The Golden Rules of Survival," awareness is extremely crucial to both crime prevention and crime survival, and it should be the cornerstone to every safety plan.

The good news about awareness is that it doesn't require any time or money. It does, however, have the capability to save your life. Awareness is like an internal watchdog that's looking out for your safety at all times. It's a decision you make to start paying closer attention to your surroundings. Awareness is making use of all five senses all the time. Imagine awareness as a small muscle. The more you exercise it, the bigger, stronger, and more natural it becomes. Your goal should be to get to

Bad Guys Beware!

To truly be aware of what's going on around you, you must begin to use all five senses: sight, hearing, touch, smell, and taste. It's also vital that you learn to use your sixth sense, which is another term for instinct.

where you no longer have to think about being aware (kind of like breathing or swallowing).

To help develop awareness, begin by practicing the little things. The next time you hear birds singing, for example, try to distinguish how many birds there are. When you're sitting in your car at a traffic light, look at the people in the vehicles around you. How many drivers are talking on a cell phone, smoking a cigarette, playing with the radio, or traveling with a child? The next time you're at the mall, look to see how many women are carrying their purse correctly or try to figure out in which pocket a man is carrying his wallet. Being aware just means getting into the habit of paying attention to the little things. Within a matter of time, it will become second nature to you.

Threats

When an employee publicly or anonymously threatens to do someone or something harm, you have a problem on your hands. This might be done verbally, electronically, physically, with a note, and so on. All threats should be taken seriously and should be reported, regardless of how trivial they might seem at the time.

When reporting a threat or incident directed toward you, start with your supervisor and give him or her a fair opportunity to resolve the problem. If your supervisor chooses to ignore the problem, don't be afraid to continue climbing the chain of command until you get the type of results for which the situation calls. Remember, we're talking about your safety here. Likewise, if you witness an employee threatening another employee, report the matter to your supervisor.

If You Spot a Problem

If someone at work behaves strangely or out of character, look further. An employee crying at his or her desk, a client making threats to hurt someone, or two co-workers challenging one another to a fight all are a big deal. These types of situations should not be taken lightly and cannot be ignored.

Stay on Your Toes

Taking the time to investigate any potential problems is the key to preventing the situation from going too far. If a problem is revealed after learning the circumstances surrounding the situation, immediate action must be taken.

Let's say you notice a co-worker crying in the women's restroom and sitting in the corner on the floor. This is something that should be considered out of the norm, and it needs to be investigated further. There are several things you can do in a situation like this, but ignoring it is not recommended. This might be a warning sign for a future violent act in the workplace, or it might be nothing at all. You won't know, however, unless you look into the matter further.

In this scenario, I suggest that you ask the woman what the problem is and if there's anything you can do to help. If she doesn't want to confide in you, make it a point to observe her behavior for the next couple of days to see if things improve. If the situation doesn't improve, you should discuss the situation with a supervisor—in private, of course. Something else you can do is talk to someone at work who knows her personally and see if that person can provide any helpful information. Remember that your goal is not to spread gossip or slander but to investigate the situation and be aware of any potential problems that might occur as a result of her emotional distress.

When to Take Action

If you investigate a minor situation and it turns out to be someone just having a bad day, no harm is done. Remember, though, with any business, the eyes and ears of the company are the general workforce. It's important that everyone takes responsibility in speaking up about worrisome behavior. In some situations, there is no time to investigate the problem further, and action needs to be taken immediately. If you notice an employee carrying a gun on company property, for example, or if a threatening incident is directed toward you, don't wait. Report it to your supervisor immediately. It's up to you to decide the best action to take for each incident, but whatever you do, take action. Warning signs are worthless unless acted upon.

Bad Guys Beware!

An employee crying in the restroom and an employee carrying a gun to work cannot be handled the same way. This is why you must use wisdom in deciding when to investigate the situation further and when to report the incident immediately. Here's a good rule of thumb: if you believe there's a chance that the situation could eventually lead to violent behavior, report it immediately. When in doubt, report it!

Disciplinary Action and Employee Assistance

Let's say that, after investigating an incident at work carefully, you determine that an employee was at fault. If so, disciplinary action might be appropriate. If the spouse of an employee or a client was at fault, you might need to get the police involved. It's not a good idea to give a mere slap on the wrist to an employee caught bringing a gun to work. (This person should be terminated from employment.)

In some cases, counseling might be the best way to resolve the problem. If a woman is crying at work because her spouse physically abused her the night before, for example, she probably would benefit from professional counseling and support.

Documentation

Another important workplace practice is keeping good documentation. Write down as many details as you can, such as

➤ Dates and times

➤ The people involved

➤ The words exchanged

➤ Any specific acts of violence

➤ Any threatening comments

Even relatively small incidents need to be documented properly. Be sure to write down what actions were taken and what the outcome was.

Stay on Your Toes

Proper documentation will prove to be invaluable in the event of an employee's termination. It also helps keep management informed of what's going on, which is a crucial part of prevention.

Putting It All Together

The following is a simple summary of steps to take in preventing and dealing with workplace violence:

➤ Look for warning signs.

➤ Take the situation seriously, regardless of how small it might appear.

➤ Investigate the matter until you have clear answers about what the problem is and why the incident occurred.

➤ Determine what must be done to prevent the problem from happening again. This might involve talking with a superior.

➤ If the incident was directed at you, report what happened by following the chain of command until you get results.

➤ Determine whether an employee was at fault.

➤ Discipline the offender if appropriate.

➤ Assist employees in getting professional counseling if appropriate.

➤ Remember to document everything in detail and keep it on file.

What Can Your Company Do?

According to the Occupational Safety and Health Administration (OSHA), every company has a responsibility to its employees to provide a safe and healthful work environment. In fact, OSHA believes this to be a company's duty. This means you have a right to speak up about these issues. Most adults spend the majority of each day at work, and they are entitled to spend this time in a safe environment without having to worry about a disgruntled employee.

Hiring Practices

The interview process should be handled with care. It's important to look beyond experience or education level and to pay attention to personality traits as well. Although you are very limited in the types of questions you can ask an interviewee, especially questions of a personal nature, you can pay close attention to behavior and personality traits. Also look for the warning characteristics previously mentioned in this chapter.

Street Talk

According to Webster's dictionary, to **disgruntle** means "to make peevishly discontented; displease and make sulky."

The following a list of things to do when in the process of hiring someone:

➤ Have him or her fill out an employee application.

➤ Call previous employers for referrals.

➤ Take the time to inquire about his or her personal interests.

➤ Ask him or her to about future goals.

➤ Ask for personal references.

➤ Do a background check for any criminal record.

➤ Request a resumé.

➤ If you hire the person, instill a probationary period so the employee can be properly evaluated before making your final decision. Most companies treat the first three to six months of employment as probationary.

Stay on Your Toes

An important rule for employers to remember is that any question you ask an applicant can be asked only out of strict business necessity. How the question is asked is very important as well. All questions asked must be directly related to the position for which the person is applying.

Training

If a company is truly serious about reducing workplace violence, quality training must be implemented. A company with a well-trained staff that is prepared for this sort of thing is the best preventative medicine money can buy.

There are several ways to go about getting the proper training, and it doesn't have to be expensive. You can do the following:

➤ Hire a consultant to come in and train management.

➤ Hire a consultant to come in and train employees.

➤ Send a capable employee out to be properly trained and then have him or her train others within the company.

➤ Educate yourself and your employees by purchasing workbooks, videos, and a list of recommended policies and procedures from a reputable source.

Evaluations

Company evaluations are an important ingredient for the success of any good safety plan. They enables a business to keep a finger on the pulse of its employees without jeopardizing company morale.

Three types of employee evaluations are effective, and they each have pros and cons. The following list contains each type along with one positive and one negative attribute:

➤ *Employees evaluating employees*
Positive: If a company has a loose cannon running around, a co-worker more than likely will be the first one to know.
Negative: Employees might be fearful about "tattling" on co-workers because of threats that have been made.

➤ *Management evaluating employees*
Positive: This gives management a firsthand look at what's going on within the company, and it helps them better connect with employees.
Negative: Most employees will guard their words for fear of looking bad in front of management. In addition, some employees are intimidated by their superiors and will not be able to answer questions effectively as a result.

➤ *An outside source hired to evaluate employees*
Positive: The hired evaluator is more likely to remain unbiased and impartial about whatever he or she learns.
Negative: Depending on how many employees a company has, this method could end up costing a great deal of money.

Whichever method you choose, remember that, for evaluations to be truly effective, they need to be conducted at regular intervals. If company policy states that every employee must be evaluated twice a year, for example, follow through by making sure it happens. Formal evaluations can act as a deterrent to threats or violent behavior. An employee probably will think twice about threatening or harassing a co-worker if he or she knows an evaluation is only a month away.

Bad Guys Beware!

Every company should have a policy that protects employees when they provide information about co-workers. Employees are much less likely to step forward with information if they think it will jeopardize them in some way.

Following Through

No matter how strong your policies toward workplace violence are, if you don't enforce them, they won't work. Whatever you decide to do must be followed through until the last step has been taken. Your plan must be consistent, must be fair for everyone involved, and can't fluctuate between employees.

If you create a company policy that any employee who carries a firearm on company property will be terminated, there is no room for compromise. If an employee breaks this policy, he or she must be terminated. If you don't follow through on these issues, your policies will not be taken seriously and will be rendered ineffective. Not only does this weaken your overall plan, some employees might construe your inconsistency as discrimination. Therefore, be sure to be consistent and fair in your follow-up of company policies.

Dangerous Occupations

Here's a little workplace trivia. The following list of the most dangerous occupations in America was taken from *The World's Most Dangerous Places* by Robert Young Pelton (published in 1997).

#1 Truck driver

#2 Farm worker

#3 Sales supervisor/proprietor

#4 Construction worker

#5 Police detective

#6 Airplane pilot

#7 Security guard

#8 Taxicab driver

#9 Timber cutter

#10 Cashier

#11 Fisherman

#12 Metal worker

#13 Roofer

#14 Firefighter

The Least You Need to Know

➤ Potentially violent behavior in the workplace must be taken extremely seriously.

➤ Learning to identify early warning signs and taking action are crucial steps for stopping violence in advance.

➤ Whatever policies your company implements regarding this issue, the level of follow-through will determine their success or failure.

➤ Quality training is essential to your company's success in combating violence in the workplace.

Part 3

Home Sweet Home

There was a time not so long ago that it was safe to leave your windows open at night and never lock your front door. You know the "I remember when … " stories. Unless you want to be the lead character in a "Once upon a time … " story, however, you need to do more today than lock your doors. Safety even has a role in where you plant your shrubs and bushes. Learn tips from the pros that make your house or apartment look occupied when you're gone. Learn how to use alarms and dogs and how to team up with neighbors to watch out for each other.

Not all entrances to our homes hang on hinges. The telephone is a vital tool we take for granted, but it can be used to invade your privacy, to harass you, and to rob you. The Internet puts the world at our fingertips. International communication, amazing sources of information, and almost-instant access to news around the world are available to the average person. The door swings both ways, however. If misused, this same technology can invade your home and cause serious damage.

Home should be a haven, the safest place to relax and be yourself. What do you do when home becomes the most dangerous place in your life? Learn the warning signs for abuse. Learn how to leave an abusive home, what to take with you, and where to get help. There are no fairy tale fix-its for life's real problems, but home can be a place where you can confidently place a doormat that says "Welcome."

Fortifying Your Castle

In This Chapter

➤ The exterior

➤ The interior

➤ Going one step further

A criminal sneaks up to your house in the middle of the night with the intention of breaking in and robbing you and your family at gunpoint. As the criminal approaches the front door, your dog begins barking loudly, your alarm goes off, and your exterior lights come on automatically because they're equipped with motion detectors. The criminal flees on foot but is caught by the police minutes later. They already were en route to your house because they were called by the company monitoring your alarm.

Whether it's trimming back a few bushes or installing $1 locks on all your windows, a little can go a long way toward keeping you and your family safe. For only a little money and a minimal amount of effort, you can safeguard your home like the pros and can sleep well at night knowing you have substantially reduced the chances of being the victim of a crime in the home.

In this chapter, I'm going to take a virtual stroll around the outside of your house to inspect it for safety. I'll show you how to check out your lighting, gates, fences, and shrubs. We'll then go inside to conduct a protection inspection for everything from doors to windows to alarms.

The Exterior

The majority of all residential crimes are committed by young people with little or no experience. (The professional cat burglar usually targets the extremely wealthy and plans his or her crime months in advance.) The novice checks out a house and, based on what he or she sees from the outside, decides whether it's worth breaking into. This is why the exterior of your home is so important. A neglected home is a likely target, but a well-lit, well-kept home is a deterrent to crime.

Making It Look Occupied

Making your home look occupied is important because criminals usually target houses where nobody's home. Most criminals don't want to contend with an angry or frightened homeowner because it increases their chances of being shot or of being caught and convicted.

The following are some things you can do to make your home look occupied even if it isn't. Keep in mind that some of these tips only apply to prolonged absences or vacations.

➤ Keep the stereo or television set on loud enough to hear from outside the front or back door.

➤ Have a trusted neighbor pick up your newspapers and mail.

➤ Don't leave notes on your door.

Bad Guys Beware!

Keep your windows covered so people walking by your house or driving down your street can't see inside. Being able to see inside your house gives criminals an idea as to whether someone is home and enables them to preview your merchandise in advance. Keep electronics such as TVs, stereos, and computers away from windows. These items are favorites for thieves because they are easy to sell.

➤ Arrange for lawn care.

➤ If you live in a small city or town, notify your police department that you're going to be away and ask them to send a patrol car by your house daily. (Unfortunately, this isn't practical advice if you live in a large city.)

➤ Inform trusted neighbors that you are going to be away and ask them to keep a watchful eye on your home.

➤ Leave a few lights on that can be seen from the street.

➤ Make sure porch lights always are on during hours of darkness. (It is best if the lights are switched on and off automatically by an electronic timer. This does a better job of giving the impression that someone is home.)

➤ Keep your garage door shut at all times.

I know that leaving lights or electronics on when you're away is not very energy effi-cient, but if you look at the trouble it's capable of preventing, you'll see that it's a wise investment. If you add it up, it's the most inexpensive alarm system money can buy.

Outdoor Lighting

Outdoor lighting is very important for a couple of reasons. First, it makes your house less vulnerable to nighttime burglaries. Second, good lighting makes it easier for you to find your keys, unlock your door, and get into your house as quickly as possible.

When choosing outdoor lighting, look for the kind with built-in motion sensors. Not only do motion sensors save electricity, they startle people who aren't expecting them. (Imagine a burglar sneaking up to your house in the middle of the night and then being surprised by a several-hundred-watt halogen lamp clicking on right above him or her. Trust me, the person's going to run.) When a light with a motion sensor turns on, there's no way to determine whether it came on by itself or was turned on with a switch.

Another type of light you might consider buying is the kind with electric timers. These automatically turn themselves on and off at the same time every day. (You can set the timer for what's best for you.) Be sure to position your lights for safety first and for appearance second. Having a house lit up at night adds to its appearance, but if the lights aren't positioned correctly, you've done nothing to deter crime. As a gen-eral rule, you should have clear illumination outward away from your house for at least 50 feet. You also should light up the main entry doors to your house, the front of the garage, and the sidewalk leading up to your front door if possible. Quality exte-rior lighting is fairly inexpensive and is one of the best investments you can make to safeguard your home and to create a deterrent to burglary.

Stay on Your Toes

If you have a fuse box or an electrical box on the outside of your house and it is not secured with a lock, criminals can cut the wires, which will turn off your lights. Secure these boxes!

Fences

If you're thinking about putting up a fence around your house, remember that, in terms of crime, the higher the fence the better. High fences are difficult to see over and are hard to climb, especially in a hurry and with your hands full. Fence gates should be left shut and latched. If you're going to be gone for several days, it's a good idea to put a padlock on your gate. While you're at it, lock up your shed. Outdoor sheds are red-hot targets because they're used to store lawnmowers and bikes and usually are left unlocked.

Shrubbery and Bushes

Shrubbery and bushes can go a long way toward making a yard look beautiful, but they also can make your home a more likely target. There are two things you need to keep in mind when it comes to greenery. First, make sure your vision isn't hindered when looking out the windows in your house. When you look outside, you need to see outside, not the backside of a six-foot plant. If you hear a noise or become suspicious, it's important for you to be able to look out your windows and check things out without going outside to do so. Your neighbor also will appreciate it if you can see whether anyone is breaking into his or her house.

The second thing you need to be careful about is making sure your foliage doesn't provide a nice hiding place or form of cover for a potential criminal. This holds especially true for bushes located next to the front, back, or garage door. You don't want someone to jump out from behind a bush and push you inside when you're entering your home.

This criminal does not have adequate cover to hide because the bushes are trimmed back properly.

Basement Windows

If your house has a basement, it probably has basement windows as well. These need to be locked and secured very tightly because they make perfect entryways for a criminal. He or she can lay down unnoticed, kick out the window, and crawl through the opening very easily. From the basement, the criminal can walk up the steps and into your home with little effort. This is why it also is important to keep the door leading into the house from the basement deadbolted at all times.

The Interior

As with the exterior, safeguarding the interior of your home is a must and can be accomplished by making only small investments of time and money.

The purpose for properly securing these areas is for protection in the event that a criminal has targeted your house. A dead bolt on your front door and a latch on your window usually are the only two things standing between the bad guy and you. Because these items could very well be your last line of defense, they need to be taken seriously.

Doors

How important is securing your doors properly? In the majority of all burglaries, the criminal gains entry into the home by kicking in the front door. The five things you need to remember when it comes to securing your doors are door quality, primary locks, secondary locks, hinges, and peepholes.

Door Quality: All entry doors to your home should be solid. Hollow doors or glass doors should never be used. It's too easy to break glass and to reach through to unlock the door. Hollow doors are so weak that they can be punched through with a fist. When it comes to choosing entry doors for your home, spend the extra money on something solid.

If you're going to use a solid wooden door, make sure it is at least 1 3/4" thick. If you really want

Safety Alert!

If you live in a two-story house and have trees near your home, keep the branches well trimmed. A tree near a house acts the same way as a ladder for helping someone get onto the second floor. Criminals know that most people don't lock their second-story windows.

Bad Guys Beware!

Never hide a spare house key in an obvious place like under the front doormat, under the flowerpot, over the door, under a rock, or anywhere else a criminal might look. If you do decide to hide a house key, be sure your neighbors can't see where it is.

something durable, buy a metal door with a metal core. Check your door frames to make sure they are sturdy and durable. The frame usually is the first thing to give when violent force is applied.

Primary Locks: Make sure all your entry doors have deadbolt locks installed. Even more important than the dead bolt, though, is the strike plate. What good is it to have a 1" dead bolt lock if there are tiny little screws going through the strike plate? When a door is kicked in, it's very rare that the dead bolt is ever broken. Instead, the strike plate is ripped away from the door frame due to inadequate hardware. Use strong screws for the strike plate that are a minimum of 1" in length.

If you choose to use multiple locks on any of your exterior doors, be sure to place the locks at least one foot apart from each other. By doing this, you maximize their over-all effectiveness. When the door locks are all concentrated in one small area, it makes it easier to focus on that area. When locks are spread apart from each other, however, it makes it very difficult for a burglar to strike multiple areas at one time.

Secondary Locks: Every door should be equipped with a latch or a chain in addition to a deadbolt lock. These help prevent the criminal from being able to push his or her way in after the door has been opened.

Stay on Your Toes

Latches and chains can't be picked or manipulated with a credit card. This makes them a great second line of defense.

Hinges: The main thing you need to know about door hinges is that they must not be accessible from the outside. Accessible hinges make it very easy for a criminal to remove the pins and then remove your door. Also make sure they are mounted to the frame with long screws of high quality.

Peepholes: Peepholes are a great investment and can be purchased for as little as $10. Having a peephole enables you to identify the person at the door before deciding whether to open it. The best kind of peephole is one that enables you to see things at a wide angle instead of only what's in front of you.

Sliding Glass Doors: If your home is equipped with sliding glass doors, don't rely on the standard locks that come with them. I recommend that you wedge something between the door and the frame such as a cut broomstick handle or a store-bought, metal brace. Also make sure your sliding glass doors can't be lifted off their tracks.

Windows

When it comes to the windows in your house, it's important to keep them locked at all times. What good does it do you to always lock your doors but to have a window that can easily be opened and crawled through? Burglars typically walk the perimeter of your home and check to see if any windows are unlocked. This is why they must be secured at all times. Choose locks that cannot be manipulated from the outside and that are durable enough to withstand a great deal of external force. Keep in mind that there are as many types of locks as there are windows and shop carefully.

Safety Alert!

Some people choose to permanently lock down their windows with either screws or nails. If you choose to go this route, keep this important point in mind: if a fire ever breaks out in your home, a window might very well be your only escape route.

Burglars are not afraid to break glass and reach through and unlock a window by hand. As a result, manufacturers have come out with numerous types of window glass that can withstand this type of abuse. Here are detailed descriptions of the four most popular types of window glass on the market:

Laminated Glass: Laminated glass has a vinyl or plastic inner layer sandwiched between two layers of glass. A burglar would have to strike the glass repeatedly in the same spot to make a small opening. Most burglars are reluctant to create this type of noise for fear of being detected.

Tempered Glass: Tempered glass is made by bringing regular glass almost to its melting point and then chilling it rapidly. This causes a type of protective skin to form around the glass. Fully tempered glass is four to five times stronger than regular glass.

Wired Glass: Wired glass has strands of metal wire inside it with the strands crisscrossing over one another for added strength. Wired glass adds the benefit of a visible deterrent. Extra effort is needed to break this type of glass and then cut through the wire located within the glass.

Plastics: Plastic material is divided into two types: acrylic and polycarbonate. The acrylics are more than 10 times stronger than regular glass of the same thickness and are commonly called Plexiglas. Polycarbonate sheets are superior to acrylics and are advertised as being 250 times more impact-resistant than safety glass and 20 times more resistant than other transparent plastic.

Garages

Most garage doors are not made with security in mind. Therefore, it's important for the door leading from the garage to the house to be of very high quality. In addition, this door needs to be secured the same way you would secure any other exterior door.

Bad Guys Beware!

If you live in a high-crime area, you might want to consider covering the outside of your windows with steel shutters and grilles or bars. They're not all that attractive, but they sure are safe. However, keep in mind that if a fire occurs, you might need to escape through a window, so plan accordingly.

Keep your garage door shut and locked regardless of whether you're home. I also recommend that you use an electronic garage door opener. Not only is this a product of convenience, it's also one of safety. Getting out of your car while it's running to manually shut your garage door makes you vulnerable to carjackings. If you ever need to get out of the house in a hurry, you might need to run through the garage, and it's much faster to push a button than to take the time to manually raise your garage door. You're also more likely to keep your garage door shut if you don't have to open and close it by hand. Do not leave garage door openers in plain view in a car parked outside. The car can be broken into and the garage door opened.

Make sure to arrange the items in your garage so a person can't hide in it effectively without you seeing him or her from inside your car. A popular tactic is for the criminal to hide in the garage, waiting for the car to pull in and the garage door to shut. The criminal then has the victim trapped. A good way to prevent this is to install a mirror in your garage that enables you to check hard-to-see areas before exiting your vehicle.

Never leave your garage door open while you're away, and arrange the items in your garage so a criminal cannot effectively hide without being seen.

One Step Further

You can take other precautions that go above and beyond the norm but that really ensure your safety. These precautions include installing an alarm, getting a big dog, and storing your valuables in a safe.

Alarms

When it comes to alarms, make sure you get one that's really loud. Noise is a great deterrent to crime because criminals will do just about anything to get away from it. Silent alarms are good for contacting the police, but by the time they arrive, the burglar could be long gone with all your valuables.

Stay on Your Toes

The purpose of an alarm system isn't just to deter a criminal from breaking into your home. It also should make sure he or she doesn't have time to take everything. When the horns start blowing, the clock starts ticking.

I recommend that you purchase an alarm with motion detectors and door and window transmitters. Motion detectors will set off the alarm if there's any movement in the room, and transmitters will set off the alarm if a door or a window is moved even slightly.

The following are some additional features you might want to consider when choosing an alarm system:

➤ A battery-powered, fail-safe backup.

➤ A re-arming capability. (This resets the alarm automatically after it has been activated.)

➤ A siren timer shut-off that automatically turns the alarm off after it has sounded for a set period of time. (This is good to have in case the alarm is set off by accident. A burglar will flee long before this feature kicks in.)

➤ A siren sounding device that can be installed on the exterior of your home to alert neighbors. If you're not home and a burglar breaks in, this will cause neighbors to investigate the noise and possibly catch a glimpse of the perpetrator and his or her vehicle.

➤ A panic button in the bedroom or bedrooms, positioned so it can be pushed by someone in bed. (This can be set to activate the alarm and to contact the monitoring company, who will then call the police.)

➤ Smoke and heat detectors.

➤ Sensors that detect broken glass.

➤ A system that can be armed or disarmed while you're away from home. This enables you to set the alarm from a remote location in case you forget to do so before you leave. This feature also enables you to turn it off temporarily to let someone in your home while you're gone without giving out your alarm code.

➤ When the alarm company installs your alarm, insist that they install the control box in the interior of the house, not in the garage. Many companies install the box in the garage because it is easy, but that makes it vulnerable to being disabled.

One last thing to remember is that an alarm system is only as good as the company monitoring it for you. Look for a professional, reputable company to monitor your alarm 24 hours a day, seven days a week, using state-of-the-art computer technology.

Bad Guys Beware!

Regardless of whether you own an alarm system, be sure to place reputable alarm system decals on your windows. This indicates that your house is monitored. It keeps the criminals guessing because there is no way they can be sure that you really do have an alarm. If they see the decal in your front window, they probably are going to assume that you have an alarm system and keep walking. Criminals are sneaky and don't play by the rules. To beat them, we're going to have to be a little sneaky, too.

Dogs

Dogs are a great deterrent to crime because fear, threats, and intimidation don't easily control them. Their loud bark alerts everyone in the house that something is wrong, and they have been known to bite from time to time. Dogs are great at hearing footsteps and sensing trouble way before people do, which is good for giving advance warning. If you're going to get a dog for security reasons, I recommend getting a medium to large dog. Small dogs are less intimidating. Some small dogs have big barks and are easier to care for, however, and this can be a good thing.

Be sure to install a few "Beware of Dog" signs outside where they can be seen by passersby. Even if you don't have a dog, I recommend that you do this for the same reason you would put an alarm monitoring decal on your window. It's inexpensive to do, and it keeps the bad guys guessing. Set a big dog dish outside and put big-dog dog food in it. You might even want to get creative and put a big dog's name on the side of the dish. (How about Brutus or Goliath?) For a water dish, use a large bucket.

Safes

If the value of small personal items warrants protection, a safe is great. If you're going to purchase a safe, you only need to know three things:

➤ Buy a safe that's fireproof.
➤ Make sure it can be bolted down so it can't be picked up and carried off.
➤ Make sure it is well hidden.

I also recommend that you insure its contents.

Stay on Your Toes

Instead of purchasing a safe, some people choose to use a secondary barrier. A secondary barrier is a small space or room concealed inside a closet. It usually is secured with a dead bolt lock and cannot be seen without someone first knowing where to look. A good secondary barrier can be created for as little as $50.

Insurance

Make sure you have adequate insurance not only for your home but for your possessions as well. Ask your insurance company whether it pays for the depreciated value of your items or for the current replacement value. This might not seem like a big deal now, but if you ever get robbed or have a fire, the difference between the two could be a bundle of cash.

It's a good idea to permanently mark your possessions and to inventory them as well. Make a list of all your valuable items and take photos. Be sure to document serial numbers next to a brief description of the item. Keep a copy of this information in a fireproof safe, with a trusted friend, or in a safe deposit box. If this seems like too much of a hassle, there are companies that will come to your home and do it for you.

If you do get robbed, don't touch anything. Leave everything as it is and call the police immediately. When you begin moving things, you begin destroying evidence and smudging fingerprints. If you don't call the police and file a report, your insurance company will not be able to assist you in the matter.

Safety Alert!

If your house has been robbed once, it's very likely that it will be robbed again. Thieves know that you'll most likely be getting an insurance settlement and will be replacing most of what they stole with brand new items. They usually will give you just enough time to replace everything and then will hit you again. Because of this, if you've been robbed, you need to take safeguarding your home even more seriously than someone who hasn't been robbed. Installing an alarm system, getting a dog, adding additional exterior lighting, and asking your neighbors to be more suspicious than usual are all great ways to prevent future break-ins.

Neighborhood Watch

If your community has a neighborhood watch program, I strongly recommend that you get involved. If your neighborhood doesn't have one, you might want to consider starting one. The National Crime Prevention Council reports that many communities that have implemented these programs have cut their crime rates by more than 50 percent. If you want to live in a safe community, you must chip in and do your part.

To start one of these programs in your neighborhood, just call your local police department and ask for information. In some cases, the police will even provide you with an officer to act as a liaison for your project.

Apartment Living

Millions of Americans live in apartments. As the price of owning a home continues to increase, apartments have become more and more popular. Apartments are not exempt from burglary, theft, or violence, which is why safety needs to be taken seriously.

Bad Guys Beware!

Before making your decision about an apartment, call the local police department and ask about crime in that particular area. Some police departments can even tell you how many calls they respond to from the complex or building you are considering. Also be sure to ask if there is any known gang activity in the area.

When shopping for an apartment, the following are a few tips to keep in mind:

➤ Look for a gated community that requires an access code, a gate card, or a remote to enter.

➤ Remember that apartments on the ground floor are more likely to be robbed.

➤ Find out whether the property is patrolled by hired security and, if so, how often.

➤ A garage usually costs extra, but it greatly reduces the chances of your vehicle being stolen or vandalized.

➤ Make sure the property is well lit.

➤ Find out if the apartment units have individual alarm systems.

The Least You Need to Know

➤ Make sure your home always looks occupied.

➤ In the majority of all break-ins, the burglar kicks in the front door, so take extra care in securing yours.

➤ Alarm systems are a great deterrent to crime.

➤ Criminals hate dogs.

➤ A good way to keep crime out of your community is to be actively involved in a neighborhood watch program.

➤ When choosing an apartment, keep safety in mind.

Chapter 14

Telephones: Thinking Before You Speak

In This Chapter

➤ Calls that raise concern

➤ Annoying calls

➤ Setting up for safety

➤ The phone as a tool

You get a call from a woman representing a marketing company. She tells you that she just needs a few minutes of your time to ask you four simple questions. She seems nice enough, so you agree to the short survey. You tell her your name, your age, that you live alone, and your profession. You hang up the phone feeling like you did a good thing. A few weeks later, you come home to an empty house. A neighbor tells you that a moving truck came during the morning and moved everything out. When the neighbor questioned the movers, they presented an invoice with your name on it, quoted the name of the company for which you work, and said your company was relocating you to California at the last moment.

In this chapter, you're going to learn about telephone safety. I'll answer questions such as how to list your name in the phone book, if at all. I'll talk about 911 and how it can be used more effectively, and you'll learn how to make an emergency breakthrough call. You'll also learn the rules for recording a conversation and getting your phone line monitored, too. Let's not forget about the ever-popular cellular phone.

Calls That Raise Concern

The phone rings in the middle of the night. Still half asleep, you answer the phone thinking it must be important or an emergency. On the other end is a man who asks you if you're home alone. You ask, "Who is this?" He replies by asking again if you are home alone. Frustrated and frightened, you finally hang up the phone only to have him call again moments later. Finally, you leave the phone off the hook. But forget about going back to sleep—you're scared!

An intimidating stranger on the other end of the line can cause serious anxiety if you don't know how to handle the situation in advance. In this situation, you should hang up without responding to the caller. Then, turn the ringer off.

Bad Guys Beware!

When you tell a caller that he or she has the wrong number, if the person asks what your number is, don't tell. Instead, ask the caller what number he or she is trying to reach. This is a popular trick for people who randomly call others in an attempt to find a voice they, for one reason or another, like. After this person has your number written down, he or she can call back anytime.

Hang-Ups

Now let's talk about those calls that raise the most concern: hang-ups. This refers to a caller who waits for you to answer and then hangs up. Some people have reported more than 50 of these calls occurring in just one day. When the calls start coming in during the night, it'll really make you worry.

Harassment: Harassment calls usually come from someone you know (although they don't identify themselves). You might have a good idea of who it is or you might not. If the harassment calls continue, look into getting Caller ID. If the caller makes threats on you or your family's life, I recommend that you get the police involved and ask them to have the line professionally monitored. By monitoring the phone lines, incoming calls can be traced. Depending on how seriously the police view your situation, they might or might not agree to this. If the police agree to have the telephone company monitor your lines, it's important that you press charges after the identity of the caller is learned.

Criminals Who Want Information: These callers are sneaky, so you have to be really careful about what you tell them. Their stories are very convincing, and they can get even the most suspicious resident to give away important information. A criminal will call several numbers out of the phone book until he finds someone who will tell him what he wants to know, usually a child who doesn't know better.

Do not, under any circumstances, tell a stranger the following information:

➤ Whether you're home alone

➤ Whether you live alone

➤ Your phone number

➤ Your address

➤ Your name

If you have children, make sure they know not to divulge this information.

Stay on Your Toes

There are various reasons a criminal might want your personal information. He or she might be targeting homes to burglarize and will want to know how much money you make and at what times you're away. The person also might be trying to find out whether you live alone.

Prank Calls

"Excuse me sir, do you have Prince Albert in a can? You better let him out so he can breathe." This is just one of thousands of prank calls kids have circulated throughout the continent in an effort to get a good laugh. To be quite honest, when I was a kid, I made a few of these calls myself. These calls are fairly innocent until it's taken a step further and results in vulgar or nasty language. If this happens to you and you know you're dealing with a kid, tell the kid you know who he or she is. Insist that you will call the police and the kid's parents if he or she calls back again. This usually will put an end to the problem.

Obscene Phone Calls

If you ever receive an obscene phone call, I'm truly sorry. Unfortunately, thousands of people each day have their day ruined by some person who enjoys this kind of thing.

If you hear something obscene on the other end, hang up right away. What excites the caller is your response. Getting upset, asking who it is, telling the person how sick he or she is, and threatening to call the police just provoke the caller to harass you even more because your reaction is motivating.

Calls from a Stalker

If a stalker targets you, be careful. These people are dangerous and should be taken seriously. The first thing you need to do is document the call. If a threat is made, call

Bad Guys Beware

The best way to get an obscene caller to stop is to take the fun out of it. How fun could it be to have a phone slammed in your ear with no response? Be sure to hang up the moment the person begins and, by all means, don't give the person an opportunity to finish. If the calls continue, get the police involved.

the police and report it. You might even consider recording the calls for evidence, but check out your state laws about this first. Any messages on voice mail or your answering machine need to be saved as well. Hold onto everything because you're going to need it to prove your case if it comes to getting this person put away.

Annoying Calls

Telemarketers, survey companies, and people asking for donations are just a few of the calls that hassle you at home. No one likes to receive these types of calls, but unfortunately, it's one of the realities that comes with being an American consumer.

It's important for you to know that many of these calls are from legitimate companies and organizations. For the most part, the person calling you is just doing his or her job. The bad news is that crooks have gotten into the action. Now it's extremely difficult to distinguish the legitimate telemarketers from the crooks. This is why you have to be suspicious of all these calls.

Telemarketers

Some companies have made fortunes from focusing on nothing but telemarketing. Unfortunately, so have a lot of thieves. There's now equipment on the market such as the Phone Butler, however, to help you with these calls.

Stay on Your Toes

The Phone Butler is a product that helps take care of annoying sales calls. As soon as you determine that it's a telemarketer on the other end, you just push the Phone Butler button. A recording will immediately begin playing that tells the caller you're not interested.

The problem with telemarketing calls is that you never know whether they're legitimate.

Because it's difficult to distinguish the honest callers from the dishonest ones, I've put together a checklist of some do's and don'ts that should help you keep from getting burned while giving legitimate companies a fair chance to earn your business.

➤ Don't tell the caller your phone number.

➤ Don't give out any banking information.

➤ Don't give out your credit card number.

➤ If the caller is promoting something you're interested in, ask him or her to mail you the information. If the person says that's not possible, hang up.

➤ Ask the caller if you can have his or her phone number so you can call the person back. If the caller won't give it to you, hang up.

➤ Ask the caller for his or her last name and write it down.

➤ Don't tell the caller where you work or how much money you make.

➤ Don't tell the caller whether you live alone, are married, or have children.

If a telemarketer calls you to promote or sell something, you can request to be taken off the call list. By law, if you make this request, the company must remove your name and number from its file. If you exercise this right, write down who you said it to and when. If the company calls you again, file a complaint.

Donations

Some of these calls come from legitimate organizations in desperate need of your support. My recommendation is that you not commit to anything over the phone. Instead, take the organization's name and number and request that information be mailed to you. Then check out the organization carefully before writing a check.

Donations for Municipalities

Be wary of police, sheriff, highway patrol, and fire department phone calls. These usually are scams. It's very rare that a police officer or a firefighter will call you asking for money. If you want to make a donation to these municipalities, there are much safer ways to do it.

What about the benevolence fund and the orphan's fund? The bottom line is that firefighters and law enforcement officers are government employees and are paid with tax dollars. They're not allowed to use their position to call citizens at home for the purpose of asking for money. I'm a strong advocate of supporting these government agencies because of everything they do for this country. Because there are a lot of crooks out there, however, it's best to avoid making donations over the phone.

Safety Alert!

Don't give out your social security number, date of birth, place of birth, or driver's license number over the phone. With this information, a person can pull up your entire life history with a few clicks of a mouse. This information, in the hands of the wrong person, has the potential to destroy your life.

Surveys

If you're interested in responding to a company's survey, tell the caller to mail it to you. If the caller tells you he or she can't do that, hang up. What kind of survey company can't mail you a survey?

If you are mailed a survey, don't answer questions relating to financial matters such as how much money you make, how much your house is worth, what kind of car you drive, banking information, or how many credit cards you have. When it comes to your money, you can't be too careful.

Setting Up for Safety

The phone companies have come a long way in developing quality features and equipment. They've developed this with the intent of making things more convenient for their customers, but they've also succeeded in making the telephone a lot safer. They have provided the public with several inexpensive features, which, if used wisely, can keep everyone a lot safer.

To Be Listed or Not to Be Listed

When deciding whether to list your number, base your decision on your circumstances and your personality. The following are a few positives and negatives to help you decide which is best for you.

Listed:

➤ If a friend or a loved one needs to reach you in an emergency but doesn't have your number with him or her, it can be obtained easily.

➤ If a long lost buddy from high school decides to give you a call out of the blue, you will be easy to find.

➤ People you don't want to hear from also can easily obtain your phone number.

➤ If you have small children and they ever become lost or scared, they can give your name to a safe person who can then call information.

Unlisted:

➤ Unless you give your number to someone, you can't be reached easily by phone.

➤ You'll get fewer unsolicited calls from companies or organizations.

➤ People who don't have your number with them will have a hard time trying to reach you.

➤ Obscene callers, stalkers, and harassers will have a difficult time getting your phone number.

If you choose to have your number listed, consider how you want your name to appear in the phone book's residential pages. Some people like to use their first initial and last name only. The only problem with this is that you take the risk of receiving a high volume of calls for someone else if you have a common last name. If someone named David Smith moves to another town without telling his creditors, for example, they will begin to look for him. The first thing they usually do is go through the phone book and call all of the D. Smiths. If your name is Diane Smith and you've listed yourself as D. Smith, you'll be besieged with calls.

If you choose to list your full name, however, you run the risk of having someone strange harass you with phone calls based on your first and last name. You must decide for yourself

Bad Guys Beware!

If you're a single female who lives alone or if you're a very private person, I recommend keeping your number unlisted. If you live in a house with other family members, you'll probably want to keep it listed. It comes down to personal preference.

which is best for you. And you can't call me to discuss this further because my phone number is unlisted.

Special Call Features

The following are some features offered by most telephone companies. They are relatively inexpensive and can go a long way to help keep you safe.

Caller ID: Caller ID is probably one of the best investments you can make when it comes to telephone safety. When your phone rings, your Caller ID box displays who is calling. This makes it your choice whether to pick up. If you get calls from people who won't identify themselves, there's a good chance you'll now have their numbers. If a stalker is calling you, this tool is invaluable.

Stay on Your Toes

The downside of this product is that, if someone calls you from a pay phone, you won't have any way to know who is calling. The caller also can punch in a code before dialing that will prevent his or her phone number from being displayed. Instead, the phrase "Private Call" shows up on your display. (In the state where I live, the code that does this is *67.) In some places, you can program your phone line to not accept calls whose numbers have been blocked. This works like a charm on people or companies that try to prevent you from seeing who they are when they call. They receive a message stating, "This phone line does not accept anonymous calls," or something similar, and the phone doesn't even ring!

When a telemarketer calls you, the person usually will punch in a special code that will cause your call box to read "Private Call" or "Out of Area." Telemarketers do this because they don't want you to know their phone number. Although Caller ID doesn't solve all telephone problems, it sure does solve a lot of them.

Call Waiting: Call waiting is a great feature for one simple reason. If a family member or a loved one ever is away from home and has an emergency, he or she doesn't have to worry about getting a busy signal when calling home for help. Can you imagine being stranded at night in the middle of nowhere but not being able to get through when you call home because someone is on the phone? Call waiting eliminates this problem.

The only way people will get a busy signal when they call is if you are talking to one person with someone else on hold. This situation never should last more than a few minutes, though, and it's a whole lot better than getting a busy signal for an hour.

Call Return: If you don't have Caller ID, the next best thing is call return. If you get a hang-up or any other call that causes you concern, just dial the three assigned digits for your area, and call return will tell you the number of your caller. (Your local phone company will be able to tell you what your assigned digits are.)

The only problem with this feature is that it can't access every number. This means that, every once in a while, you'll get a recording saying something like "We're sorry, we can't help you find this number."

Safety Alert!

Call waiting is useless if the person who hears the beep doesn't switch over. Make it a rule in your home that everyone must take other calls. Otherwise, someone could be in a serious emergency and not be able to get through.

The Phone as a Tool

The telephone is a tremendous tool that has assisted the police with the apprehension of thousands of criminals. If you're ever in a life-or-death situation, you can use the phone to get help in a hurry. Tracing a call can determine who is targeting you and where the person is located (if done legally). The phone is a valuable resource for safety as long as you're aware of its capabilities. Some stiff laws are attached to a few of these uses, however, so it's important to know your limitations. You don't want to get yourself into trouble with the law in an attempt to catch a criminal.

Dialing 911

911 has saved more lives than can be counted. Before 911, people would frantically try to get through to the police department by calling the operator. This wasted valuable time, and in a life-or-death situation, a few seconds can make all the difference.

If you truly are in a life-threatening situation in which every second counts, dial 911 and leave the phone off the hook. You don't need to hang on the line, explaining your situation and giving directions to where you live when a strange woman is waving a gun in front of you. Dial the phone, leave it off the hook, and run. The police can trace the call instantly (unless you're calling from a cellular phone). If you have the time, though, stay on the phone and give the dispatcher the information he or she needs.

Life Savers

If you're going to call 911, make sure your situation is truly an emergency. It doesn't count as an emergency if your cat's in a tree, if you're locked out of your house or car, or if you have a really important question to ask the police. Calls like this to 911 could cost someone else his or her life. For every officer that responds to a ridiculous, nonemergency call, that's one less officer to respond to the real thing. For every dispatcher that has to tie up a line talking to someone with a question, that's one less operator and available line to take a life-saving call.

Emergency Breakthrough

If you're in an emergency situation, you can call the operator and request that he or she interrupt a busy line. The operator will ask whether it's an emergency before agreeing to do this and might even ask for a brief explanation. If he or she feels your request is valid, the operator can cut into the call and tell the person on the phone that you're trying to get through.

Tracing a Call

As you probably know from television and films, one thing the police can do if they feel your situation is serious enough is have your phone line monitored with special equipment. This enables the police to locate where calls are coming from. In most cases, you have to stay on the line with the caller for a certain amount of time so the call can be effectively traced.

Recording Conversations

As Linda Tripp knows, recording telephone conversations is tricky business, and there are laws to make sure people don't cross the line. You can easily hook up a tape recorder to your telephone for very little money, but you must know the rules.

Stay on Your Toes

A telephone bill can be a valuable tool in solving crimes. Phone bills are used in courtrooms as evidence every day and are considered a valid source of proof.

If you're going to record a telephone conversation, you must tell the person with whom you're speaking that he or she is being recorded. If the person hangs up, that's his or her right. If you don't let the person know about the recording, it's very unlikely that you can use the tape as evidence in a court of law. If you record a person admitting to committing a felony, however, you can get around this.

Cellular Phones

These technological wonders have done a great deal for safety over the years. If you've ever been in an emergency and had to hunt down a phone, you know what I mean. Time is everything when it comes to life-or-death situations. That's what cellular phones do—save precious time.

The biggest problem with cellular phones is criminals and scanners. A special scanner can be purchased for a few hundred dollars that enables criminals to listen in on your call and to retrieve your phone number and serial number in just a few seconds. The criminal then can sell this information to someone who will run up your bill to an astronomical amount. The victim doesn't have the slightest idea that anything is wrong until he or she gets the next phone bill. By then, it's too late. Unfortunately, there's not a lot you can do to prevent this from happening, although some states are trying to pass stiffer laws to help combat this problem.

The most important thing to remember is that your telephone is for your convenience. Having a phone should be a good experience, one that makes your life easier and safer.

The Least You Need to Know

➤ It's difficult to know whether a telemarketing call is legitimate.

➤ Do not give out personal information about you or your family over the phone.

➤ Avoid giving money to charitable organizations that call you unsolicited. Have them mail you information instead.

➤ Don't agree to be surveyed over the telephone. Have the survey mailed to you instead.

➤ Be sure to use 911 only in emergencies. Otherwise, it might not be available to someone who really needs it.

Chapter 15

Not Getting Burned on the Internet

In This Chapter

➤ Protecting yourself

➤ Surfing

➤ Staying safe and secure

➤ Viruses

➤ Online annoyances

You're browsing around on the Internet one evening, shopping for a camera. After about 30 minutes, you find the deal of the century. The same camera you saw in the mall last week for $300 is for sale on the Internet for only $75. You have to act now, though, and you can only pay with a credit card. You've never heard of the company before, but you're fairly sure it's legitimate because it has a beautiful, eight-page Web site that's very professional looking. You type in your credit card information and press Enter, congratulating yourself on the money you're saving.

A month goes by. You still haven't received your camera, but you have received your credit card bill. Thousands of dollars have been fraudulently charged to your card. By taking a few simple precautions, you could have prevented this from happening.

The Internet is a public network of millions of computers, and it is growing at an astronomical rate. Enormous amounts of information are moving faster than the blink of an eye across public phone lines. This creates a huge security risk for both the sender and the receiver of information. If you're going to use the Internet, you need to know how to protect yourself from a variety of different problems.

In this chapter, I'm going to give you some useful information about how to not get burned on the Internet. I will discuss Web privacy and how it works, as well as encryption as it relates to being online. I'll also cover how to use the Internet to do your shopping and banking. How important are passwords when it comes to protecting your information? What about viruses? I'll go over this information, too. Finally, I'll discuss online harassment and some great ways to keep your children out of trouble. Like the Internet at its best, this chapter is filled with information that can save you a lot of time and money.

Protecting Your Personal Information

The World Wide Web exposes you to a wealth of public information that travels all around the world, 24 hours a day, without ever taking a rest. What you need to remember is that, every time you decide to log on and take a ride on the information highway, you become vulnerable to Internet crimes. Remember, if you can see their address, they can see yours. Here you will learn about specific safeguards. Your personal information—credit card numbers, bank account numbers, home address, telephone number, and so on—is valuable to a crook, so you need to know how to protect it.

What About Privacy?

Keep in mind that you can only enjoy a certain amount of privacy on the Internet. Remember, the Internet is a public network. This means you must use caution and wisdom when giving out information. You should exercise the same precautions before giving out your personal information on the Web as you would before giving it out any other time. Internet information is transferred through public phone lines, and eavesdropping is an easy and common practice.

When you sign up with an Internet service provider (ISP), you're assigned an address. Every time you visit a Web site, that site can immediately tell who your provider is, where it's located, what site you last visited, and what browser you're using. Fortunately, this does not give the site access to personal information about you such as your personal mailing address, email address, phone number, or name. The only way for the site to obtain this information is if you provide it.

Safety Alert!

The majority of people who surf the Web give information out way too easily, putting themselves at risk. Your information is only as private as you make it. It's important that you practice caution when giving out information on the Internet.

Before You Enlighten

Before giving your information to someone on the Internet, the first thing you need to know is whether it's going to be shared with others. Anytime you are asked for personal information, you need to check out that particular Web site's privacy policy. This will let you know whether your information will be shared with anyone else, and it should tell you exactly how your information will be used. If the site doesn't have a privacy policy (or doesn't have one you're comfortable with), don't give out your information. Because this has become a significant issue with consumers, most sites have them readily available.

Bad Guys Beware!

When visiting a site, check for fine print that asks whether you want to be put on the site's mailing list. If you don't want to be put on this list, click No; otherwise, the site most likely will assume that your answer is Yes, and on the list you'll go.

Want a Cookie?

A cookie is information about you that your computer might store after you've visited a Web site. Anytime you go back to revisit that particular Web site, the Web browser you are using will send your information cookie back to the site as well. The reason for this is so the cookie can provide useful information about you to the site you're revisiting.

If you like to frequent a certain Web site to purchase compact disks or cassettes, the cookie will keep track of the music you buy. The next time you visit a site, the cookie will pass along your information to the site you are visiting so they can learn about you for the purpose of trying to make more money off of you. If you want to know exactly when all of this is happening (it only takes seconds), you should be able to adjust the setting on your computer so you're alerted when a cookie is being stored on your hard drive.

Street Talk

According to the official AOL Internet Guide, a cookie is "a small text file created by a Web server and stored on your computer to keep track of the sorts of things you do on the server."

For the most part, cookies are safe. The only information a cookie can contain is what you provide to it, so be careful about what information you give out about yourself when visiting Web sites. This primarily is used as a sales and marketing strategy in an attempt to get you to buy more of what the site's selling. Nevertheless, you need to be aware that this information is stored and then passed along.

Encryption Description

Encryption is a way of scrambling personal or sensitive information to stop others from gaining access to it. Currently, there are two levels of encryption as it relates to the Internet. There is a 40-bit and a 128-bit level, both of which are intended to make things very difficult for hackers. With the 40-bit encryption, there are billions of possible keys to weed through to decipher the protected information—and only one of them works. If you think that's tough, the 128-bit level of encryption requires the deciphering of hundreds of trillions of times as many keys as the 40-bit encryption does. Does that sound safe or what? This makes finding the right key to decipher your information nearly impossible.

Stay on Your Toes

Encryption puts sensitive information in a secret code so it cannot be read or understood by others. The United States government, financial institutions, and credit card companies all use encryption to send and receive information. Of course, this means that buying and selling technology that can break encrypted codes (or can create codes that can't be broken) has become a very big business.

So what does all this encryption stuff mean? It means that passing along information on the Internet has the potential to be extremely safe, but it's up to you to check the security level of the Web browser you're using. You need to make sure encryption is being used; if it's not, keep surfing.

Let's Go Surfing Now

You can spend all day on the Internet and never run out of exciting sites to visit. You can get caught up on your shopping, do your banking, get the best price on a new car, even plan a trip to Hawaii. Not only that, your feet won't hurt at the end of the day, and you don't have to fight traffic or hassle with waiting in long lines.

Shopping and Banking Online

If you're going to get scammed on the Internet, there's a good chance it will happen while you're shopping or banking. If you can learn to be careful when doing these two activities, you can stay safe on the Internet.

You might find this hard to believe, but using your credit card on the Internet is much safer than using it around town. (Of course, this is taking into consideration that you are following some basic guidelines.) The reason for this is that a lot of Web sites now work together with your browser software to encode your information to prevent eavesdroppers from being able to read it.

There also is technology in use called Secure Sockets Layer (SSL) that counters security threats in three ways:

> **Data Integrity:** This is what makes sure your information isn't tampered with by another party while it's being transmitted.

> **Authentication:** This is what is used to verify that the party receiving your information is who it claims to be.

> **Encryption:** This is what scrambles the information into a secret code so it can't be read by eavesdroppers.

Safety Alert!

Your two main concerns when on the Internet should be impersonators and eavesdroppers. Impersonators make you believe they are a legitimate company so they can get your credit card or banking account numbers. Eavesdroppers "listen in" on your transaction to steal information. They both can pose a serious threat if you don't take proper precautions.

To find out whether a site uses SSL, check the Web address line for an *s* at the end of *http*, which means it will read *https*. If you're about to surrender your personal information to a site that does not use SSL, your Web browser will warn you in advance by displaying a message on your screen.

Stay on Your Toes

Your credit card number is actually safer on a secure Web site than it is when you hand it to a cashier or a waiter. It's fairly easy for a sales clerk to write your account number down without you noticing. There is no sales clerk on the Internet.

When you're visiting a particular Web site, you can tell whether the site is in its secure mode by looking for the security icon, which usually is a picture of a key or a padlock that appears at the bottom of the screen. If the padlock is closed, you are in secure mode. If it's open, you aren't. If there's a key on the screen and it's solid, you are in secure mode. If the key is broken, you aren't. It's important that you learn to pay close attention to these icons.

Digital Certificates

For increased security and to make things easier, I recommend that you get a digital certificate. A digital certificate is software you can purchase and install into your Web browser. A digital certificate consists of an attachment to an electronic message, used for security purposes. The most common use of a digital certificate is to verify that a user sending a message is who he or she claims to be, and to provide the receiver with the means to encode a reply. The following are some of the things it does:

➤ It improves your overall security when on the Internet. Your certificate cannot be guessed, forged, intercepted, or forgotten.

➤ It eliminates the need for you to remember a bunch of different passwords. The digital certificate automatically becomes your new password for all the Web sites you visit.

➤ It enhances the security of all emails you send and receive.

➤ It logs you into Web sites automatically without you having to register each time.

➤ After a Web site recognizes that you have a digital certificate, it can customize information for you in a matter of seconds, according to your interests.

Children and the Internet

Take the time to explore the Internet with your children, teaching them about the potential dangers and setting firm guidelines. Keep the following in mind:

➤ Teach your children to never give out personal information over the Internet, including their name, address, phone number, age, and the name of the school they attend.

➤ Keep your computer in a nonprivate area where you can monitor what your child is doing. (I don't recommend putting a computer with Internet access in your child's room.)

➤ Don't give your children their own email address. By having only one address in your home, you can better monitor the emails your children are sending and receiving.

➤ Don't allow your children to arrange a meeting with someone they meet on the Internet.

➤ Make it a rule in your home that your children can never order or buy anything from the Internet without first getting your permission.

➤ Purchase a filtering program that prevents your children from visiting inappropriate Web sites (some ISPs provide some filtering features as well).

Safety Alert!

Don't allow your children to visit chat rooms or news groups. Pedophiles can use these sites to pick up children by pretending to be young themselves and then befriending your child. A man in his 40s might pretend to be a 13-year-old girl to develop a relationship with your 13-year-old son. After he has earned your child's trust, he then might try to set up a private meeting.

Staying Safe and Secure: Passwords and Viruses

Passwords are an important key to your privacy while on the Web, so they need to be chosen with safety in mind. If you're going to be sending or receiving emails, you need to know some of the basic precautions to take as well. What about those ugly viruses passed along on the Internet? One of these cyberspace diseases can completely infect and destroy your hard drive and all the information stored on it in a matter of seconds.

Passwords

Sometimes a password is the only thing standing between all your personal information and a total stranger who wants it. Internet passwords are your first line of defense and should be taken seriously.

Stay on Your Toes

Choosing and using passwords with safety in mind is what makes them effective. Choosing them for convenience and not for security will only put you at risk and will not be nearly as effective.

When someone learns your password they can give it to others. The easiest way to learn someone's password is to look over their shoulder when they are typing it in. Having someone's password is like having one of their account numbers because people have passwords to sign on, to access bank accounts, and so on.

The first thing you need to know is how to create a safe password. The following is a list of things to avoid:

➤ Avoid using any part of your name.

➤ Avoid using any part of a name belonging to a friend, pet, or family member.

➤ Don't use birthdays.

➤ Don't use addresses or telephone numbers.

➤ Don't use your social security number (or any part of it).

➤ Avoid using the same password that you use for other things.

➤ Avoid using letters or numbers in sequences (like 9876).

➤ Don't use your username or login name.

➤ Avoid using the names of places you've been.

➤ Don't use different variations of any of the above, such as spelling words backwards.

The following are some ideas to help you create a secure password:

➤ Make up words that aren't in the dictionary but that are easy for you to remember.

➤ Try to always use at least six characters in your password.

➤ Instead of using only letters and numbers, try incorporating special characters (!$&*+).

➤ Mix upper- and lowercase letters.

Make it a rule to never give out your password to anyone. If you can, change it every few months. When you're entering your password, make sure no one can see you. If you believe someone might have learned your password, change it immediately.

EMail Security

A good rule of thumb is to protect your email address the same way you protect your home phone number. This is private information that doesn't need to be shared with everyone. Unless your email address is listed in a directory or you give it out to someone, unauthorized people shouldn't be able to get hold of it.

The following is a list of some practical tips for using email:

➤ Don't give out your email password to anyone.

➤ Continually update your browser so it contains the most up-to-date security technology.

➤ Log out of your account when you finish surfing. Don't walk away from your computer while you are logged on, and get into the habit of closing your browser before signing off.

➤ If a Web site asks for your email address, check out its privacy policy first to see whether your address will be shared with others.

➤ If you receive spam email, don't respond. (By responding, you let the sender know that your email address is valid.)

➤ Be careful about giving personal information to people you meet online.

➤ Keep in mind that, once you e-mail someone, that person will know your email address.

➤ If you participate in Internet newsgroups, know that these groups are public. You may be revealing your email address to total strangers.

➤ If you get an email from someone you don't know and it contains an attachment, don't open it. (It could contain a nasty virus.)

Bad Guys Beware!

The best way to protect the information you send through email is by obtaining a digital certificate.

Street Talk

According to the official America Online Internet Guide, **spam** is "unsolicited email or newsgroup postings, generally considered to be a waste of time, bandwidth, and disk space."

Those Ugly Viruses

One morning you walk into your office, sit at your desk, and log on to the Internet to check your email. You have three new messages, one of which has an important document attachment that you've been waiting for from a client. You download the document onto your hard drive, and along with it you unknowingly download a virus. In no time at all, your computer begins to malfunction. It freezes up so badly that you have to unplug it from the outlet just to get it to reboot. Before you know it, the virus has completely wiped out your hard drive and has deleted hundreds of hours of hard work along with it.

What Is a Computer Virus?

The first thing you need to know is that computer viruses are ugly computer programs created intentionally by humans to aggravate others. A lot of people are under the assumption that viruses are just something that happens as a result of technology growing so fast. The truth is that viruses are a type of vandalism that specifically target computers. Viruses are capable of completely erasing your hard drive as well as causing you a great deal of frustration. Viruses can replicate themselves many times over and then attach themselves to other programs, infecting everything they touch.

Stay on Your Toes

Currently, more than 7,000 computer viruses for PCs have been identified, and two or three new viruses are being added to this list nearly every day.

Catching an Internet Virus

Unfortunately, it is possible for a virus to be transferred to your computer through the Internet. The good news, however, is that these viruses cannot travel independently. They have to attach themselves to a file you download onto your hard drive. Think of a computer virus on the Internet as an electronic leach that is only a threat when it is attached to a life source such as a file.

A virus cannot do any damage to your computer until the file to which it has attached itself has been executed. This is why antivirus software is so effective in combating the problem. In addition, your Internet browser sometimes will warn you in advance that you run the risk of obtaining a virus if you download a particular file. This gives you the opportunity to scan the file for viruses.

Protecting Yourself from Viruses

Antivirus software can be used to scan all drives and files on your computer, and it usually is inexpensive to purchase. It also can save you from potential disaster. For some people, their computer is a way of life. If it is damaged or if important information is lost, it can affect their livelihood the same way a robbery or a burglary could. Some viruses not only wipe out your hard drive, they also erase all your memory as well. Getting this fixed can cost a great deal of money.

The following are some of the advantages of having antivirus software:

➤ It can detect viruses already present.

➤ It can detect viruses attached to something you are about to download.

➤ It can do complete scans of your entire system.

➤ It can do isolated scans of specific areas or drives.

➤ It can scan specific files only.

➤ Scans are done very quickly, and reports can be printed.

➤ If a virus is found, most of the time the antivirus software can remove the virus and correct the problem immediately.

Bad Guys Beware!

Be extra cautious about short emails that ask you to download an attached file. Don't download files from sources you don't know.

➤ Scans can be scheduled to run automatically at times you set in advance.

➤ Scans can be set to run automatically every time your computer is turned on or rebooted.

Remember that new viruses are created daily. To protect yourself properly, you need to continually update your antivirus software so it can combat new viruses as well as existing ones.

Types of Viruses

Although there are many different types of computer viruses, each one can be categorized as one of the following:

➤ **Macro-Type Virus:** This infects document files.

➤ **File-Type Virus:** This infects computer files and can spread when you open an infected file.

➤ **Boot Sector Virus:** This infects boot sectors and is very difficult to pick up from the Internet. (Boot sector is short for Master Boot Record, a small program that is executed when a computer boots up. Typically, the MBR resides on the first sector of the hard disk. The program begins the boot process by looking up the partition table to determine which partition to use for booting. It then transfers program control to the boot sector of that partition, which continues the boot process.)

➤ **Multipartite Virus:** These nasty viruses play no favorites and will infect files and boot sectors alike. This type of virus is a combination of the other two types.

Online Angst

As the Internet continues to grow in popularity, unfortunately, the number of online troublemakers increases along with it. There are people on the Internet who find great pleasure in causing others grief. They can accomplish this by cyberstalking, by making threats, or by being obscene (for example, imagine that every time you log on to check your email there is an obscene message from a stranger or a death threat). Regardless of what their method is, it can make your life miserable in a hurry. You need to know what to do in case you get put on a harasser's list.

Harassers

For the most part, online harassers are harmless, but every once in a while, one crosses the line and takes things too far. Finding out where you live, calling you at home, making threats on your life, and following you are just a few ways a harasser can take things too far. This is why all online harassers must be dealt with seriously. It's very difficult to distinguish the harmless ones from the dangerous ones. If only one weirdo out of a thousand is capable of physically attacking you, that's one good reason to treat all incidents seriously.

Stay on Your Toes

One reason that harassing people online has become an increasing problem is because the harasser can be as brave as he or she wants to be behind the "mask" of the computer. The person can remain anonymous and doesn't have to deal with the victim face to face. This enables the harasser to say things he or she usually would never say. The person also can pretend to be anyone he or she chooses to be.

The following are the most common origins of online harassment or cyberstalking:

➤ E-mail

➤ Usenet newsgroups

➤ Message board postings

➤ Internet Relay Chat (IRC)

I can't stress it enough. Avoid giving out personal information to a stranger. Just because you befriend someone on the Internet doesn't mean the person is safe. (How do you know if your new friend is who he says he is?) In fact, it has become very common for prison inmates to develop relationships online with women while pretending to be someone else and not revealing the fact that they're incarcerated. (They especially target women running singles ads.) Some government officials are now lobbying to pass a law that will make it mandatory for a Department of Corrections screen to come up anytime you begin corresponding with a prisoner.

Because the majority of people victimized by cyberstalking, harassment, and obscenity are women, women should use gender neutral names to disguise their gender. If the harassment becomes obscene, don't read it. Just save the evidence on a disk or print a copy of it and file it away.

Cyberstalkers

Cyberstalking is not much different than other forms of stalking except the stalker uses a computer to harass his victims. Sometimes the stalker meets his victim online; sometimes he already knows the victim. In some instances, a cyberstalker already is actively stalking his victim using other methods and then adds the computer to his list of tools.

It is important for you to differentiate between someone who is harassing you and someone who is just annoying or bothering you. Annoying, immature people are not what I'm preparing you for in this section. I'm talking about criminals who cross the line by frightening you, threatening you, or intimidating you. With that in mind, the following are guidelines to follow if you're being harassed or stalked online:

Bad Guys Beware!

If you are being cyberstalked, keep in mind that your stalker's objectives are to intimidate you, to frighten you, and most of all, to provoke a reaction from you. This is why it is so important that you don't react or respond to an online harasser.

➤ Don't keep the situation a secret. (Share what's going on with a friend, a family member, or a co-worker.)

➤ Change your email address and abandon any chat rooms or newsgroups you visit that the stalker might know about.

➤ Either print a copy or store to a disk anything that can be used as evidence.

➤ Don't react by making threats or by being rude. (If you have something you must say, respond firmly but without emotion.)

Online Authorities

Depending on how you're being harassed online, the following are a few online authorities you can contact:

➤ The harasser's Internet service provider (ISP)

➤ The newsgroup administrator

➤ The Internet Relay Chat (IRC) administrator

➤ The harasser's postmaster

➤ Your employer (if the harassment is taking place on your computer at work)

➤ The police (if you feel that you or your family are in danger of being hurt physically)

When you contact the authorities, you will need to provide evidence that you are being harassed. This is another good reason to keep good records of everything sent to you.

The Least You Need to Know

➤ When on the Internet, be very careful about who you give your personal information to.

➤ Obtaining a digital certificate is one of the best ways to protect yourself.

➤ Choose a password with safety and security in mind, not convenience.

➤ The best way to protect yourself from computer viruses is by purchasing antivirus software.

➤ Treat all online harassers seriously and keep a record of all evidence.

➤ If you are physically threatened on the Internet, report the incident to the police immediately.

Chapter 16

When Home Is No Longer Safe

In This Chapter

➤ Defining the problem

➤ Planning for safety

➤ If you decide to leave

A mother of three children is being violently victimized, and the offender is her husband. She knew he had a problem controlling his anger while they were dating, but she thought he would change after they were married. Unfortunately, he has only gotten worse. At first, his outbursts consisted of just yelling at her, but eventually, he began to throw and break things. Now he physically hits her when he gets angry, and she is worried that her children might be next.

Each year, millions of Americans are victimized by violence behind closed doors. In this chapter, I'll discuss domestic violence in the home and how to prevent it from happening to you. If this type of abuse is affecting you or a loved one, you'll learn how to get out of it. I will discuss child abuse as well as emotional, sexual, physical, and psychological abuse. I also will show you how to read the warning signs, how to get help, and, if necessary, how to start over.

Defining the Problem

When most people hear the term "domestic violence," the first thing they think of is a man physically abusing his wife or girlfriend. This is a common stereotype but an inaccurate one. Domestic violence affects both genders and every age group. It also affects family members and friends. In fact, statistics show that women abuse men, teenagers abuse parents, and relatives abuse other family members.

Stay on Your Toes

Anger, stress, jealousy, revenge, mental illness, and drug or alcohol addiction all are factors that can be related to domestic violence.

The following are some different scenarios involving abuse:

➤ A husband physically beating his wife

➤ A mother hitting her children

➤ A woman emotionally abusing her boyfriend

➤ A relative sexually abusing a younger family member

➤ A teenager hitting his mother

➤ A boyfriend psychologically abusing his girlfriend

It's important for you to remember that domestic violence is not an economic or class issue. This abuse has been known to affect all Americans regardless of how much money one has earned, where one lives, or the color of one's skin.

A Few Numbers

The following are some shocking statistics relating to domestic violence and its victims in the United States:

➤ There are more than 4 million cases each year of severe domestic violence in the United States (stabbing, shooting, punching with a closed fist).

➤ More than 25 percent of American households experience a mild domestic violence problem (slapping, scratching, shoving, hitting).

➤ In some instances, domestic violence has been known to account for more than 50 percent of all late-night calls made to police.

➤ According to the National Victimization Survey, a person is more likely to be injured by a family member than by a stranger.

➤ Twenty-three percent of assaults committed by strangers result in injury, but 57 percent of assaults committed by a spouse result in injury.

➤ Seven percent of assaults committed by a stranger require medical attention, but 24 percent of assaults committed by a spouse require medical attention.

Safety Alert!

If someone you know is being physically abused, lovingly confront the person and suggest that he or she tell someone and take steps to get help. Ignoring the problem is the worst thing you can do.

Source: Statistics taken from Domestic Violence FAQs

Women Hitting Men

How many women are hitting men behind closed doors? According to a national survey taken in 1980, women are just as likely to resort to violent behaviors as men. The big difference lies in who is getting hurt as a result. Domestic police reports from the Santa Barbara Police Department in California were carefully analyzed, and when it came to reports in which injuries were reported, this is what they revealed:

➤ Women received 90 percent of all injuries reported.

➤ The remaining 10 percent of injuries reported were received by both parties (male and female) in the dispute.

➤ In nearly every case reported in which both parties received injuries, the woman's injuries were more severe than the man's.

Partner Abuse

Partner abuse, or violence between intimates, includes murders, rapes, robberies, or assaults committed by spouses, ex-spouses, boyfriends, or girlfriends. This type of abuse is difficult to measure accurately because most incidents take place in private, and there is no way to know how many incidents go unreported.

Types of Abuse

Domestic abuse isn't limited to someone hitting someone else. Several different types of abuse take place behind closed doors. Some leave physical scars; some leave scars that can't be seen, but still qualify as abuse.

The following are the most common types of abuse that take place:

➤ Physical abuse

➤ Emotional abuse (criticisms such as "You are fat, ugly, stupid, and so on")

➤ Sexual abuse

➤ Psychological abuse (threat-oriented words such as "I'll kill you," "You better not tell," and so on)

➤ Child abuse

Warning Signs

If someone you know is being abused, it is very unlikely that they'll make you aware of it. Shame and embarrassment are the most common reasons people keep abuse a secret, but they are not the only reasons. There also is a reluctance to get the abuser in trouble because of love or a sense of loyalty. Some victims don't tell anyone because they are afraid their abuser will increase the abuse or even kill them. Another reason is denial. Many victims are convinced that what is happening to them either is normal behavior or is their fault.

Because most victims don't share, the following are a few warning signs to look for if you suspect someone is being abused. Be suspicious if the person

➤ Almost always has bruises.

➤ Poorly explains injuries.

➤ Has a high absentee rate from school or work.

➤ Never invites you inside his or her home.

➤ Has very little freedom to come and go.

➤ Has become very quiet, shy, or timid.

➤ Is easily frightened or startled.

➤ Gets very uncomfortable when you ask about his or her home life.

Planning for Safety

If you currently are involved in a physically abusive relationship with a spouse, a loved one, a relative, or a friend but don't know what to do, this section will help you. I am going to teach you how to plan for safety if you're in an abusive relationship or are trying to get out of one.

Stay on Your Toes

More than 50 percent of defendants accused of murdering their spouse had been drinking alcohol during the time the offense took place.

If You Have Been Victimized in the Past

If a person you know has physically or sexually abused you in the past and you are concerned that it might happen again, you must prepare as if the likelihood of it happening again is definite. Having a plan can mean the difference between life and death.

The following are some things you can do to reduce your risk if another incident occurs:

➤ Plan a route of escape so you can quickly evacuate (study the doors, windows, elevators, emergency exits, stairwells, and so on).

➤ Place your keys and purse where you can grab them in a hurry (preferably by an exit).

Bad Guys Beware

A great deal of the information discussed in this chapter was derived from information disseminated by the Metro Nashville Police Department on Domestic Violence and Abuse. The department is taking great steps to reduce this problem and to educate the public.

➤ Explain your situation to a trusted neighbor and request that he or she call the police if suspicious noises are coming from your residence.

➤ Teach your children how to contact the police or fire department in the event of an emergency.

➤ Teach your children a secret command word and tell them to call 911 if they hear you say it.

➤ Work out the details in advance regarding where you will go if you have to leave in a hurry.

➤ Keep some cash on hand in case you have to leave and your abuser cancels your credit cards.

➤ If possible, reasonably comply with your partner until he or she begins to calm down. (Your goal is not to win the fight but to get out safely.)

Life Savers

If you are in an abusive relationship, find a safe location within your residence that you can move to if an argument ensues. Slowly move to this safe area before things get too heated. This should be a location near an exit, with a telephone, and away from objects that could be used as potential weapons. Try to avoid arguing in the bathroom, the garage, or the kitchen. Too many readily available objects could be used as weapons in these places, and it will be difficult for someone to hear you if you yell for help. By planning for the worst and hoping for the best, you begin to lower your risk of getting injured if an incident occurs.

If You Throw Someone Out

If you throw someone out, there are some precautions you should take, especially during the first few months, to ensure your safety in case the abuser returns. Keep in mind that if he or she does return, there's a good chance he or she will become angry or violent. This is why it is so important for you to take some precautions to safeguard your home.

The following are some things you can do to your home to make it much safer:

➤ Change the locks on your doors, even if the person has returned your keys. (He or she might have had copies made.)

➤ Install a peephole, a dead bolt, and a safety latch on your main entry door.

➤ Keep your windows locked.

➤ Consider having an alarm system installed.

➤ Install smoke detectors and fire extinguishers. (These are important items to have whether you've thrown someone out or not.)

➤ If your residence has a second floor, install a rope ladder. (These are inexpensive and can prevent someone from being trapped upstairs.)

➤ Install a pole or a bar on sliding glass doors and windows for extra security.

➤ Make sure your exterior lighting is adequate. (Exterior lighting with motion detectors and timers is most effective.)

➤ Have your children memorize the phone number of a friend or a family member to call after calling the police.

➤ If you have trusted neighbors, ask if it's okay for your children to run to their residence in an emergency. If they agree, incorporate this into your children's escape plan.

➤ Tell the people who take care of your children not to allow them to leave with anyone other than yourself.

This information is covered in greater detail in Chapter 13, "Fortifying Your Castle."

Safety Alert!

If someone who has physically abused you in the past shows up on your doorstep, do not let him in. Tell him that, if he has anything to say to you, he can say it over the phone or through the door, but don't let him into your residence under any circumstances. Don't let a sincere apology or a few shed tears change your mind either.

The Restraining Order

A restraining order, also known as an order of protection or a protection order, is a valuable tool when it comes to protecting yourself from a past abuser. A restraining order prevents the offender, by law, from being able to approach you physically. This document usually specifies how many feet away from you the offender must remain. Let's say you file a restraining order against your ex-girlfriend, and it states that she cannot come within 200 feet of you. If she shows up a couple weeks later where you work, she has violated the protective order and has broken the law. If you notify the police and report the incident, it is very likely that she will go to jail.

To get a restraining order, you must fear that you are in danger of imminent bodily harm. To file a restraining order you can either go to the civil department of your county courthouse or have your lawyer file it for you.

The following are some things you can do to ensure the effectiveness of your restraining order:

➤ Keep your restraining order near you.

➤ Give a copy of your restraining order to your local police department as well as to police departments in towns or communities you frequently visit.

➤ Call the county registry in advance and make sure your restraining order is in the registry. If a past abuser violates the order and you call the police, the officer can call the county registry to validate the document. The county registry is the place where all records of restraining and protective orders are kept on file. Having your order listed in the registry means that it is legally active.

➤ Inform your employers that you have a restraining order in effect so they are aware of the situation and can call the police for you in an emergency.

➤ Inform your close friends and family members about the restraining order.

➤ Make copies of the order in case your abuser destroys the copy you carry with you.

Bad Guys Beware!

If you obtain a restraining order against a past abuser and he or she violates it, report the incident to the police immediately. If you don't enforce the order the first time it is violated, the abuser will cease to obey it. If the police ignore the violation, report it to an attorney, to the courthouse, or to the chief of police.

The only way an officer can arrest the violator is if they commit a criminal act, and this is difficult for the victim to prove. If a violation of the protective order occurs, you also should be allowed to file a private criminal complaint with the district attorney in the jurisdiction where the violation took place.

Note that just because you file a complaint doesn't mean that you can file a restraining order; one is much more severe than the other.

When Battery Affects the Workplace

When separating yourself from a batterer, you should take preventative measures to help you stay safe at work as well. If you have a job, you might want to take the following precautions:

➤ Apprise your supervisor of the situation, especially if there's a chance the batterer might come to where you work.

➤ If possible, have someone at work screen your phone calls or use voice mail to do the screening.

➤ When leaving work, have security or a co-worker walk you to your car.

➤ When driving to and from work or other destinations, take alternate routes.

➤ Deposit your paycheck and do your banking at a different branch (or at least on different days) than you used to.

➤ Park your car in a different location than you usually do. Ask your supervisor if there's a place to park that's very close to the building until your situation is resolved.

➤ Avoid staying at work late by yourself.

Stay on Your Toes

Unfortunately, many women who live in a physically abusive environment end up losing their jobs. This often is the result of frequent absenteeism due to inflicted injuries or illnesses, frequent court appearances, and having to move a lot.

If You Decide to Leave

More women are injured as a result of being battered than in auto accidents, rapes, and muggings. If your situation is becoming increasingly dangerous for you or other family members, leaving might be your only option. If this is the case, there are some things you can do to prepare yourself in advance. Remember, preparing for the worst means using wisdom in a situation in which someone might become violent, is emotionally unpredictable, is abusing alcohol or drugs, or has uncontrollable anger.

According to the U.S. Department of Justice, up to 75 percent of domestic assaults reported to law enforcement agencies were inflicted after the separation of the couple took place. This means that deciding to leave an abusive situation might not be easy. Batterers tend to escalate their level of violence to convince or frighten their partners into coming back. Sometimes the violence escalates because the batterer feels rejected or betrayed and chooses to retaliate. In fact, one study shows that more than 70 percent of battered women seeking emergency medical attention received their injuries after leaving their batterer.

Items to Take with You

If you are preparing to leave or just want to be prepared, there are some things you definitely will need. Waiting until a crisis occurs to put these items together is not a good idea. The following are some key items to compile in advance:

➤ Personal identification
➤ Drivers license and vehicle registration
➤ Social Security card
➤ Birth certificate

➤ Passport

➤ Green card and/or work permit

➤ Bank statements

➤ Checkbook

➤ Cash

➤ Credit cards

➤ House, car, and office keys

➤ Medical records

➤ Prescribed medication

➤ Important documentation (such as the deed to your house or rental/lease agreements)

➤ A few items of clothing

➤ Address book

Bad Guys Beware!

If you are planning to leave an abusive environment, you're going to need money. After you leave is not the time to try to go to the bank if you share a joint account with your abuser. Preparing yourself financially in advance is a must; otherwise, you might find that your account has been closed or emptied out. Find out what the law in your state says about how much money you can take. Some states allow you to take one-half of the funds out of the account whether you work or not.

If you aren't planning to leave your abuser but you want to be prepared in case you have to evacuate in a hurry, it's still a good idea to keep some clothes, cash, and important documents at a friend's or family member's home.

If Children Are Involved

If you will be taking your children with you, the following are some additional items to keep in one place:

➤ Child's birth certificate

➤ Child's social security card

➤ Child's medical records

➤ Child's prescription medication

➤ Child's school and vaccination records

➤ Child's favorite blankets or toys

Getting Help

If you are in a situation in which you are being abused, you must get help. Talking to family and friends is important, but you might need to seek help from a professional. Numerous organizations throughout the United States are dedicated to helping victims of domestic violence and abuse. Many of these organizations will provide counseling as well as other means of support for little or no money. Support groups, shelters, and professional counseling all should be available to you, and you should seriously think about taking advantage of them.

Stay on Your Toes

If you've been victimized by physical or sexual abuse and you aren't sure where to go for help, call your local police department. The police can give you the telephone number of a shelter that will take you in or a program you can begin attending.

Depending on the severity of your situation, you also might need to hire an attorney or an advocate, especially if children are involved. Divorce proceedings, custody disputes, and financial matters all are serious issues and might need to be handled by a professional. If you can't afford an attorney, talk to the counselors at the program you are attending. They should be able to discuss some other options with you. Every state differs on this, so your options might vary depending on where you live.

The Least You Need to Know

➤ Men are victimized by domestic violence, too.

➤ Emotional and psychological abuse are just as severe as physical abuse.

➤ If you are living with an abuser, plan your escape in advance.

➤ Restraining orders are valuable only if you enforce them.

➤ If you are trying to get out of a physically abusive situation, let your employers know so they can work with you.

➤ If you've been victimized, get professional help.

Part 4
Safe Drivers Wanted

Carjacking doesn't always happen to the other guy. Your vehicle can be stolen quietly in the night while you sleep, or it can be taken when someone bumps into your car, you get out, and they get in. Find out why car theft is so popular. Learn how to protect your valuable vehicle and stay safe doing it.

So you forgot to get gas, you're on a lonely stretch of road, it's almost dark, and … . You can fill in the remaining blanks. Now what? Should you stay with the car, leave the car and walk, or wait for help from a stranger? Maybe being out of gas isn't your problem; maybe it's a flat tire or mechanical problems. No one answer fits all problems. Life goes on and so do we—every day for thousands of miles all over the country. Use the keys in this section to make your miles safe ones.

Public transportation might be an ordinary part of your life or an occasional experience. Trips with strangers all around you require forethought and a little planning. The bus, subway, and train present different challenges (more than just catching one on time). Learn how to choose a safe seat, how to guard your valuables, and how to recognize dangerous passengers. Find out how to enter—and exit—without becoming another victim that tomorrow's passengers will read about on their way to work.

Chapter 17

Protecting Your Pride and Joy

In This Chapter

➤ An overview of vehicle theft

➤ Carjackings

➤ Protecting your car from theft

You've just enjoyed a wonderful lunch at a nice restaurant, but when you return to your parking space, your car is not in it. You walk around for a little while, thinking you must have forgotten where you parked it. You begin to get nervous. You think maybe it was towed. Surely no one stole your car in broad daylight and from a busy parking lot. Who would take the risk of stealing a car with so many people around and during the middle of the day? Not only is your day ruined when you realize that, in fact, your car has been stolen, you also might be out a lot of money, you have to deal with your insurance company, and you have to find a ride.

In this chapter, I am going to teach you how to prevent this scenario from happening to you. Auto theft is a serious problem that affects millions of Americans, and you need to know how to protect yourself. What about those crazy carjackings that seem to be so popular? I'm also going to teach you how to protect yourself from being victimized by carjackings in the first place, and I'll tell you what to do if you find yourself in the middle of one.

Cars cost thousands of dollars and represent a huge investment for most people. Vehicles usually rank as either the first- or second-largest investment made. In addition, many Americans depend on their car to get them to and from work daily, which makes it a necessity as well as an investment. If you lose your car, you might end up losing your job along with it. As a result, antitheft products for vehicles are a big business and earn manufacturers hundreds of millions of dollars each year. These products can be expensive. Before you buy, you need to know which ones work and which ones don't. Don't worry, I'm going to give you an overview of all the major products available.

Street Talk

Chop shop is the street name for an illegal garage where stolen vehicles are taken to be disassembled. The parts then are sold individually for huge profits.

An Overview of Vehicle Theft

A stolen vehicle can cost you a whole lot more than just a hassle. It can affect your job, your finances, and your insurance rates. The most important reason you need to take this crime seriously, however, is because it can greatly affect your safety. The majority of vehicles stolen are done so by thieves who take them to chop shops.

Car Theft Statistics

Some crime statistics can be misleading or unrealistic because there is no way of knowing how many incidents go unreported each year. With auto theft, however, nearly everyone who has their car stolen reports the incident to the police. They do this for two reasons. First, they want to get their vehicle back. Second, your insurance company won't work with you until you provide a police report. Both of these are strong incentives, don't you think?

Here are some statistics that relate to auto theft in the United States:

➤ The FBI estimates that approximately 1.7 million vehicles are stolen each year.

➤ The chances of your car being stolen or broken into are 1 in 40.

➤ Older model cars are stolen more often than newer models.

➤ One vehicle is stolen approximately every 18 seconds.

➤ Two-thirds of vehicle thefts occur at night.

➤ Only half the vehicles stolen are recovered.

➤ Auto theft is the most costly property crime in America with a total loss of about $8.5 billion per year.

Your Finances

Your car gets stolen, you fill out a police report, you call your insurance company, and your insurance company mails you a check, right? Unfortunately, this isn't how it works.

Let's pretend you buy a new car and finance $20,000 from the bank (with interest) for 60 months. After driving it for only a few months, someone steals it from your driveway. You owe the bank $20,000, but it's your insurance company's policy to pay only market value, which is $15,000. Now, not only do you not have a car, you owe the bank $5,000 (due immediately), and you owe your insurance company its deductible. This doesn't include any valuables you might have lost that were in the car when it was stolen.

If you lease a vehicle and it's stolen, you might be expected to pay off the full lease amount. This means that if you're leasing a $20,000 vehicle for two years, your lease agreement probably states that you're responsible for the full $20,000 if anything happens to the car.

Street Talk

Many insurance companies now offer what's called **gap insurance**. If your car is stolen, gap insurance covers the difference between what you owe the bank and what your car is worth. Gap insurance raises your annual premiums a little, but it is a wise investment.

Your Insurance

If you have a vehicle that is stolen and you file a claim with your insurance company, your annual rates most likely will increase. Your insurance company also might decide to cancel your coverage after it pays your claim. Auto theft costs insurance companies a tremendous amount of money each year, which in turn drives rates up for everyone. This means that your insurance premiums are affected by vehicle theft whether it's your vehicle that's been stolen or not.

Your Safety

How does auto theft affect you and your family's safety? You must keep in mind that the value of most vehicles exceeds thousands of dollars. Something this valuable is going to be attractive to a thief. If a thief decides to steal your vehicle, he or she might be willing to put up a fight for it. This is why carjackings are so common. The crim-

Safety Alert!

If you notice someone trying to steal your vehicle, don't make physical contact with the person. It's very likely that the thief is carrying a weapon, and you don't want to provoke the person into using it. Your only two objectives should be to get a good description of the thief and to startle the person so he or she flees the scene (without your vehicle). Too many times, people get injured or killed while struggling with a thief.

inal decides to take your vehicle from you whether you like it or not. Carjackings have resulted in people losing their lives. There's also the risk of catching a thief trying to steal your vehicle. Most people's natural tendency is to try to stop the thief, but this can easily lead to violence.

Carjackings

You're sitting in your car at an intersection, waiting for the light to turn green. You're adjusting the radio when, all of a sudden, your door flies open and there's a gun pointed in your face. A stranger is yelling at you, telling you to get out of the car! You don't move fast enough so he hits you in the head with the gun, causing you to bleed. Within a matter of seconds, you're lying on the pavement with a severe head injury, and your car is gone. Now imagine that you had a small child or an infant in the back seat of the car. This would represent a whole new set of problems.

Carjacking is a vicious crime—and is now categorized as a federal crime. It's armed robbery with a fancier name and, sometimes, higher stakes. It's violent, it's serious, and innocent people are beaten and killed every day as a result. (The majority of carjackers are armed with either a gun or a knife.) The average carjacking takes fewer than 15 seconds to complete, so you've got to know what to do in advance.

Why Is Carjacking So Popular?

Law enforcement officials now are calling carjacking the growth crime of the '90s. Why is the number of carjackings increasing so rapidly in the United States? The answer is simple. Carjacking is easier and even safer for the criminal than the usual methods of automobile theft. What could be simpler than walking up to a person with car keys and asking him to hand them over? In addition, if the thief gets pulled over, having the keys in the ignition looks less suspicious than having a broken steering column with wires hanging down and twisted together by hand.

Stay on Your Toes

In J. J. Bittenbinder's book *Tough Target,* he states that "Most carjackings occur between 8 and 11 P.M., more often on weekends than during the week. The most active month is December, when over 25 percent of carjackings take place. Over 90 percent of carjackings take place in 15 metropolitan areas."

Entering and Exiting Your Vehicle

Some carjackers like to move in when you're either approaching or exiting your vehicle. They try to time it so they catch you off guard and you already have the door open. This means the car keys probably are already in your hand, and the carjacker doesn't have to mess around with opening the door himself.

The following are some ways to prevent this from happening to you:

➤ Try to avoid parking next to large trucks or vans. (They provide cover for a carjacker.)

➤ Get into the habit of surveying the area surrounding your vehicle while you're approaching it. If someone is loitering near your vehicle, don't approach it until the person leaves.

➤ Before shutting off the engine, unlocking your door, or exiting your vehicle, get into the habit of looking around and surveying the area for anyone who looks suspicious.

➤ When approaching your vehicle, have your keys in your hand and be ready to unlock the door. This enables you to get into the car much faster.

Sitting Duck

Some carjackers prefer targeting people who are already in their vehicle with the engine running. Carjackers have been known to tap on the window with a gun, to yank the door open, or to shatter the glass by striking it with the gun. Grabbing the driver by the hair and pulling him out of the car also is a popular technique.

The following are some things you can do to reduce your chances of being carjacked while in stopped or slowed traffic:

➤ Keep your doors locked and, when in slowed or stopped traffic, keep your windows rolled up.

➤ Don't stand outside the car while buckling up a child. Instead, get into the vehicle together, strap the child in with the doors closed and locked, and then get into the driver's seat. When the door is open and you're leaning in the vehicle, you're easy to surprise from behind.

➤ If someone frightening approaches your car, drive away.

Life Savers

If a carjacker approaches your vehicle and demands that you get out and give him or her the keys, do so without hesitation and without argument. If you have a child in the car, however, you cannot let the carjacker leave with your vehicle until the child is out safely. Tell the carjacker you will fully cooperate as soon as your child is safely out of the vehicle but not until then. If the carjacker refuses to let the child out of the vehicle, toss the keys. When the carjacker retrieves the keys, get the child out quickly. If you let the carjacker leave with the child, you might never see the child again.

➤ Be extra cautious about people who approach your vehicle asking for spare change, wanting to wash your windows, selling flowers, taking donations, or asking for directions.

➤ When using drive-up ATMs at night, be extra cautious of your surroundings.

➤ Don't be afraid to lean on the horn to draw attention to yourself.

➤ Get into the habit of checking your rearview mirrors frequently, especially when you are in slowed or stopped traffic.

➤ Never stop for a stranger, especially at night.

➤ Park in well-lit areas.

➤ When in slowed or stopped traffic, pay attention and be aware of your surroundings. (This is not a good time to change your radio presets, read the newspaper, or apply makeup.)

Keep a Safe Distance

Whenever you are in slowed or stopped traffic, try to keep a car length between your vehicle and the vehicle in front of you. A good rule of thumb is to make sure you can see the rear tires of the vehicle in front of you. This gives you an escape route if a carjacker approaches your vehicle. It also reduces your chances of rear-ending another driver.

By stopping too close to the vehicle in front of you, you make yourself more desirable to a carjacker.

The Bump and Ruse

The bump and ruse technique involves a carjacker in another vehicle that hits you from behind while you're in your car. When you get out of your car to assess the damage and trade information, the carjacker makes his move. At this time, the carjacker jumps into your vehicle and drives off. Sometimes it's just one carjacker looking to switch vehicles. Other times, it might be two or more thieves driving around, looking to pick up another vehicle. This can be very dangerous because the carjacker usually is armed and isn't prepared to take no for an answer.

To protect yourself, you must first create a plan. You must decide in advance how you're going to respond if someone hits you from behind. I recommend that, if you are hit from behind while in your car, be very selective about where you choose to pull over. Pulling over immediately isn't a good idea because this is exactly what the carjacker wants you to do. Turn on your hazards, roll down your window, and drive slowly as you wave for the driver who hit you to follow you. Drive to a location that is well lit, well populated, and with which you are familiar, if possible. Driving to a police station is ideal, but this might not be feasible. If it is a carjacker, the person won't follow for long. If it isn't a carjacker, you can explain your actions when you pull over.

Bad Guys Beware!

The best way to avoid being victimized by a carjacker is to be prepared. Carjackers are looking for drivers who aren't paying attention. By looking alert, having your windows rolled up, and maintaining proper distance from the vehicle in front of you, you are less likely to be carjacked because you have sent a message to the criminal that you are prepared. This is exactly what a carjacker is trying to avoid.

When it comes to trading information with the person who hit you, I recommend that you write down your information in advance on a 3 × 5 index card. You can role your window down slightly and hand this card through the opening. Find out what information your state requires you to provide to the other party and keep this on the card.

A Flat Tire

A polite driver pulls up next to you and signals that you have a flat tire. When you pull over, the polite driver steals your vehicle.

If someone tells you that you have a flat tire, don't pull over. Drive to a safe, well-lit, well-populated area such as a service station and check it out there. This rule applies to every instance in which someone tries to get you to pull over.

The Smash-and-Grab

The smash-and-grab technique has become quite popular with thieves over the past few years, especially young ones. Here's how it works: The criminals hang out at a location where they can discreetly peer into your vehicle without being noticed. They are looking for easy-to-grab valuables lying on the passenger seat such as laptop computers, purses, briefcases, or cell phones. If they see something they like, they throw a small, solid object at the passenger window such as a round, steel ball bearing about the size of a marble. This shatters the glass on contact. While you're sitting there trying to figure out what just happened, the thief reaches into your vehicle, grabs what he wants, and takes off on foot. The entire process takes only a few seconds.

Preventing this crime is simple—keep your valuables out of sight. Place them on the floor or, better yet, in your trunk. If the criminal doesn't see something worth taking, you shouldn't have a problem. If the criminal does see something he likes but it is tucked away on the floor, he will be less likely to go for it because of the time and effort involved. These criminals are looking for valuables that can be snagged quickly.

Protecting Your Vehicle from Theft

Most vehicles are targeted for their accessories such as expensive wheels, stereos, speakers, and so on. Airbags also have become a real hot item. (They are removed and resold to the public.)

The best thing you can do to prevent your vehicle from being stolen or broken into is to keep your doors locked. In addition, keep valuables out of sight at all times. Leaving briefcases, cellular phones, purses, laptop computers, or shopping bags in your vehicle and in sight is like painting a bull's eye on your windshield. If you can't take these items out of the vehicle, at least lock them in the trunk.

Numerous products on the market are designed to protect your vehicle from theft. The following sections discuss the most common products available. To better assist you, I have rated each product's effectiveness and price.

Stay on Your Toes

Of all the vehicles stolen each year, 20 percent have keys in the ignition and 80 percent have unlocked doors.

Alarms

Rating: Good
Price: Moderate to expensive

The best alarms to buy are the ones that flash your headlights, honk your horn, and are equipped with motion and impact sensors.

The bad thing about alarms is that many models can be disarmed with an Electronic Scan Box (ESB), which a professional car thief is likely to have. An ESB is a scanner that can disarm an auto alarm. Before purchasing an alarm for your vehicle, find out whether it can be disarmed with a scanner.

Steering Wheel Locks

Rating: Good
Price: Inexpensive to moderate

This large, steel lock goes over the steering wheel and prevents a thief from being able to turn the wheel enough to steer the vehicle. The good news is that these are very visible and act as a great deterrent to theft. The bad news is that a professional thief can remove one of these locks in seconds. One way is to spray the lock with a special aerosol that freezes it and then strike it with a hammer. This breaks the lock into pieces. Other criminals just pick the lock.

Bad Guys Beware!

If you decide to buy a steering wheel lock for your vehicle, spend the extra money to purchase one with an advanced locking system. The inexpensive ones usually have cheaper locks that are very easy to pick.

Tracking Devices

Rating: Excellent
Price: Expensive

Tracking devices are great for recovering a missing vehicle quickly, but they don't do a great deal to prevent it from being stolen in the first place. A decal that says the vehicle is equipped with a tracking device can be very effective against theft. The tracking device is a chip is hidden somewhere on the vehicle. If the vehicle is stolen, it can be tracked electronically by satellite.

Security Glass

Rating: Excellent
Price: Expensive

Security glass is very expensive, but it is an excellent investment. It doesn't do a great deal to prevent your vehicle from being stolen, but it goes a long way toward protecting whoever is inside the vehicle. Security glass looks ordinary, but it is extremely difficult to break. Led pipes, hammers, and tire irons can't break through it. This is great for stopping carjackers.

Stay on Your Toes

Many high-profile people and government officials have security glass on their vehicles. Some security glass is even bulletproof.

VIN Glass Etching

Rating: Good
Price: Moderate

In VIN glass etching, the vehicle's identification number (VIN) is permanently etched into all the vehicle's windows. This will deter some thieves because it increases their chances of getting caught after they've stolen your vehicle; when a car is stolen the VIN ID plate on the dashboard can be changed quickly, but the windows can't. If pulled over, the officer can make sure the VIN numbers match. If they can get the vehicle to a chop shop, however, the windows will come out immediately.

Kill Switches

Rating: Good
Price: Inexpensive

A kill switch is a switch hidden inside a vehicle that needs to be flipped before the vehicle can be started. It can affect either the starter, the flow of electricity, or fuel flow. Kill switches are moderately effective and are simple to install. A professional car thief can get around kill switches, but an amateur can't.

Steering Column Armored Collars

Rating: Good
Price: Moderate

This product prevents a vehicle from being hot-wired by protecting the steering column with a durable, protective collar. I like the ones that are permanently installed. Stay away from the kind that has to be manually installed every time you get out of the vehicle. Armored collars act as a visual deterrent as well.

Security Keys

Rating: Excellent
Price: Moderate

Security keys have a small computer chip installed inside the top of the ignition key. If any other method is attempted to start the vehicle, it will shut down. The chip communicates with the vehicle's onboard computer and alarm system; without it, the vehicle will not respond. These keys are great, but if you lose one, it can cost as much as $100 to order a new one, which must be ordered from the dealer.

Decals and Blinking Lights

Rating: Good
Price: Inexpensive

It's surprising how effective a $5 blinking red light on your dashboard can be. An alarm decal that looks legitimate also is a great deterrent. These products can be purchased for very little money and can make a thief think twice because he won't know whether an alarm is really installed. If you're looking for an inexpensive deterrent, these products are definitely the way to go.

The Least You Need to Know

➤ Billions of dollars are lost each year as a result of auto theft.

➤ Unless a child is with you, be quick to give a carjacker your vehicle without resistance.

➤ The best deterrent to carjackings is to be aware and alert.

➤ Removing valuable items from your vehicle is a great way to prevent theft and vandalism.

➤ The easiest and most inexpensive way to prevent your vehicle from being stolen is to keep the doors locked at all times and never leave the keys in the ignition.

➤ The best vehicle antitheft devices are the ones that act as a visual deterrent as well.

Chapter 18

Roadside Assistance for the Stranded Driver

In This Chapter

➤ The dangers of getting stranded

➤ Knowing your options

➤ The big three

➤ Reducing the risks

You're driving on an unfamiliar highway late one night, and all of a sudden your engine light comes on. The next exit is four miles away. You keep driving, hoping you can make it. Unfortunately, thick steam begins rising from under the hood, the engine dies, and you're forced to pull over to the side of the road. To make matters worse, it's cold outside, you have no way to call for help, and you don't know the area. You're stranded.

In this chapter, I will discuss the dangers of getting stranded and how to best protect yourself if this happens to you. I also will teach you how to reduce the chances of ever becoming stranded. There are several options you can take, and the pros and cons of each will be discussed in detail. Being stranded puts you and anyone who might be with you at serious risk in several ways, so it's important for you to know how to protect yourself.

I also will teach you about road rage and the dangers associated with giving strangers a ride. Violent acts of road rage are becoming more frequent on our streets and highways, and you need to know how to handle this type of aggression. You will learn all you need to know to protect yourself on the open road. So buckle-up and let's go!

The Dangers of Getting Stranded

Being stranded is a terrible predicament to be in, and it can put you in great danger. Stranded drivers have been the victims of murder, kidnapping, violent assault, rape, robbery, and hit-and-run drivers. Not only does being stranded make you more susceptible to crime, you also have to guard against other vehicles. Any way you look at it, getting stranded makes you vulnerable and jeopardizes your safety. Unfortunately, many people don't prepare for getting stranded because they don't view it as a serious problem. To help demonstrate the severity of this problem, the following sections provide a few examples of the dangers that can stem from being stranded.

Being stranded can be a frightening experience, especially if you don't know what to do.

Car Crimes

When stranded, some people choose to leave their vehicle behind and set out for help. Upon returning, many people have found their vehicle to be broken into, vandalized, stripped down, or even stolen. A stranded vehicle with no one around is an easy target for a thief, especially if it's dark outside and no one is around.

If you ever have to leave your vehicle on the side of the road, try to have it removed as quickly as possible. This is why a program such as the American Automobile Association (AAA) is so great. One phone call and a tow truck will be on the scene right away. The longer your vehicle sits unattended, the greater the potential of something happening to it. A lot of criminals will leave your vehicle alone the first time they see it and then come back a little later to get on with their business. They do this because they know if a vehicle isn't picked up within the first hour, it will usually sit there overnight.

Violent Crimes

Some criminals drive up and down highways and interstates looking for stranded drivers to victimize. People have been abducted and never seen again because they

weren't prepared and didn't make good decisions. Many times, a criminal will pose as a Good
Samaritan who just wants to help. The criminal
knows you are in a vulnerable situation, and this
is why he or she is interested in you. The criminal also knows you are much more likely to
accept help from a stranger because of your lack
of options. This is why you must stay on your
toes and have a plan. In this situation, you have
several options, which I will be discussing later in
this chapter. Regardless of how nice a stranger
seems in offering you assistance, stay on your
guard and be very suspicious. Follow your
instincts and don't be afraid to offend.

Bad Guys Beware!

If your vehicle breaks down, the
best thing you can do to protect it
is call for a tow truck right away.
Don't leave it sitting unattended
unless you absolutely have to.

Getting Hit

On occasion, inebriated, sleepy, or distracted drivers have been known to hit parked
vehicles, including police cars. As a result, when your vehicle is parked on the side of
the road (or in the middle of the road), you run the risk of being sideswiped or rear-
ended by another driver. You need to protect yourself from this. You also are susceptible to being hit by flying objects thrown out of the windows of passing vehicles. I
know this sounds cruel, but it happens all the time. Some people think it's entertain-
ing to hit stranded bystanders with flying objects while driving by. This might not
seem like a big deal, but keep in mind that the speed at which the object is traveling
will be the same as the speed at which the vehicle is traveling. Getting hit by a beer
bottle traveling 60 mph can kill you instantly. With this in mind, choose where you
stand carefully.

Every year, innocent people are killed by moving
vehicles that hit them when they are sitting in or
standing near a parked car. The following are
some precautions you can take to protect yourself
and your vehicle from other drivers:

Safety Alert!

If you need to stop your vehicle
because of car trouble, pull over to
the right as far as possible. Park on
the grass if you have to, but don't
block traffic. Leaving your vehicle in
a traffic lane is very dangerous and
puts you, your vehicle, and other
drivers at serious risk.

➤ Turn your hazard lights on immediately and
leave them on.

➤ Don't stand close to your vehicle. (If another
driver hits your vehicle and you're standing
too close, you might be hit as well.)

➤ Stand in a place where your vehicle is
between you and traffic. This can act as a
shield and can help protect you from anything thrown by passersby.

➤ Place flares, reflective triangles, or cones around your vehicle (if you have them).

➤ Strive to stop your vehicle in the safest place possible.

Knowing Your Options

If you get stranded, several options are afforded to you. Unfortunately, none of these options are 100 percent foolproof, but one option might be safer than the others, depending on your circumstances. The more options of which you are aware, the more likely you are to get home safely. Remember, applied knowledge is power.

Things to Consider

One positive thing about being stranded is that you are afforded the luxury of time—time to make good decisions based on circumstances and surroundings, not fear. You don't have to do anything rash, and you can stop to carefully think things through.

When making decisions about what steps to take and how best to handle the situation, you first need to take into consideration your exact circumstances. No two scenarios are the same because the circumstances are never exactly the same. Ask yourself the following questions before you make any decisions:

Stay on Your Toes

Your number one priority is to get home safely as soon as possible. Taking care of your vehicle should be your second objective. Decisions need to be based on your welfare and safety, not your automobile's.

➤ Do you consider your location to be safe or dangerous?

➤ How many cars are driving by (several, few, or none)?

➤ How far are you from an open business?

➤ What are the weather conditions?

➤ What time is it?

➤ Are you alone or with someone?

➤ Do you have any way to place a call?

➤ What kind of essential items do you have with you (such as flares, a gas can, a blanket)?

Staying with Your Car

Remaining with your vehicle can be your safest choice, or it can be the most dangerous thing you can do. Again, it depends on the circumstances.

If you choose to stay, keep in mind that your car is not an invincible fortress. The only thing standing between you and someone who wants in is a piece of glass, which can easily be broken. Rolling up your windows and locking your doors is a must, but don't put false hope in the level of protection this provides. Being prepared by knowing your options will do a much better job of protecting you and keeping you safe than a piece of glass will.

It might be a good idea to stay with your vehicle if any of the following circumstances exist:

➤ You've placed a call, and you know that help will arrive shortly.

➤ You have a child with you.

➤ The weather conditions are extreme, and going to get help could be dangerous.

➤ Police frequently travel the road or highway on which you're stranded.

➤ A stranger has agreed to call for help for you.

➤ The nearest place to go for help is too far to walk.

➤ You've placed a Need Help—Call Police sign in the window where it can be seen by passersby.

➤ You happen to know that waiting a little while will give your car enough time to settle down and run again, at least long enough to get to safety.

➤ You're parked in a safe, well lit, well traveled area.

Walking to Safety

Depending on your situation, walking to get help might be your safest option. The following are some circumstances that might justify leaving your vehicle on foot to retrieve help:

➤ You have no way of calling for help.

➤ There is a safe location within reasonable walking distance.

➤ Your vehicle doesn't provide you with adequate protection from the weather (convertibles, motorcycles, and so on).

➤ Your vehicle could draw dangerous attention to yourself (such as a new Mercedes Benz stranded in a crime-ridden or dangerous part of town).

Because every situation is different, you have to use your best judgment in determining what is the safest course of action for you to take. Just remember, follow your instincts and don't make decisions based on fear.

Hiding

Every once in a while, a situation arises when staying with your vehicle is not a safe option and neither is walking off to get help. If this is the case, you might want to consider hiding. (You can hide either inside the vehicle or near the vehicle.) Hiding is a good idea if one of the following circumstances exists:

➤ You're in a dangerous area but have called for help.

➤ Someone you are suspicious of is approaching your vehicle.

➤ An activity is going on nearby that makes you nervous (such as a group of people drinking alcohol).

➤ Someone passes you and then stops to turn around.

Stay on Your Toes

If you're going to stay with your vehicle and hide, it's a good idea to have a plan of action. Hiding and hoping the problem solves itself is not a good idea. You might only need to hide for a few minutes until someone goes away, and this is fine. Hiding for hours with no purpose won't help you.

Strangers

If you become stranded, it's very likely that a stranger will stop to ask if you need help. If a stranger approaches you offering assistance, ask him or her to call the police for you and nothing else. If the person is truly concerned for your safety, he or she will have no problem doing this for you. If the person insists on giving you a ride instead, you might have a problem. If you're out of gas, it's okay to ask the stranger to bring you back some fuel in a container. Just don't accept a ride from a stranger. Getting into a vehicle with a stranger is dangerous business, regardless of how nice, kind, innocent, and harmless the person might appear. The only time this can be justified is when *not* accepting a ride will put you in greater danger. You might be frightened, for example, because the same suspicious car has driven by several times, slowing down as it passes. In a situation such as this, it might be better to take the ride than to stick around to see what happens next. Use your judgment, but keep in mind that getting into a vehicle with a stranger should be your last option in a bad situation. Take into consideration who is offering a ride—a gang in a car, surely not; a family, possibly.

The Big Three

When you and your car are stranded, it's usually for one of three reasons. The car either has run out of gas, has a flat tire, or is experiencing mechanical problems. Preparing for these circumstances in advance will help reduce your chances of being stranded in the first place.

Out of Gas

Running out of gas has stranded more vehicles than can be counted. This is something, however, that can easily be prevented. I know stopping to fill your gas tank is an inconvenience, but so is sitting on the side of the road.

Flat Tire

Unlike running out of gas, getting a flat tire isn't as easy to control. You *can* prepare yourself, though. A lot of flat tires can be repaired quickly with a $5 can of tire sealant. Tire sealant is a small can filled with air and a rubber sealant. All you do is screw the end of its little rubber hose onto your tire, and it does the rest. It puts enough air in the tire to get you to safety, and it seals any small holes or leaks you might have. It also is a good idea to make sure you're not driving around on unsafe tires that could blow anytime. If your tires are bald or if you can see steel chords poking through the rubber, you're asking for a flat tire or, worse, for a terrible accident. If your tire blows while you're driving, you can lose control of the vehicle.

You also need to carry a spare tire (properly inflated), a jack, and a lug nut wrench. If you've never changed a tire before, take the time to learn how. Take the tire off your car and put it back on at least once at home. You don't want to be stranded with a flat tire and not know how to change it yourself. In many areas, there are classes especially for women to learn how to do this.

> **Bad Guys Beware!**
>
> The best way to prevent running out of gas is to retrain your brain. Convince yourself that one quarter of a tank is equivalent to an empty tank. This way, every time your fuel gauge reads one quarter of a tank, you'll stop to fill up.

Stay on Your Toes

An oil change every 3,000 miles, checking your vital fluids, scheduled tune-ups, and routine checkups once in a while can go a long way toward keeping you from sitting on the side of the road in the middle of nowhere.

Mechanical Problems

The best way to prevent mechanical problems is to keep your vehicle in good working order.

If you hear a strange noise, notice a warning light, smell a strange odor, or see a gauge with an unusual reading, get it checked out. You'll be glad you did. You might think you can't afford to fix this stuff, but if you don't, it will only get more expensive and could end up costing you more than just money.

Reducing Your Risk

Proper planning is vital to your safety. Being stranded is not nearly as dangerous when you've taken the right steps. Take the time to prepare for emergencies. That way, if they occur, you won't be so vulnerable. This section will help you equip yourself with options.

Cell Phones and CB Radios

There's nothing more valuable to your safety if you're stranded than a cell phone or a CB radio. This equips you to call the police, an ambulance, a tow truck, a family member, a friend, or your office. A cell phone or a CB radio also enables you to call on someone else's behalf who might need help or if there's been an accident.

Owning a cell phone used to be expensive but not anymore. There now are roadside assistance packages for as low as $15 per month. They give you 30 minutes of calls each month, which is more than enough air time if you're only going to use the phone for safety reasons and emergencies. If you sign a one-year contract, most companies will even throw in the phone for free.

Things to Have in Your Car

The following is a list of items you might want to consider carrying in your vehicle at all times:

➤ Everything you need to change a flat tire

➤ A one-gallon gas container

➤ A blanket

➤ A warm coat, gloves, and a hat

➤ A comfortable pair of walking shoes

➤ Flares and reflective triangles (or small orange cones)

➤ A "Need Help—Call Police" cardboard window sign

➤ Water

➤ Jumper cables

➤ An umbrella

➤ Tools

➤ A flashlight

Bad Guys Beware!

I strongly recommend that you keep a small container of mace in your vehicle at all times, separate from the one you carry with you. Knowing you have it in the car will ease your mind, especially if you have to walk to get help or are approached by a stranger.

Roadside Assistance Programs

Roadside assistance programs are great. For very little money, you can have access to a toll-free phone number that dispatches help immediately to wherever you are. AAA is probably the most recognized roadside assistance program, but there are others. Sometimes this service is offered for free as an incentive to purchase a new vehicle, a new cell phone, or a new vehicle insurance policy.

Stay on Your Toes

When dispatched, most roadside assistance companies will help you if your battery is dead, if you run out of gas, if you have a flat tire, if you need a tow, or if you've locked your keys in your vehicle.

Police Call Boxes

Police call boxes are emergency phones placed on the sides of some highways. They were designed specifically for calling the police if you become stranded. If you have a choice between traveling on a road that has call boxes and a road that doesn't, I recommend the road with the call boxes. Even if it's going to take a few extra minutes to get somewhere by traveling the route with call boxes, it's well worth the time. If you ever need one, you'll know what I mean.

Life Savers

If someone gets angry with you on the road, don't retaliate. Angry drivers have been known to run their victims off the road, to follow them home, to pull over to fight, and to shoot their victims from their vehicle. They also have been known to get their victim's license plate number so they can deal with it later, which is even worse. Drive away, stop and turn around, gesture an apology, do whatever it takes. If you have to, turn somewhere you don't need to just to get away from them. Whatever you do, don't participate! If they follow you, don't drive home or to someone's residence. Instead, drive to a police department, a fire department, a hospital (there often are police officers at hospitals), or somewhere else you consider safe.

Other Roadside Dangers

The following sections discuss two other roadside dangers with which you need to be familiar: road rage and giving rides to hitchhikers. Road rage has become extremely popular—and extremely dangerous—and can appear in your rear-view mirror without warning. Also, the days of safely picking up hitchhikers are long gone, unfortunately.

Road Rage

Road rage is what takes place when one driver becomes angry with another and decides to get revenge. A good way to describe it is to imagine uncontrollable anger traveling at 60 mph while sitting behind a few thousand pounds of steel. This can be sparked by cutting someone off, not letting them cut in front of you, driving too slow in the passing lane, or not letting someone pass you. Whatever the reason, it's very dangerous, and people have been killed as a result.

Hitchhikers

When it comes to giving rides to strangers, don't! This is extremely dangerous and can even get you killed. If you see someone who needs a ride and you really want to help, call a cab and pay for it. Give the person bus fare, buy the person a bottle of water, or give the person a few dollars—don't give the person a ride. I know this sounds cruel and unkind, but people get killed doing this.

Stay on Your Toes

Picking up hitchhikers is such a dangerous practice that many states have passed laws making it illegal.

The Least You Need to Know

➤ When stranded, getting home safely should be your number one priority.

➤ Decisions need to be made based on circumstances, not fears.

➤ Accepting a ride from a stranger is dangerous and is not recommended.

➤ There are steps you can take to greatly reduce your chances of becoming stranded, such as properly maintaining your vehicle.

➤ Cell phones are one of the best investments you can make to ensure your safety when in your car.

➤ Road rage has cost many innocent people their lives.

Chapter 19

Safely Getting Across Town

In This Chapter

➤ Traveling by taxicab

➤ Braving the bus system

➤ Surviving the subway

You're visiting a large city to which you've never been before, and you need to take a taxicab back to the airport. You signal a cab from a busy corner and it stops. The driver puts your luggage in the trunk and away you go. Ten minutes pass and you begin to wonder whether you're heading in the right direction. You might not know the area, but you do have a sense of direction, and you're pretty sure you're going the wrong way. You ask the driver, and he assures you that he knows what he's doing. He tells you he's avoiding heavy traffic by going another route. A few minutes later, the driver pulls over on a vacant street and points a gun at you, demanding that you lay all your valuables on the seat. After you comply, the driver makes you get out. You're left standing in the middle of nowhere without your money, identification, credit cards, or airline tickets. To make matters worse, your luggage is still in the trunk.

Whether you're traveling by taxicab, bus, or subway, this chapter is filled with life-saving wisdom that can help keep you safe. I will discuss the most common dangers associated with commercial transportation, and I'll prepare you for the worst of situations. Whether you use public transportation every day or once a year, you don't want to miss this practical information that will keep you in the driver's seat.

Taxicabs

For the most part, taxis are a safe way to travel. Unfortunately, not all cab drivers are honest and well meaning, which is why this chapter is so important. In fact, some of them are downright dangerous. Because the few that are bad don't drive around town with a sign on the top of their cab that reads "Criminal for Hire," it's important for you to know how to spot them in advance and how to protect yourself from them.

Stay on Your Toes

Driving a cab is one of the most dangerous professions in the United States.

Choosing a Taxi

The best way to order a taxi, if you can, is to order one by phone to come and get you. That way, you know what company to look for.

Bad Guys Beware!

If you share a cab, make sure that, when the other passenger exits, he or she doesn't take one of your bags. Believe it or not, this scam has been around for years. Sometimes the driver and the passenger are working together, and sometimes the passenger is working alone.

Most people usually just hop into the first taxi that's available. After all, aren't all cabs the same? How can you tell by looking at a cab whether it's going to be safe?

If for any reason you're suspicious of the driver, trust your instincts and don't get in. Simply say "No thank you" and walk away. You don't have to have a good reason for not getting in, and it doesn't have to make sense. Your instincts are an internal alarm system that needs to be trusted. Another thing to take into consideration when choosing a cab is other passengers. If another passenger is in the cab already, or if one jumps in with you, get out. Don't share a cab unless you're short on money and it's the only way you can afford it. The other passenger probably is completely harmless, but why take chances if you don't have to? The other passenger also could be a partner in crime with the driver, and this would make robbing you extremely easy.

Things to Look For

The first thing you need to do is look to see whether a company you recognize owns the cab. I recommend staying with familiar cab companies whenever possible. The larger, more reputable cab companies usually have hiring practices that check an applicant's criminal record before hiring him or her. Some of the smaller, privately owned companies might not.

Before getting into the cab, look to see whether a photo ID of the driver is displayed. This photo usually is located near the glove box or meter and only takes a second to glance at. If there isn't a photo, or if the photo is of someone other than the driver, wait for another cab. Also glance inside to make sure there's a CB radio and a meter. If the cab doesn't have these two important items, it probably is not legitimate.

It also is a good idea to check the cab's identification number, which should be located in large numbers on both sides of the vehicle. If these numbers don't exist or if parts of the number are missing, don't get in. This cab probably is someone's personal vehicle.

Stay on Your Toes

There's nothing wrong with an individual owning his or her own cab, but if the person doesn't have it legally registered, what does this tell you about the driver? This rule also applies to an expired inspection sticker or tags. Any cab that is part of a legitimate company will be current and legal. Remember, it only takes a second to find another cab.

Baggage

Keep your luggage as close to you as possible. Only let the driver put your belongings in the trunk if there isn't room for them inside. By placing these items in the trunk, you put yourself at a disadvantage. If there's a dispute over how much money the driver wants to charge you, if the driver doesn't want to give you the proper change, or if the driver is a thief, having your belongings locked in the trunk of the cab greatly reduces your options. It also is a good idea to keep these items in the back seat with you and not up front with the driver.

If you must put some of your belongings in the trunk, put the least valuable items there and keep the important ones with you. Watch the driver put your bags in the trunk before entering the cab. Some drivers run a scam in which they leave one of

227

your bags lying behind the cab. After you leave, a thief who is working with the driver will come by and pick it up. A good rule of thumb is that, if you can't afford to lose it, make sure it stays within an arm's reach.

Once You're in the Cab

Where you sit is important. The safest seat in a cab is in the back seat directly behind the driver. If the driver is a criminal and decides to point a gun at you to rob you, he would have to stop the vehicle and reposition himself first. It's virtually impossible for a driver to hold a gun on someone sitting directly behind him. In addition, if you're sitting in this seat, the driver can't see your face without looking in the rearview mirror. If the driver is going to pull a gun or try something stupid, it is likely that he or she would want to look at your face first to make sure you aren't paying attention.

Don't ever take food, candy, or beverages from a cab driver. If the driver offers you something, you can politely accept if you want to be nice, but don't eat it. There's a good chance the driver is just being kind, but unfortunately, some drivers have used this tactic to drug their passengers, resulting in crimes such as rape and robbery.

If you become suspicious of the driver for any reason, write down his or her information so that, if something does happen, you can report it to the police or to the cab company. You need to write down the driver's name, which should be printed on the photo ID, and the cab's identification number, which should be publicly displayed as well.

Giving Out Information

Be careful not to give out any information to the driver. Dishonest drivers can give this information to thieves or can come back and rob you themselves.

The following is a list of questions you should avoid answering:

➤ Are you from out of town?

➤ Where are you from?

➤ How long are you staying?

➤ What do you do for a living?

➤ Are you married?

➤ Do you have any children?

You'd be amazed how much someone can learn about you just by asking a few simple questions. Keep in mind that this driver might be taking you to your home, your office, or your hotel. If the driver decides to target you based on the answers to the preceding questions, you probably won't be too hard to find.

Going the Wrong Way

Sometimes a dishonest cabby will take you to a drop point where others are waiting to rob you. The driver also could take you to an isolated location to rob you himself and then leave you stranded afterwards. This is why it's a good idea to pay attention to where you're going when riding in a cab. Don't be afraid to ask questions about the route the driver is taking.

Paying the Fare

It's always a good idea to have change (small bills) on you before getting into a cab. When it's time to pay a $13 fare and all you have is a $20 bill, a dishonest driver can easily tell you he doesn't have change. If this happens to you, tell the driver either to take you to get change (without the meter running) or to wait while you go inside somewhere to get it. If the driver doesn't have change, it's his responsibility to tell you. By having smaller bills, you can avoid this hassle.

Bad Drivers

If a cab driver does something illegal—for example, if he begins driving you in the wrong direction or taking the long way until you say something about it, or if you fear that the cab's meter is fast (they can be tampered with)—do something about it. Depending on the situation, you might need to call the company for which the cab driver works, or you might even need to call the police. By ignoring the situation, there's a good chance other passengers will be victimized by the same dishonest behavior.

Life Savers

If you are familiar with the area and notice the cab driver heading the wrong way, bring it to his or her attention immediately. If the driver doesn't stop and turn around right away, insist that he or she stop the cab and quickly get out.

If the cab driver refuses to stop to let you out, you might have to do something drastic like reach over his or her shoulder and grab the keys out of the ignition or throw the car into park. If the cab has a security partition installed and you can't reach into the front, you might have to let the driver know how serious you are by opening a rear door or breaking out a window. I know this sounds drastic but remember, if you tell a driver he or she is going the wrong way and the person keeps going, you have a serious problem. If you tell the driver to stop the car and he or she refuses, you're in serious danger.

Buses

Buses are a popular form of transportation because they're one of the cheapest ways to travel. If you're going to ride the bus, however, you'll need to know a few things to help keep you safe in the process.

The Bus Stop

The only thing you really need to be careful about when standing at the bus stop is theft. If you're going to be setting your valuables down, keep a careful eye on them. Also be mindful of pickpockets. If someone standing at the bus stop causes you concern, don't get on. If three rowdy gang members are yelling obscenities at passersby and are harassing other people at the bus stop, they're probably going to act the same way on the bus. The only difference is that, if you get on the bus with them, you're stuck with them. If they make you nervous and you want to get away from them, wait for the next bus.

Choosing Your Seat

When choosing your seat, safety should be your first priority. Seats closest to the exit are the safest because you can exit quickly if necessary. Don't get a seat that's so close to the exit, however, that everyone who gets on and off the bus ends up brushing up against you and your valuables. This is a great way to lose your belongings. I also recommend choosing an aisle seat over a window seat. Again, the quicker you can get off the bus in an emergency, the better.

Guarding Your Valuables

When you're on the bus, be sure to guard your valuables. An aisle seat is ideal when the window seat next to it is vacant. That way, you can put your valuables beside you on the window seat. The safest place to put your belongings, however, is on your lap. If you can't put them on your lap, put them somewhere you can easily watch them. Placing items by your feet or between your legs usually is pretty safe.

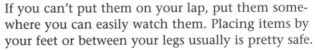

Safety Alert!

Avoid putting anything valuable under your bus seat. The person sitting behind you can easily go through your bags without you knowing it.

Dangerous Passengers

When you're on a bus, it's important that you be aware of who is on the bus with you. Discreetly look around to see whether anyone causes you concern. If everything looks fine, continue to quickly scan the area every few minutes. If you notice someone or something suspicious, don't be afraid to ask the driver to stop the bus and let you out, or you can wait until the next stop and get out there.

When Exiting the Bus

When exiting the bus, double-check to make sure you have all your belongings with you. When standing up in the aisle, hold your belongings in front of you and not by your side. Holding your possessions by your side makes it too easy for thieves who are sitting. Be suspicious of anyone who bumps into you and avoid getting to close to the person in front of you. The safest thing to do is remain in your seat until the majority of the people pass by and then get up to exit.

Subways

For many major cities around the world, subways are the lifelines of transportation. Millions of people use subways daily, so it's inevitable that subway crime is a problem.

Bad Guys Beware!

The best time to look the bus over for troublemakers is when you're getting on. It appears to other passengers that you're just looking for a seat when, really, you're making sure it's safe to stay. Aware people make difficult targets. Never be afraid to turn around and walk off the bus. However, be sure to go by a passenger's behavior and not their appearance.

Subways, as with most forms of mass transportation, are filled with a variety of races, age groups, social groups, cultures, and people with different religious beliefs. This can create tension. This section teaches you how to stay safe while riding the subway and what kind of dangers to keep an eye out for.

Subway trains are filled with a variety of different cultures, age groups, and social classes, and this sometimes can cause tension.

Stay on Your Toes

New York City has an estimated 648 miles of tracks, 469 stations, and nearly 6,000 train cars in use.

Subway Stations

Pickpockets and thieves love subway terminals because they're crowded and because it's fairly easy to make a quick escape. Therefore, carry briefcases and purses firmly. Don't flash your cash when buying tokens and make sure you don't look like a tourist (especially if you are one). Expect to see a few homeless people who might ask you for loose change. Don't worry, though, panhandlers usually are pretty safe. Gang members are who you really need to keep an eye on, especially several of them together. When walking through the terminal, try to look confident, aware, and alert. It's the best deterrent to crime there is.

Bad Guys Beware!

If you see an empty seat between two people who look safe, take it. This way, you're choosing who your neighbors are going to be. If you take a seat next to another vacant seat, you never know who you'll end up sitting next to.

Where You Sit

A seat needs to be chosen with safety in mind. If you have to choose between sitting near a person who makes you uncomfortable or standing for 10 minutes, it's better to stand. Your safety should be a higher priority than your comfort.

Here are a few more helpful tips:

➤ Avoid riding in empty cars.

➤ Avoid riding alone late at night.

➤ Conceal jewelry in order to not make yourself an easy target.

Guarding Your Stuff

Like when riding the bus, keep your belongings close to you at all times and keep an eye on them. Try to find a compromise between securing them close to you and keeping them out of sight, especially items that appear to be valuable. An expensive leather briefcase or a Gucci purse can draw the attention of a thief with an eye for quality. I'd place the Gucci purse on my lap with my arms laying over it, and I'd place the briefcase on the floor between my legs. Never leave your belongings unattended, not even for a second.

Be careful of any distractions that occur while on the train. This very well could be a diversion technique used by a few thieves working the train together. Let's say a woman drops her purse in front of you. She knows you probably will bend over to pick it up for her and so does her partner sitting next to you, who is waiting to steal your wallet when you bend over. If you notice a distraction or want to assist someone on the train, keep an eye on your possessions while you do so.

Entering and Exiting the Train

Before entering the subway, take a second to peek inside the train and see if anyone makes you feel uncomfortable. If so, move down to the next car. Remember, trust your instincts!

When it comes time to exit the train, you need to be careful of pickpockets. Subway pickpockets love to take people's possessions while everyone is gathered at the exit. You are much less likely to be suspicious of a bump from a pickpocket when you're exiting, and even if you do notice, the pickpocket probably has already disappeared into the crowd.

The Least You Need to Know

➤ Taxicabs can be a safe way to travel as long as you know what precautions to take.

➤ Giving out too much information to a taxicab driver can lead to trouble.

➤ Your biggest concern when riding the bus should be guarding your belongings.

➤ Never be afraid to get off a subway or bus earlier than you expected if you feel uncomfortable.

Part 5

Face to Face with the Enemy

You've learned ways to prevent becoming a victim of a crime by planning ahead, by recognizing danger, and by avoiding risky situations. Now let's turn to actions you can take when face to face with the real thing—your enemy. Your objective is not to defeat your enemy in combat; your objective is to escape from him. It is vital that you remember this. Victory is a safe escape.

"But I can't fight a criminal." Is that what you're thinking? "I'm too weak … " or "I'm too old … too young … too out of shape." You don't have to be strong, young, older, or in shape to use the techniques described in this section. They are simple, practical, and—most importantly—effective. You can quickly learn how to instinctively use this system of self-defense. This is not a commercial; it's a reality. Thousands of people in all walks of life already have learned it. It's a way to fight back and create the time you need to get away safely.

If you ever face a criminal, there are four steps to survival. You will learn them along with other factors to consider: Is there a weapon? Do you have children with you? What does the attacker want anyway? What should you do if you are ordered to relocate? Get in the car or go to another place? You have the advantage. (Didn't know that, did you?)

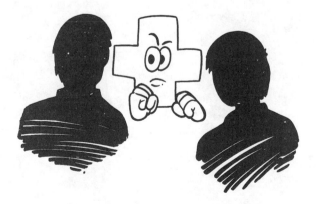

When You're Confronted by a Criminal

You've just enjoyed a long day at the new mall. The mall is closing, and you start to head back to your car, exhausted. You're looking forward to going home and propping your feet up with a good book. As you walk through the parking garage, a strange man quickly steps out from behind a van holding a large hunting knife. Within seconds, he has grabbed your arm with one hand and is pointing the knife in your back with the other.

The stranger tells you to get into the van or he'll kill you. He promises that he won't hurt you as long as you cooperate, but he threatens to kill you again if you don't. You're more frightened than you've ever been in your life, and you don't know what to do. You definitely don't want to get into the van, but what if he kills you if you resist?

In a life-or-death situation such as this, there's no room for mistakes. The decisions you make in these few seconds will affect the rest of your life, so it's vital that you know what to do.

In this chapter, I'm going to teach you what to do if a criminal confronts you face to face. I will discuss several helpful scenarios and will give you some practical options for what to do in seemingly helpless situations. Personal safety experts agree that the first three seconds of an encounter with the bad guy are the most crucial in determining the outcome. This is why you must know the answers in advance if you're going to survive. If you're not sure what to do when confronted by a criminal, you definitely don't want to miss the life-saving information in this chapter.

The Four Steps to Survival

To increase your chances of survival, you first must prepare your mind. You also must know the risks involved and make good decisions based on them. Once you know all the risks, you can better assess the situation and determine all your options. This is what leads to the safest plan of action possible. These four steps are

➤ Prepare your mind

➤ Know the risks

➤ Know the options

➤ Know the objective

Prepare Your Mind

For most people, the very thought of being attacked by a criminal makes them uncomfortable. The reason it's so uncomfortable to think about is because it touches one of our greatest fears, the fear of being physically injured, raped, or killed. The truth is, by confronting these hard-to-deal-with issues, you begin to increase your chances of surviving a crime scene.

Stay on Your Toes

To come out of a crime scene unscathed, you have to know what to do in advance. The people committing these acts are hardened criminals who allow no room for mistakes. Hoping it will never happen to you does nothing to improve your chances of survival.

The best way to prepare your mind is to visualize yourself being confronted by an attacker and to picture your response. If you see a story on the news about a recent crime that took place, for example, imagine yourself in that situation for a brief moment and visualize yourself making good decisions and winning.

This does a whole lot more for your safety plan than turning the channel. If you read a story in the newspaper about someone who was robbed at gunpoint while coming out of the mall, for example, stop to think about what you would do in that same situation. Don't visualize yourself doing things that are unrealistic such as over-powering the attacker, taking the gun, and holding the person there single-handedly until the police arrive. See yourself responding with wisdom and not acting out of fear, keeping a clear head, and surveying your surroundings. Imagine finding the perfect opportunity to escape, such as the criminal being distracted by a passerby, and taking it. Think of surviving, not losing! Preparing your mind in advance is crucial to your survival.

Know the Risks

Before you can make good decisions, you first must know the risks involved. After you determine the risks, your decisions will be based on odds of survival rather than a fear of getting hurt. If deciding not to give a robber the keys to your new car increases your risk of getting shot, for example, and handing your keys over lowers your risk of getting shot, the safest choice is obvious.

Know Your Options

Choosing the best option can be done only after you have determined the risks involved. The following are some of the most common options you probably will have to choose from if confronted by a criminal:

➤ Should I try to escape?

➤ Should I scream?

➤ Should I cause a scene?

➤ Should I comply?

➤ Should I resist?

Life Savers

Let's pretend a criminal has jumped into the back seat of your car while you're sitting at a stoplight. The criminal holds a knife to the back of your neck and tells you to drive. You are stopped at an area that has lots of traffic, but you know the area straight ahead is very isolated. What are the risks in doing what the driver says and driving forward? What are the risks in jumping out of the car? What are the risks in staying right where you are and refusing to drive at all?

In this situation, your greatest risk would be to drive because you would be moving to a more isolated area. Based on risk, your best option would be to jump out of the vehicle while it's still stopped. If you base your decision on the immediate fear of getting hurt, however, it is more likely that you would do what the criminal told you, only to find yourself in a worse situation than before.

➤ Should I become aggressive and attack?

➤ Should I comply now and wait for a better opportunity to escape?

Know the Objective

In a crime scene, you should have only one objective—to get home safely. If you have to choose between getting hurt and losing your life, there is no choice. Some people will do whatever it takes to prevent from being physically injured and end up losing their life for it. Some people have gotten into the car with their attacker, for example, simply because they didn't want to be punched again. This logic is the opposite of how you need to be thinking. Your first priority is to stay alive, and this is the objective by which all decisions must be measured. Your number one objective is to stay alive!

Factors to Consider

No two crime scenes are exactly the same because the circumstances surrounding these events are always different. The following sections discuss the six most common factors to consider before making your decision about what course of action to take.

Safety Alert!

If criminals ask you to surrender your money, jewelry, car keys, or anything else that can be replaced with money, hand it over. Don't make a fuss about it either. Give them what they want and let them be on their way.

What the Attacker Wants

Is the attacker requesting just your valuables? Or does he want your cooperation beyond a reasonable level? If the individual wants more than just your valuables, you might need to try to escape or scream for help. This will be discussed later in this chapter.

Too many people have lost their lives defending items that can be replaced with money. This goes for items that have sentimental value, too. Don't put your life in danger just because your grandmother gave you your wedding ring or your grandfather gave you your watch. As long as you remember your number one objective, letting go of your valuables shouldn't be a problem.

The Location

The location where a crime takes place usually plays a key role in deciding what to do. If you are in a deserted location, your options are going to be different than if you are in a parking lot with lots of people coming and going. This is why it's so important to avoid being in dangerous, isolated locations alone, especially at night (see Chapter 6, "Dangerous Places," for more information). These places not only make you more susceptible to crime and violence, they also remove many of your options. Just remember, the more people that are around, the greater your chances of getting home safely.

The Time

The time at which an incident takes place is important as well. If a criminal decides to target you at three o'clock in the morning, it doesn't matter whether you're standing in the middle of Grand Central Station. The number of people who might hear or see what is going on and possibly help you is going to be very limited during late hours. The time factor can work to your advantage, too. If the incident takes place at three o'clock in the afternoon in the middle of Grand Central Station, you are equipped with all sorts of options. The time at which the incident takes place will seriously affect the number of options you have, so try not to be out alone when it's really late.

Weapons

The most important factor that needs to be considered is whether a weapon is involved. There are literally hundreds of things a criminal can use as a weapon, but not all of them pose the same threat. A gun, of course, is the most dangerous weapon you could be faced with, but it isn't the only weapon considered lethal. Three of the most common weapons used by criminals are guns, knives, and objects that can be used as clubs (for example, a crowbar, a baseball bat, a golf club, a tire iron, and so on). If a knife is involved, you have more options than if a gun is being used. If a club is used, you have even more options available. Because a club offers the user a reach advantage, it is more desirable. With a knife, the attacker must be within arm's reach, but with a club the attacker can stay several feet away while attacking.

Bad Guys Beware!

The kind of weapon the criminal is using, if any, should definitely play a major role in your decision-making process when deciding what to do. Always take this information into account before taking action.

The Number of Attackers

If there is more than one attacker, you have to think differently than you would in a one-on-one situation. A situation involving multiple attackers really complicates things and affects any plans you might have for fleeing the scene. You still have options, however, and believe it or not, there are even a few advantages.

241

Although escaping will be more difficult, the good news is that the situation will naturally draw the attention of others in the area. Several suspicious-looking characters standing around in a group will easily grab the attention of passersby. People also are more likely to call the police if they see several people surrounding one person than if they see only two people facing one another.

Stay on Your Toes

If you are attacked by more than one criminal and you must use lethal force to defend yourself, it will be much easier to justify your actions in a court of law. Convincing a judge that your life was in danger when you were surrounded by a group of thugs shouldn't be too difficult unless, of course, you're an ex-Navy Seal or Green Beret.

Children

If you have a child with you when you are confronted by an attacker, everything changes. You can't take the same risks as when you are alone. In a situation such as this, even the objective changes. Now your primary objective is to get both you and the child home safely. This means you have to respond, react, and think differently than you would if you were alone. In some instances, however, having a child with you can improve your mindset. The following scenarios assist in proving my point.

Scenario #1: Without Child   You're walking through a parking lot one afternoon when a gang of teenage thugs surround you. What is your mindset? In this situation, it is likely that fear will come over you and you will begin to think like a victim. Your normal reaction will be to base decisions on not wanting to get hurt rather than on surviving.

Safety Alert!

Never go anywhere with a criminal—no matter what!

Scenario #2: With Child   You're sitting in your living room watching television one evening while your 10-year-old son is outside playing in the front yard. Suddenly, you hear a loud scream. You jump out of your chair and quickly run outside to investigate. In your driveway, you see three teenagers standing in a circle around your child, taking turns kicking and punching him. Immediately, you begin tearing through the teenagers like a wild animal, pulling them away from your child with no fear of being injured whatsoever. The only thing on your mind is protecting your child. The teenagers flee the scene immediately because they sense your survival mindset and don't want anything to do with you. In this situation, you thought like a survivor and not a victim. You weren't basing your decisions on your fear of getting hurt.

Stay Right Where You Are

It's one thing to be confronted by a criminal who wants to rob you, but what do you do when that's not all the criminal wants? What do you do when you hand over all your valuables and the gun is still pointed at you? What do you do when the criminal gives you an ultimatum such as "Get into the vehicle or be killed"? In a situation such as this, you must make smart decisions. Believe me, there is no room for error. Make no mistake about it, the decisions you make during this sort of crisis will affect the rest of your life. You have to make smart decisions based on your objective to survive. Leaving with a criminal usually is a one-way trip, and second chances rarely are given. Whether it's stepping into the alley or getting into the criminal's car, you can't win.

You Have the Advantage

Remember, if a criminal is trying to get you to relocate, you have him or her at a disadvantage. Think about it: If the person was comfortable committing a crime in your present location, would he or she be trying to get you to go somewhere else? Keep this advantage—it works in your favor.

Playing the Odds

If you were in Las Vegas and you had only $1,000 to gamble with for the entire weekend, where would you bet your money? You probably would bet on the game that gives you the highest odds of winning, right? If your chances of

Life Savers

J. J. Bittenbinder does a great job of defining your odds in his book *Tough Target.* Here's what he has to say:

"If you break and run immediately, out of one hundred times, how many times do you think this guy is going to shoot? ... I'll give you half. Fifty times out of one hundred he'll shoot. So out of that fifty times, how many times do you think he's going to hit you with his little pistol while you're running down the street, yelling "Fire"? ... I'll give you half again. ... Out of that twenty-five times, how many times will it be a serious or fatal injury? I'll give you half again. So, now we're down to twelve and a half times ... That means eighty-seven times out of one hundred you're okay. ... The real number, according to the justice department, is less than 5 percent. Now 5 percent is clearly better than twelve and a half percent, but in either case you can live with those odds. But if you get into the car, he's holding all the aces and your odds are lousy. Why would he be taking you somewhere else? The odds are in your favor. So you have to understand your options. You've got to deny privacy."

winning the game on your left were 10 to 1 and your chances of winning the game on your right were 3 to 1, which one would you play?

To survive a crime scene involving a criminal who wants you to relocate, you have to play the odds and make the choice with the least amount of risk. If a criminal is standing in front of you holding a gun and telling you to get into the car, there's going to be risk involved no matter what you do, so pretend you're gambling for a moment.

The following are some statistics related to armed robbery:

➤ Less than 5 percent of armed robbers shoot their victims.

➤ Criminals carrying a knife either cut or stab their victims approximately 20 percent of the time.

➤ It is estimated that criminals with guns hit their targets less than 4 percent of the time.

➤ Approximately 10 percent of armed robbers murder their victims.

Source: *Strong on Defense* by Sanford Strong

Criminals Are Liars

One important fact you must remember is that criminals are liars. Don't believe a single word that comes out of their mouths. Too many victims have based their decisions in a life-or-death situation on promises made by their attacker. Promises such as "Get into the car or I'll kill you" or "Don't scream and I won't hurt you." Before you decide to base your decisions on promises made by a criminal, remember who you're making deals with. We are talking about the sort of people who go around robbing, raping, assaulting, and murdering innocent people. These individuals couldn't care less that you are someone's mother, father, son, daughter, brother, or sister.

Stay on Your Toes

How many times do you think police officers hear the words "He promised he wouldn't hurt me if I got in the car and cooperated?" The people usually saying this are victims who still have tears streaming down their faces from their recent ordeal. These are the fortunate victims, if you compare them to the ones who are never heard from or seen again. You must base your decisions on circumstances, not empty promises made by professional liars.

Right This Way

A common ploy of criminals is to try to get you to move to a location nearby so they can't be seen or heard by passersby as they commit their crime. I know this doesn't sound like a big deal, but you'd be amazed at how much you empower your attacker when you step a few feet toward a more private location. If you are standing on the corner where people are coming and going, there's a good chance someone will notice what's going on and help you. When you step out of sight, however, you seriously reduce the chances of someone coming to your aid or being able to hear you scream.

Never allow a criminal to talk you into moving to another location, no matter how close by it is.

Criminals know the importance of not being seen or heard. This is why they are so persistent when trying to get you to move. Comply with criminals until the point when they request that you move. The chances are very slim that criminals will become lethal as a result of your choosing to take a stand because they are not comfortable with the current level of privacy. If they were, would they be trying to get you to go somewhere else? When it comes to relocating, stand your ground.

Get in the Car

A criminal requesting that you get into his or her car is probably one of the most dangerous scenarios with which a person can be faced. You don't want to say yes because you know that, once you're in the car, your chances of surviving become very slim. You don't want say no either because you fear the wrath of an angry criminal who is threatening to kill you if you don't comply.

It doesn't matter how angry the person becomes; you cannot get into the car. If you do, you must know that you probably will be taken to the middle of nowhere to be badly hurt or even killed. If you're fortunate enough to only be badly injured, it is unlikely that the criminal is going to give you a ride back to civilization. This means you'll lay there alone and with no help in sight. If the criminal does decide to become violent toward you for refusing to get into the car, at least you'll be in a location where you are likely to be found by someone who can call the police or an ambulance. Look at it like this: would you rather face the wrath of an angry criminal in a parking lot or in the middle of the woods?

Life Savers

When you're trying to make your escape, there are two important things you need to be doing. The first thing you need to do is scream loudly. A criminal is less likely to give chase to someone frantically screaming and drawing a bunch of attention to the situation. The second thing you need to do is zigzag back and forth while you're running. This way, if the criminal has a gun and decides to shoot at you, it will be very difficult to hit you. Hitting a stationary target is difficult enough for most people. Trying to hit a moving target that is getting further away from you is nearly impossible for an inexperienced marksman.

When to Escape

Many victims who chose to get into a vehicle with a criminal shared the same reasoning behind their decision. They didn't feel like they had a chance to escape at the time but thought that, if they got into the car with the criminal, a better opportunity to escape would present itself later. This logic rarely works. In fact, quite the opposite is true. The further you and the criminal get from civilization, the worse your chances of being able to get away become. The best time to make your escape is right away. If you've given the criminal everything he or she has requested and the person is still standing in front of you with a weapon in hand, this probably is the best time to get out of dodge and make your daring escape.

Be Quiet or Else

It's very common for criminals to try to get their victims to be quiet. In most instances, being quiet is the worst thing you can do. First, a criminal wouldn't want you to be quiet unless he or she thought there was a chance someone might hear you. By screaming, you cause the criminal to begin worrying about getting caught. When criminals are worried about getting caught, they usually flee. Second, when you scream, it helps you block out any pain you might be experiencing.

The Least You Need to Know

➤ Learning to think like a survivor instead of a victim is a vital part of your safety plan.

➤ If what the criminal is requesting can be replaced with cash, hand it over.

➤ Base your decisions on the objective of getting home safely, not the fear of being injured.

➤ Leaving with a criminal is never an option.

➤ Escapes must be attempted sooner than later.

➤ Criminals are liars, and decisions never should be based on their promises.

Chapter 21

The Basics of Fighting Back

In This Chapter

➤ The basics of blocking an attacker

➤ Kicking to keep them away

➤ Give yourself a hand—using handstrikes

➤ Getting out of their grasp—breaking holds

➤ Hitting below the belt—fighting dirty

What would you do if you unexpectedly were attacked by a criminal? What if you were forced to physically defend yourself, but the only weapons available to you were your hands and feet? Would you be capable of defending yourself long enough to get away? Or would you be in serious trouble? Imagine an attacker choking you with his bare hands while you stand there helpless, not knowing what to do. Now imagine the same scenario, but this time, you deliver a swift blow to the attacker's nose, causing him to let go long enough for you to safely flee the scene.

In this chapter, I am going to teach you how to physically defend yourself when you are left with no other option but to fight back. Sometimes, knowing how to throw one or two simple techniques can mean the difference between being victimized and getting away safely. I'm going to teach you how to throw some basic but effective blocks, kicks, and handstrikes. In addition, you'll learn how to break an attacker's hold and how to fight dirty if necessary. Fighting back is the last thing you ever want to have to do, but if a situation arises in which it's your only option, you need to know what you're doing. When it comes to fighting back, it's definitely better to know it and not need it than to need it and not know it.

Footwork

Footwork is probably the most important fundamental skill you can learn when it comes to defending yourself. From your footwork comes your balance, your ability to evade, and the basis for a good offense. Without good footwork, defending yourself is very difficult. This is why you should have a good understanding of the footwork taught in this section before moving any further.

Bad Guys Beware!

When you're in your ready stance, make sure you always stand where other people can't reach you. This way, if they want to hit or kick you, they must first step toward you, which gives you more time to react.

Stances

The wonderful thing about stances is that they enable you to be prepared for an oncoming attack while, at the same time, not giving away the fact that you're ready. Stances also play a key role in protecting you from an attacker by positioning your body in a way that reduces the number of targets the attacker can pursue. If you're standing up straight while facing your attacker, for example, he or she can easily strike your ribs, stomach, throat, knees, groin, head, and face. By turning your body sideways to your attacker and getting into your ready stance—which is like standing normally, but turned sideways—you can conceal all these targets by placing them further away, turning them to an angle at which they are difficult to injure, or protecting them by covering them with an arm.

The ready stance.

When you're in your ready stance, make sure to keep the majority of your body's weight on your back leg. This enables you to throw a very fast kick with your front leg (the one closest to the attacker), and it enables you to evade your attacker quickly if necessary by taking a step backward. I recommend that you keep 80 or 90 percent of your body weight on your back leg.

Evading

Evading by stepping out of the way is the best way to avoid getting hit, kicked, or grabbed by your attacker. To evade properly, you need to know how to step in four directions: front, back, left, and right. When a person advances toward you with the intent to cause you harm, evasive footwork can keep you out of harms way without having to raise a finger.

A good way to practice your evasive footwork is to stand up straight with your feet together while another person stands in front of you and calls out directional commands (front, back, left, or right). When the command is give, your objective should be to step in that direction as quickly as possible without hesitating. After doing this for a while, begin having your partner step toward you from a variety of directions while you practice stepping quickly out of the way. It will become instinctive for you to step quickly out of the way.

Evading is simple to learn and can protect you from even the largest of attackers. Remember, your goal is to look for an opportunity to make a run for it, not to evade attack after attack until your luck eventually runs out. Get out of the way and then run as fast as you can!

Shuffling

Shuffling is the footwork used when throwing an offensive attack at someone trying to hurt you. When you throw offense, such as handstrikes or kicks, you have to be close enough to your attacker to be able to reach him. Because your goal is to always stay out of arm's reach, however, how are you going to be close enough to throw offensives while staying away from your attacker at the same time? It isn't possible, and this is why you need to know how to shuffle properly.

To shuffle correctly, you first need to be standing in your ready stance, turned sideways to your attacker, with the majority of your weight on your back leg. You then step toward your attacker while staying in your ready stance, throw your offense, and quickly step back to where you were. Again, shuffle in, launch your attack, and step back out while maintaining your ready stance. The entire process should only take a second at the most. It's very quick and very effective, and it enables you to do your business and get out in a hurry. It also enables you to stay far enough away from your attacker that he or she can't reach you, but you can still step in and reach the attacker if you need to. Isn't shuffling great?

Stay on Your Toes

Shuffling in and out to launch offensive attacks without getting hit is a popular technique in professional boxing.

Blocking

Blocking is defense, and defense wins fights. It doesn't matter how good your offense is, if you can't stop a punch from hitting you in the face or prevent a kick from plowing into your ribs, your offense isn't going to do you much good. Blocking can protect you while intimidating your attacker at the same time. Imagine trying to hit someone as they instinctively throw a strong block, which really hurts your arm. This sends a clear signal to the bad guy that you know what you're doing and that you don't plan to go quietly, which is the exact opposite of what a thug wants. Blocking wins battles because it protects you while buying you valuable time.

Safety Alert!

When throwing blocks, it's vital that you always keep your eyes on your attacker and never look at the punches themselves. If you watch the punches instead of the attacker, you won't know if a weapon is being pulled. It also makes it very easy to fake you out with one hand and hit you with the other.

Keeping It Simple

Keep in mind that, when I teach my students how to block, I don't teach them different blocks for different attacks. Instead, I teach different blocks for different areas of the body being attacked. This means that, if a punch is coming toward your left side, there's only one block you need to throw to take care of the problem. It doesn't matter what the attack is; all that matters is where it's coming from. If it's a kick, a punch, a push, or a grab, it still doesn't affect which block you should throw. The only thing that affects which block is thrown is the direction from which the attack is coming.

I believe it is better for students to know how to effectively throw four blocks that will stop just about anything than to know how to throw 15 different blocks that will only end up confusing them in a real-life situation. The less information you have to remember, the better. Every block in this section can be thrown from a ready stance or while standing with your feet together, facing your opponent.

Outward

The outward block is probably the most frequently used block because it's designed to stop attacks that come from the side. One of the most commonly thrown punches is a hook punch, also called a hay maker, and it is loved by brawlers all over the world because it's simple to throw and because it generates a tremendous amount of power. Because this punch generally is thrown toward the side of the head or the jaw area, the outward block is the best defense against it. By the way, if you get hit with one of these bulldozers, there's no telling where you'll wake up. In professional boxing, they call this a knockout punch. The good news is that these punches are easy to block because they generally are pretty slow and can be seen coming from a mile away.

Stay on Your Toes

You should use the forearm to block because it's one of the hardest bones in the body. This means the defender will hardly feel the impact of a blocked strike. The attacker, however, will definitely feel it for days.

An outward block.

To throw an outward block, put your hand up by the side of your head like you're raising your hand in class to ask a question. Your arm should be positioned at 90 degrees (a right angle) with your forearm pointing up (perpendicular to the ground) and your triceps muscles parallel to the ground. The part of the arm you block with is the elbow and forearm area, not the hand and wrist area, so an open or closed hand

253

doesn't affect the block. If you were to use your hand or wrist area to block, the force of a strong punch easily could cause your block to collapse inward toward your head. If you use your forearm and elbow area to block, however, nothing will collapse. This means less strength is required to stop the attack.

Upward

The upward block is designed to defend against any overhand attack thrown toward your head. With an upward, the same part of the arm is used to block the attack as with the outward block.

To execute an upward block, simply throw your forearm over your head to block an overhand punch, a bottle, a club, or anything else that might come from that direction. Remember, you're protecting a particular area of the body, in this case the top of the head. You're not trying to block a particular attack. Again, make sure you use your forearm to block the strike and not your wrist or hand; otherwise, your block will collapse into your forehead, which will really hurt. Trust me, I'm speaking from experience on this one.

An upward block.

Downward

Downward blocks are used to defend against kicks and punches that are thrown low and toward the ribs, groin, or midsection area. If someone tries to attack this area of your body, all you need to do is use your forearm to stop the attack the same way you would if you were using an upward or outward block. In this situation, however, your forearm is parallel with the ground and is positioned just below your waist.

Safety Alert!

If you try to stop a kick by blocking with your hand or wrist, it is very likely that you will break a bone.

254

A downward block.

Elbow Blocks

Have you ever seen one fighter charge another with a flurry of wild punches? How in the world do you block something like this? Elbow blocks were designed specifically for this type of attack. When a professional boxer is stuck in a corner with another fighter pummeling him, the fighter in the corner usually uses elbow blocks to ward off the flurry of blows long enough to get out of the corner. (Hey, if these blocks are good enough for a prizefighter, they're good enough for me.)

To throw elbow blocks, just put both hands behind your head and keep the insides of both forearms pressed up against the sides of your head. Your elbows will be pointed out in front of you, and if you step forward, they will act like little spears, pushing into the face of your attacker and driving him backward. If you step into the attack while throwing elbow blocks, you take away the other person's power. Why? You do this for the same reason a pro baseball player tries to make contact with the ball using the middle or end of the bat—there's no power near the handle.

Elbow blocks.

Make sure you keep your forearms pressed tightly against your head for the best possible protection. These blocks are great for protecting the head area from an offensive tornado, but you have to remember to keep your eyes on your opponent at all times. In other words, don't look down at the ground while you're throwing elbow blocks.

Stay on Your Toes

Complicated and high, fancy kicks are not designed for the street and aren't practical for real-life situations.

Kicking

When it comes to kicking, I've got two simple rules. Keep them low and throw them where it hurts the most. This is why I'm only going to teach you how to throw two kicks: the front kick to the groin and the knife edge kick to the knee.

A front kick.

Front Kick

To throw a good front kick, take either your front or rear leg (if you're standing in a ready stance) or your right or left leg (if you're standing with your feet together) and throw the kick straight ahead toward the attacker's groin. This works best if you kick the underside of the groin where the greatest collection of nerves is located. When you throw the kick, it's important that you kick through the target instead of just hitting the target and pulling the kick back. This kick works great if the attacker is standing still or is advancing toward you. Either way, the stopping power of this kick is phenomenal if you hit your target.

Knife Edge Kick

The knife edge kick has one purpose—to blast the attacker's knee. To give you an idea of just how sensitive the knee is, set a small pebble on a hardwood or tile floor and then kneel on the pebble. You'll be back on your feet faster than you can say yowza!

To throw this kick, take the heel of your foot and place it on or near the kneecap of your attacker as quickly and as hard as possible. If you want the knife edge kick to work, you have to put your body weight into it. To do this, raise your foot really high and drop it like a sledgehammer—with all your weight coming down with it—right on top of the attacker's knee. If you don't get the results you're looking for, do it again. Believe me, something will give.

Bad Guys Beware!

If you miss your target, the kick is worthless. If you're going to practice throwing it, practice your aim. Also make sure you raise your knee slightly higher than the kick itself. This will give it more snap and power and will make it more difficult for the attacker to block because he or she will think you're throwing the kick higher than you actually are.

A knife edge kick.

Handstrikes

When it comes to handstrikes, I'm very careful to teach only the ones that can't injure the wrist or hand. I also stick with handstrikes that don't require much size or strength behind them to be effective. This is why you're going to learn the hammer fist and a good front elbow. The great thing about these two handstrikes is that they're quick, powerful, and effective. They're also really easy to learn.

Hammer Fist

The hammer fist got its name because the mechanics of it are the same as swinging a hammer. This strike can be thrown to the attacker's groin area or to his nose. To throw the hammer fist, just make a really tight fist and use the bottom of your closed hand to strike the target, just like swinging a hammer. It's much more difficult to injure your hand throwing this strike than if you throw a traditional punch, striking with your knuckles. If you punched a door with your knuckles you probably would break your hand, but if you hit a door with a hammer fist, you would hardly feel a thing.

Stay on Your Toes

To practice the hammer fist, simply make a fist with your right hand and, using the bottom of your fist, strike your other hand while it's in the opened position. Make sure you use the same arm you would use to throw a baseball so you get all the power you can. That's all there is to it.

A hammer fist.

258

Front Elbow

Although there are several different types of elbow throws, I believe the most practical one for self-defense is the front elbow. The front elbow is thrown at the attacker's face. Aim for the nose, but anything close will do such an eye or the mouth.

To throw a front elbow, bend your strong arm (the one you write with), take your forearm, and swing it really hard like you're trying to throw a baseball with the tip of your elbow. Throw the imaginary baseball at your opponent's face and hope you make contact. If you make contact, the results will amaze you. Don't try to hit the attacker with your actual elbow, though. Instead, let your forearm do the striking. This gives you more room for error than your elbow does. Keep in mind that the front elbow is a close range weapon. This means your attacker needs to be right in your face for it to be effective. (This happens quite frequently when a criminal turns violent.) Finally, when you throw the front elbow, be sure to step forward and directly into the attacker while you're throwing it.

A front elbow.

Breaking Holds

For some reason, most criminals don't attack men and women the same way. When a criminal attacks a man, he usually hits, kicks, or wrestles the man to the ground. When a criminal attacks a woman, however, he usually tries to grab and control or restrain her. For this reason, I've included a section about how to break holds.

Face Plant

If you find yourself pinned on the ground with an attacker on top of you, here is what you can do:

Bad Guys Beware!

If someone tries to grab your arm or wrist in an attempt to restrain you, kick the person in the groin or in the knee until he or she lets go.

➤ **Step 1:** Bring your left foot up close to your body and plant it so it doesn't move. This will cause your left knee to be pointed up in the air.

➤ **Step 2:** Take your right knee and aggressively throw it into your attacker's back side, causing him to launch forward.

➤ **Step 3:** As the attacker is being thrown forward, begin to roll toward the left side of your body (the one that has the foot planted).

➤ **Step 4:** As you're rolling toward your planted foot, the attacker will have to let go of you with at least one hand to try to catch himself from falling forward. This is when you take your free hand and use it to push on the attacker's chest.

➤ **Step 5:** Push the attacker in the same direction you are rolling.

➤ **Step 6:** Get up quickly and run for your life.

Step one: Plant your left foot firmly up close to your body.

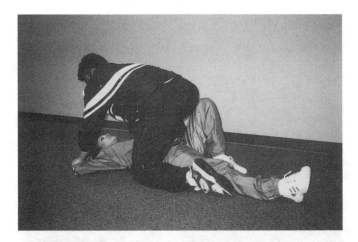

Aggressively throw your right knee into the attacker's backside as you begin to roll toward your planted foot and push the attacker off you.

Stay on Your Toes

If you don't plant your left foot close to your body before throwing your other knee into the attacker's backside, the rest of the technique won't work (and you probably will make your attacker angry).

Surprised from Behind

If you're grabbed from behind, use these simple techniques to make your attacker let go in a hurry:

➤ Scrape the edge of your shoe down the attacker's shinbone.

➤ Stomp on the attacker's foot repeatedly.

➤ Throw your elbows into the attacker's rib cage.

➤ Throw the back of your head into the attacker's face repeatedly.

➤ Throw multiple hammer fists into the attacker's groin area.

➤ Kick the heel of your foot up between the attacker's legs and into the underside of his groin.

➤ If you can reach it, bend down and bite the attacker's arm.

Choking

If you are in a situation in which someone is trying to choke you, it's important that you know what to do and that you act fast. Within seconds, your air supply will be cut off, and you will either pass out from a lack of oxygen or die. Fortunately, this is a very simple hold to free yourself from if you're facing your attacker because you have both legs and both arms free. Your attacker, on the other hand, has both hands on you. This makes defending himself extremely difficult (unless he lets go, which is the idea). The following are a few simple offensive techniques you can use to free yourself from a choke:

➤ Gouge the eyes with a finger or a thumb.

➤ Throw a front kick to the groin.

➤ Drop to your knees and throw a handstrike to the groin.

261

Safety Alert!

If someone is choking you, don't waste valuable time trying to pry the person's hands off your throat. This technique rarely works, and it can cost you your life in the process. Time is crucial when your air supply is being cut off, so take the offensive and begin attacking immediately.

➤ Punch the stomach or solar plexus.

➤ Throw a knife edge kick to the knee.

If you are being choked from behind, grab the attacker's pinky fingers and bend them backward until he lets go.

Fighting Dirty

This section is dedicated to breaking all the rules. Criminals don't play by the rules. If they did, they wouldn't be robbing, raping, assaulting, and murdering innocent people. Sometimes the only way to survive a violent attack is to fight dirty. Remember, there are no rules when it comes to saving your life.

Eye Gouges

Regardless of how big, strong, or fast an attacker is, it is very unlikely that he can endure a finger shoved in his eye socket. Gouging an eye is a very simple procedure—just take your finger or thumb and place it in the eye of your attacker. This technique works even better if you have long fingernails. Don't be concerned about blinding the person either. Remember, this person is trying to hurt or kill you. This is no time to be concerned about affecting the person's long-term vision. If the attacker closes his eyes tightly in an attempt to protect them (which he probably will), keep poking as hard as you can. A closed, squinted eye is no match for your finger or thumb, and eventually, you'll get the results you're looking for. I know this seems gross, but you'll be amazed at what you can do when your life is in danger. If you're not sure how effective an eye gouge is, ask people who have been poked in the eye accidentally before. They'll tell you how long it took before their eye quit tearing and they could open it again without needing a tissue.

Biting

This technique brings a whole new meaning to the "Take a bite out of crime" campaign. A lot of pressure can be generated with a few small jaw muscles. (The jaw is what makes your teeth such an effective weapon.) When it comes to biting, no training is required to become an expert. A 3-year-old can bite hard enough to make a grown man cry. Biting is great for getting someone to let go of you in a hurry. It's simple. If someone grabs you, bite his or her hand. If someone chokes you, bite the person's arm. If someone pins you to the ground, bite his or her wrist. If you're going to bite someone trying to hurt you, bite as hard as you can and don't let up until the person lets go.

Choking

If your attacker can't breath, your attacker can't fight. Dogs know this well; when they fight, they always go for the throat. The first dog that locks on to the other's throat usually wins the confrontation. Do whatever it takes to get your arms or hands around your attacker's throat, and don't let go until he or she either passes out or lets go of you.

Hair Pulling

Hair pulling might not be proper etiquette for a professional wrestling match or a karate tournament, but when it comes to staying alive in the hands of an attacker, it's perfectly legitimate. Grab a handful of hair and don't let go until the attacker does.

The Least You Need to Know

➤ Don't fight with your attacker unless it's your only option.

➤ One of the advantages of a good stance is that it reduces the number of available targets your attacker can strike.

➤ To execute a block properly, it's important that you use your forearm and elbow to stop the blow, not your wrist or hand.

➤ High, fancy kicks are not practical for self-defense and should be avoided, especially when you're in real danger.

➤ The best handstrikes protect your hand from injury and generate a lot of power.

➤ Although chokes are very dangerous, they also are very simple to get out of if you know what to do.

Weapons and Gadgets: What Really Works?

A woman is walking through a parking garage one afternoon when a thief approaches her, intending to rob her and make a quick getaway. Just before he grabs her, she holds a can of mace up by her shoulder with her finger on the trigger ready to spray. The robber steps back quickly, almost losing his balance. He knows what she's about to do, and he doesn't want any part of it. He runs for the exit without looking back. Thanks to a few ounces of mace that were readily available and in the hands of someone who wasn't afraid to use them, a crime was prevented and an innocent life might have been saved.

Hundreds of personal safety products are on the market, and if you don't know what you're doing, you could end up with a product that won't work for you when you need it the most. Many of these products claim to be able to save lives, but the truth of the matter is that some of them are worthless gadgets that could get you hurt. The last thing you want to do is put your trust in a product that doesn't work.

In this chapter, I am going to give you an overview of the most popular personal safety products on the market today. I'll tell you what they do (or what they are supposed to do), and I'll give you my professional opinion of each product. If you ever are in a life-or-death situation, you might be banking your life on whatever product you chose to buy, so you need to know what you're doing. You are about to get an unbiased and impartial critique of the products that claim to keep people safe.

Firearms

Unlike all the other nonlethal products mentioned in this chapter, firearms are lethal weapons and are intended to kill. Before deciding whether to own a firearm for personal protection, you need to ask yourself a simple question. Can I take another human's life to protect my own life or the life of a family member in a do-or-die situation? If you're not sure you could do it, don't get a firearm. They are a tremendous responsibility. If you don't think you could kill a criminal, don't buy a gun.

Prepare to Shoot

When it comes to using guns for personal protection, you need to remember a few guidelines. First, never put your finger on the trigger unless you're planning to pull it. Second, don't pull the trigger unless you're prepared to kill the person standing in front of you. Guns aren't designed to maim the bad guy, and they definitely aren't designed to intimidate a criminal. If you threaten a criminal with a gun that you aren't prepared to use, you run the risk of having the gun taken from you and then used against you. In addition, the criminal might flee the scene only to come back another day with a gun of his or her own.

Safety Alert!

If you're going to own a firearm, it's very important that you learn how to properly use it. I recommend that you take a gun safety class and spend some time at a shooting range. If you're going to carry a firearm with you or on your person, find out what the laws are in your state and obey them. Getting caught with a gun when you're not licensed to carry one can get you into a lot of serious trouble with the police.

If Your Partner Isn't Comfortable

If someone you live with isn't comfortable with you having a gun in the home, take the person to the firing range and teach him or her how to use it properly. Teach the person about gun safety and give the person an opportunity to turn his or her fear of the firearm into respect. Telling someone to "get over it" and never educating the person about how to safely use the gun only makes matters worse.

Of course, there is always another option if your partner is uncomfortable with the idea of having a gun in the home: Don't purchase one.

Handguns

Handguns are compact, effective, easy to use, and affordable. For personal safety, however, I recommend that you buy a revolver instead of a semiautomatic. Revolvers are less likely to jam when fired, and they are easier to use when you're scared or under pressure. They also are less expensive to buy. Revolvers hold fewer bullets than semiautomatics, but six bullets should be more than enough.

Stay on Your Toes

One of the problems with handguns is the likelihood of bullets traveling through walls and hitting innocent people. I've heard terrible stories about family members in other rooms getting shot through a wall.

As with all firearms, you must be careful about keeping the gun safe and secure in a location where children can't get to it. If you're going to carry a gun in your purse or in your car, you need to be extra careful when other people are around. Handguns are a full-time responsibility. If you don't want the inconvenience of having to be responsible all the time, buy pepper spray instead.

Shotguns

It's real hard to miss your target when using a shotgun. If you do miss, you don't have to worry about a bullet flying through a wall and hitting a family member in another room or going into the adjoining apartment. There are two downsides to using a shotgun: its big, bulky size and the fact that it isn't good for hitting someone far away because the ammunition begins to spread and scatter as it travels. The effective range of a shotgun depends on the type of shotgun and the type of ammunition being used.

Shotguns also are very hard to safeguard from curious children unless you keep them unloaded, which defeats the purpose of having one around for safety. (Most criminals will not give you time to load.) Overall, I don't recommend using a shotgun for home protection.

Peashooters

Peashooters are tiny little guns that people carry for personal protection. They usually are small enough to fit into the palm of your hand. Some people carry them in their pocket, purse, boot, or car. Peashooters can be bought to look like common accessories such as belt buckles or wallets. They hold one to six bullets on average and are relatively inexpensive to purchase. They aren't good for target practice because they're

Safety Alert!

If you're going to carry a peashooter, you must treat it with the same level of responsibility as you would a large handgun. The law demands that you do. Peashooters are guns, not toys.

so small. They'll hurt your hand if fired repeatedly, but in a life-or-death situation, an uncomfortable hand will be the least of your concerns.

These miniature guns are ideal for close-range defense (if your attacker is within a few feet of you), but they aren't very effective from mid- to long-range.

Pepper Sprays

When it comes to nonlethal personal safety products, pepper spray is at the top of my list. I've seen a two-second burst of pepper spray drop a grown man to his knees in less than five seconds. Not all pepper sprays are equal, though. Some sprays are cheap mixtures that couldn't deter a cocker spaniel; others can clear a room of 30 people in less than a minute. The best sprays are the ones that contain 10 percent cayenne pepper.

Stay on Your Toes

Pepper spray gets its name from cayenne pepper. Some pepper sprays consist of up to 10 percent cayenne pepper, which can affect an attacker three different ways: burning and skin irritation, swelling of the mucous membranes (which makes it difficult to breathe), and swelling of the veins in the eyes (this is blinding). The effects usually last for 20–30 minutes.

The Downside of Pepper Spray

The following are some disadvantages of pepper spray:

➤ If your attacker has certain medical conditions (heart, respiratory, and so on), a blast of pepper spray could kill him or her.

➤ If the wind is blowing, you very easily could spray yourself by accident.

➤ A criminal can take it from you and spray you in the face.

➤ If you have small children, you run the risk of them spraying themselves by accident.

➤ It doesn't affect all attackers the same way. Some might drop to the ground immediately; others might not react to it for several minutes if at all.

Carrying Pepper Spray

Pepper spray is meant to be a deterrent to crime. In other words, carrying it should make you less susceptible to an attack. The only way this can happen, however, is if it is visible and ready to use. Carrying it down by your side or in your purse with the safety on is not going to do you any good. The criminal knows that, in this case, he can take it from you before you can spray him with it.

For pepper spray to be a deterrent, you must make sure people can see it. Carry it up by your shoulder with your finger on the trigger ready to spray. Make sure the safety is turned off and the case is unsnapped. Of course, you only need to carry it like this when you're in a situation or a location where extra caution is called for or when your instincts tell you it's a good time to prepare your mace.

When mace is carried correctly, it acts as a deterrent to crime and greatly reduces your chances of being attacked.

Streams, fogs, foams, and dyes are the four main categories you'll have to choose from when buying mace.

Streams

Streams shoot a steady stream of liquid directly at whatever you are aiming at when you pull the trigger. The good thing about streams is that they are extremely accurate, and you can hit your attacker from several feet away. The bad thing about streams is that they're like a water pistol in the sense that only a small area of your target is hit at a time. This is definitely the best product

Bad Guys Beware!

Be sure to replace your mace about once a year. This way, you'll know that, if you ever need to use it, it will do what it's supposed to.

269

to fire into the wind, however, because you have a much smaller chance of it blowing back into your face.

Fogs

The best thing about fogs is that, when sprayed, a large cloud of pepper spray fogs up the area. It's really hard to miss your attacker if he's standing close to you, but fogs aren't very effective if he's standing several feet away—but it will help to keep the attacker away from you! The worst thing about fogs is that it's very easy to spray yourself by accident, especially if the wind is blowing. When it comes to personal use, I prefer streams.

Foams

When sprayed, foam pepper sprays look like hair mousse. The good news is that the foam stays with your attacker, and when he tries to rub it off, it will only spread. This makes getting it off very difficult and time-consuming. The bad news is that, if your attacker touches you, you'll join him on the ground gagging. I don't recommend foams for personal use unless you're a fast runner and have great aim.

Dyes

A colored dye can be added to pepper spray to mark your attacker. This way, if your attacker gets away and you call the police, they can look for someone marked with colored dye. This stuff doesn't come off for days regardless of how hard you scrub. Even if the police don't find your attacker, someone who sees the person wearing dye might become suspicious of what he or she has been up to and might take the initiative to call the police.

Stay on Your Toes

It only costs a few dollars more to get a spray with dye added, and it's well worth the investment. Stopping the attacker from hurting you is what mace is for. Stopping the attacker from hurting someone else is what dyes are for. Some brands of mace now come with ultraviolet identification dye. Put the attacker under a black light and watch him glow.

Miscellaneous Products

The following sections discuss miscellaneous personal safety products currently on the market that don't necessarily fit into a category of their own.

Personal Alarms

Personal alarms are designed to draw attention to your situation. This, in turn, should cause your attacker to flee. Whether it works out this way depends on your location. If you're in the middle of downtown Los Angeles, you could be in a lot of trouble if you're counting on someone to hear your personal alarm and come running to your rescue. If you're in the middle of a grocery store parking lot, however, you might summon the help of several good Samaritans.

What I don't like about personal alarms is that they don't do anything to stop an attacker. Mace will drop someone, but a loud noise won't. "Step back or I'll make noise" might not be the most effective threat you can make. In short, I love the idea of having a personal alarm to call for help, but I hate the idea of people thinking that an alarm can protect them. If you're going to buy one, just keep in mind its limitations and you'll be fine.

I don't recommend whistles or air horns because you have to either press a button or blow continuously to get them to make noise. All the criminal has to do is take the noisemaker away from you and voilá, no more noise. Get a personal alarm that doesn't shut off for a while after it's activated and that has an internal energy source. I like the ones with a metal pin attached to a small chord that you pull. Until the pin is placed back into the small hole located on the alarm, it doesn't shut up. A criminal isn't going to take the time to try to place a pin into a small hole.

Stun Guns

When it comes to buying a stun gun, the more voltage the better. A few years ago, I let a student use his stun gun on me (because I knew it wasn't a good one). It was uncomfortable for a second, but it definitely wouldn't stop me. I've seen some stun guns, however, that would drop a horse. If someone that makes you nervous is approaching you, just push the button once or twice. The flashing blue arc of electricity and the popping sound should be enough to make anyone think twice about getting any closer.

Life Savers

If you are in a situation in which you're face to face with a criminal and you are carrying a personal alarm, activate it and then throw it behind the criminal. If you keep it in your hand, your attacker can take it from you and shut it off. By throwing it behind the criminal, he or she has to turn around and go get it, flee the scene, or stay but take the chance of getting caught. If the criminal tries to retrieve the alarm, run for your life and don't look back.

The part of the attacker's body that you hit with the stun gun makes a big difference. Go for bare skin whenever possible: A stun gun isn't as effective if it has to go through clothing. The cheek, neck, arm, hip, and hand all are great locations to send a few volts.

A stun gun can be bought on the Internet, in some drug stores, and in some specialty stores. I recommend the ones that are 300 volts (try army surplus stores, spy shops, and so on).

Knives

The biggest problem with knives is that most people don't like the idea of cutting someone, even a dangerous criminal. Plunging a knife into another person's body is a pretty disgusting act, and just the thought of it can be disturbing. Pulling a knife is easy, but if you really had to use it on your attacker, could you? If your answer is no, I don't recommend carrying a knife for personal protection.

Stay on Your Toes

Walking down the street with a knife in your hand could be construed as a challenge to someone looking for a fight. If a police officer sees you, you can bet you're going to have some questions to answer. If you conceal the knife, you probably won't be able to get it out fast enough to protect yourself with it. Overall, I don't recommend carrying a knife for self-defense purposes.

Kubotans

The kubotan is a self-defense device used for joint manipulation, striking, and key flailing (swinging your keys at someone, using them as an offensive attack). It's several inches in length (about the size of a magic marker), and it usually is carried as a key chain. If an attacker grabs you, you're supposed to place the kubotan on the person's wrist or hand and start cranking. It can cause severe pain by digging into the bones of the hand, wrist, or forearm, and it gives the user a strength advantage because of the additional leverage that the length of the kubotan provides. This makes it ideal for performing wristlock techniques (bending the wrist back).

Its bottom end can be used as a striking surface when it sticks out past the bottom of your fist. (Remember the hammer fist I taught you in Chapter 21, "The Basics of

Fighting Back"?) If used as a key chain, you also can flail your keys at someone. The striking and flailing techniques are easy to perform, but to perform the joint manipulation techniques, you'll need some training. This product has a lot of potential as long as you take the time to learn how to use it properly.

Expandable Batons

Expandable batons are clubs that are several inches in length in the closed position but, with the flip of a wrist, can expand to three or four times their normal length. After they're expanded, you have a club specifically designed for striking your attacker. Their capability to expand enables them to be concealed in a purse or a pocket.

I don't think expandable batons make good self-defense devices for the general public for the following reasons:

➤ It takes too much time to retrieve it and place it into the ready position.

➤ The law doesn't look very kindly at civilians clubbing their attacker with metal batons. (It makes it difficult to prove you were only defending yourself.)

➤ It can be taken from you very easily because of its length.

➤ It's easy for a criminal to block, while stepping toward you.

➤ You might have to strike a criminal several times before getting results.

➤ It takes too long to swing a club at someone, leaving you vulnerable in between swings.

➤ A club does not intimidate most criminals.

Light Flashes

The flash of light is a product that is supposed to temporarily blind your attacker by flashing a quick burst of light into his or her eyes. It's kind of like looking directly at a camera flash but a lot worse.

I consider this to be one of those ideas that looks great on paper but not on the street where it counts. I watched a live demonstration of this product once, and the results were embarrassing. The man who was supposed to be blinded by the light grabbed the woman using the product and pinned her to the ground in a matter of seconds. He held her there until he regained his sight.

Products for Children

Your main priority when purchasing a product for your children should be to prevent them from being abducted. Keep in mind that none of these products can actually prevent your child from being abducted, but they can alert you immediately or help you find the child after the fact.

Computer Chips

The computer chip is placed under your child's skin. If your child is missing, a satellite will track his or her approximate location. Some chips are even configured so that the monitoring company can tell whether the child is still alive. The problem with a computer chip is that it has to be inserted into your child's body, which raises some ethical and moral concerns for some people. This process costs several thousand dollars.

The chip can be inserted anywhere in the body, and doctors always use different locations so kidnappers won't know where to look.

Bad Guys Beware!

Teach your child to drop his or her hat, backpack, schoolbooks, pager, or anything else he or she can think of in the event of being abducted. This lets police know where to begin looking, which is crucial when it comes to finding missing children.

Satellite Monitors

This product does the same thing as the computer chip (tracks the child's location), but with this product, the chip is concealed in a device that resembles a pager. The only way this product can work is if the child is carrying it during the abduction. If the abductor sees it, it is very likely that he or she will destroy it or will place it in a false location to confuse the police. If your child is going to have one of these devices, it must be hidden in a location where the kidnapper can't see it.

Safety Alert!

If you decide to have your child equipped with a computer chip, it's a good idea not to let the child know. If the child tells his or her abductor that there's a chip tracking their location, the abductor might hurt the child trying to locate and remove the chip or might kill the child and flee. Remember, kids aren't the best at keeping secrets, especially when they're scared.

Personal Monitors

This monitor lets a parent, guardian, or baby-sitter know when a child has exceeded a certain distance from that person. If the parent sets the monitor at 100 feet and the child moves 120 feet away, the parent's unit will make a loud noise. The good thing about this product is that it can work through walls. The bad thing is that, although you might be alerted immediately that your child no longer is in the front yard playing, you still might have no idea where the child is. Some of these monitors are so advanced that, if your child falls into water, a special alarm will sound. This is great if you have a swimming pool.

The Least You Need to Know

➤ Firearms are designed to kill, not merely intimidate.

➤ Pepper spray only is effective if it is quickly accessible or is being carried in the ready position.

➤ The best pepper sprays are 10 percent cayenne pepper and contain an identification dye.

➤ The best personal alarms are the ones that, once activated, can continue to sound on their own.

➤ Knives are not ideal for personal protection.

➤ Personal safety products for children work well for alerting adults to a potential problem or for tracking children down if they've been abducted, but these products aren't effective at preventing abductions.

Part 6

Defense for Special Situations

We all find ourselves home alone from time to time, even if we don't live alone. Being safe can be a challenge. How do you prevent unwanted guests? How can you make it look like you're not alone? Learn how to answer the door and how to handle unexpected company without being intimidated into a dangerous situation.

The safety of our children strikes the heart of every parent. Just like we teach them bicycle safety or water safety, we need to train them in self-defense. They don't come dumb; they just come small. Use their bright little minds to teach them what a stranger is. Create passwords and special commands and practice them. You'll also learn ways to prepare children for times when you are not around. It's possible for even a small child to get away from a much larger adult. Just add self-defense to the daily list of other important things you are teaching your children.

Two more groups that criminals like to target are senior citizens and the physically challenged. There are ways, however, to prevent the types of scams and thefts that criminals often use to prey on them. Sometimes physically limited people and seniors look weak, but that's not how they should see themselves. They need to concentrate on their strength. If you fit into one of the special groups in this section, you can learn some simple self-defense moves that are surprising and effective.

LAST LINE
OF DEFENSE

Home Alone

You're sitting at home by yourself late one afternoon when the doorbell rings. As you're walking to the door, you're thinking to yourself, "I'm not expecting anyone. I wonder who it could be?" You say "Who is it?" and the person on the other side responds by saying "You have a package." Excited and curious, you open the door for the delivery man. You invite him to step inside for a moment while you sign the receipt, but when he steps in, so does another man you didn't know was there. Now you have two criminals in your home that want to rob you—and you're home alone. What do you do?

In this chapter, you're going to learn all about staying safe when home alone. If you're going to be home by yourself, you need to know how to stay safe and secure from any criminals that might want to get in, with or without your permission. Unexpected visitors, delivery people, repair people, salespeople, solicitors—it doesn't matter. You've got to set some guidelines to protect yourself when you're the only one around. What if someone enters your home when you're there? What if you wake up in the middle of the night with someone in your house? This chapter is filled with life-saving information for anyone who ever has been or ever will be home alone.

Stay on Your Toes

Living alone can be a wonderful experience as well as a safe one. You need to take a few extra precautions, however, to help keep the bad guys away.

Knock Knock

If you're home alone and hear a knock at the door, you need to know what to do. No two situations are the same, but walking up to the door and blindly opening it never is the right choice. Regardless of who is knocking, you've got to play it smart.

Before You Open the Door

Here are some safety precautions that should be followed prior to opening the door:

➤ Look out the peephole or window to see who it is. (A peephole is one of the best $10 investments you can make.)

➤ If what you see through the peephole doesn't cause you concern, ask who it is.

➤ If what you see raises concern, ignore the knock and don't ask who it is.

➤ If you don't know who it is that's knocking, ask the person what he or she wants.

➤ If you're not satisfied with the answer, don't open the door.

Safety Alert!

Make it a rule to never open your door for someone who's knocking until you see who it is and until you know exactly what the person wants. If you're not satisfied with what you see and hear, don't open the door.

Unexpected Visitors

If someone you know comes by your home unexpectedly, don't feel obligated to let him or her in. It's one thing if it's your mother or your best friend, but if it's someone you used to date or an old co-worker, that's a different story. Tell acquaintances that you're a safety-conscious person and that you'd appreciate it if they would call before they dropped by. There always will be one or two people who get a little offended, but the majority will understand, especially if you live alone. Besides, calling before you drop by someone's home is a courtesy most people have forgotten.

If someone you know is at the door but you're not comfortable being home alone with the person, here are some things you can do:

➤ Step out of the house and talk to him or her outside.

➤ When you step out, close the door behind you so you can't be physically pushed inside.

➤ With the door closed, tell the person that it isn't a good time. Ask the person to come back later or give you a call.

➤ Ignore the knock.

Stay on Your Toes

A high percentage of rapes, murders, and assaults are committed by people who know the victim. This is why you must be careful around acquaintances that drop by your home unannounced. It's better to offend an unexpected visitor than to let the person in and put yourself in a dangerous situation.

Special Delivery

What about an unexpected delivery person who has a package for you? A large box, an envelope, or maybe even a dozen roses? The person looks legitimate through the peephole because he's holding a package in his hands.

The first thing you should do is look to see if the person is wearing a uniform. Then look to see if he's driving a personal vehicle or a company vehicle. If it's a personal vehicle, write down the license plate number if possible and ask the person to leave. Of course, you're doing all this by looking through your window or peephole and not with your door open. If everything checks out, ask the person to leave the package in front of your door and retrieve it after he drives off. If he says you must first sign for the package, you need to ask whom the package is from. If it's

Bad Guys Beware!

If you have to crack the door open slightly with a secondary lock in place, keep your foot and hip up against the door for added protection. If you buy one of these locks, don't get the chains. The solid metal levers are much safer and are harder to break.

281

from someone you've never heard of before or if the delivery person tells you the sender is anonymous, don't open the door.

If you have a mail slot in your door, you can have the delivery person slip the receipt through the door so you can sign it. Secondary locks also work well in this situation. These locks enable you to open the door a few inches. Keep in mind that secondary locks cannot withstand a great deal of force, but they do help deter someone from trying to push their way in.

Just because someone is holding a package doesn't make them legitimate or safe.

Common Tricks

Here are a few scenarios that involve impersonators pretending to be delivery people in an attempt to be invited into your home. This should give you an idea of just how sneaky these con men can be.

Scenario #1/Out of Ink: The impersonator intentionally carries a pen that's out of ink. When you try to sign the receipt and see that the pen is out of ink, either you'll invite the person inside while you get another pen or you'll tell the person you'll be right back and go inside. The only problem is that, when you go inside, chances are high you'll leave the front door open because you don't want to be rude. This is when the criminal comes in.

Scenario #2/Bad Weather: The impersonator knocks on your door with a delivery when the weather outside is terrible. If it's raining, snowing, or is 20°F outside, there's a good chance you'll invite the delivery person inside.

Scenario #3/Wrong Address: The impersonator asks you to sign for a package addressed to someone other than you. When you bring it to the person's attention, he or she will ask permission to use your phone to call the office and get the problem straightened out.

How would you respond in these situations? Would you let the delivery person in your home? Would you leave the door open while you go inside?

Salespeople and Solicitors

It's hard for me to give unbiased advice about this group because I don't answer the door for uninvited solicitors (unless it's a child selling cookies or candy for their school). For me, a "No Solicitors" sign takes care of this problem. If someone knocks on my door wanting to sell something, I just remind the person of the sign on the door and that's the end of that. Don't get me wrong. It's not because I'm a Scrooge or enjoy turning people away. It's just that crime and violence in our country have escalated to the point where you just can't let total strangers into your home. Unfortunately, there's no way to distinguish the legitimate salesmen from the criminals. For this reason, when a stranger knocks on my door, I politely say, "No, thank you."

For those of you who care to entertain door-to-door sales calls, I recommend that you get as much information as possible before opening your door. Ask the person what company he or she represents and what product is being sold (with the door still closed, of course). Even if you're interested, I don't suggest inviting the person into your home. Step outside with the door closed behind you and let the person show you what is being offered. If you're really interested but the person needs to come inside to give you a demonstration, ask if you can schedule an appointment. This way, you can have a friend in the house with you for the demonstration. If you set up an appointment for a later date, ask the person for a business card and call the number to make sure he or she is legitimate.

Service and Repair

If you schedule a repair person to come to your home, try to have a friend with you at the time

Safety Alert!

Don't invite a delivery person into your home and don't leave the door open if you have to retrieve something.

Bad Guys Beware!

If you are suspicious of salespeople or solicitors for any reason, watch to see where they go after leaving your home. If they really are selling something, they'll probably go to your neighbor's house. If they're crooks, they'll probably walk to their vehicle and leave. If this happens, be sure to get a license plate number and report the incident to your local police. It might turn out to be nothing, or you could be saving someone's life. Remember, whenever you're in doubt, check it out.

of the repair. Don't let the repair person do work when you're not home—that's asking for trouble. If the person has to do work in a part of your home that contains valuables, remove the items before the person arrives and put them somewhere safe and out of sight. Otherwise, you'll have to stand over the person's shoulder the entire time, which is not a good idea.

A great way to prevent this type of theft is to suddenly appear every few minutes and ask questions like "How's it going?" or "Have you found the problem?" A repair person is going to be less likely to steal something if he or she thinks you could pop in any second.

Stay on Your Toes

Most repair people are honest and perfectly safe, but you still need to exercise caution because it only takes one bad experience to ruin your day or life.

Before the repair person arrives, it's a good idea to walk through your home and open all the blinds and curtains, especially in the bedrooms. If you have a dog, keep it inside with you until the person leaves.

Intruders

Having an intruder in your home is dangerous, not to mention scary. Reacting properly in this situation could mean the difference between life and death. Don't worry, though. I'm going to teach you how to make good decisions and how to react correctly if an intruder ever enters your home.

If You Think You Hear an Intruder

If you think you hear an intruder, it's not a good idea to boldly walk around investigating the situation. Be extremely careful and very quiet and, by all means, don't walk into the room where the noise originated and yell, "Who's there?" If someone is in your home, the last thing you want to do is startle him or her. They probably don't know you're home, and it's best to keep it that way.

If you can't evacuate your home because the noise is coming from a location that would put you at risk if you tried to exit, you need to get to a phone. Try to sneak into a closet to call 911. If that's not possible, dial 911 and leave the phone off the hook. The important thing is to not let whoever is in the house know that they are not alone. Most burglars are looking for a vacant house to rob, not an occupied one. They want to grab your valuables and make a clean getaway without confrontation. If you startle the thief, however, he or she likely will become violent.

If Someone Is in Your Bedroom

If you wake up in the middle of the night and see a stranger standing in your bedroom, your greatest challenge is going to be controlling your fear. In this situation, a phone and a weapon are two very important items to have readily available. Mentally, you need to prepare yourself to do whatever it takes to survive. Either you need to get out of the bedroom, which probably will require a struggle, or you need to give the criminal a reason to want to get out.

Whatever your weapon of choice is—mace, a stun gun, a baseball bat, and so on—it needs to be near where you sleep. This is why so many people keep a weapon in their night stand drawer, under their mattress, or under their pillow. If they wake up to a stranger hovering over them or if they hear a noise in the other room, they're prepared.

If You Come Home to an Intruder

If you come home and believe that someone uninvited is inside, don't go in. Turn right back around and run to the nearest phone. The last thing you want to do is interrupt a thief pilfering through your stuff. Don't let the person know you've spotted him or her, either. You want the person to still be there when the police arrive.

If you see that your house has been robbed but you don't think the person is still in the home,

Safety Alert!

If you hear a noise and think it might be an intruder, the best thing to do is be still for a few moments and make sure it's not just your imagination. If you still think you hear something, try to sneak out of the house quietly and go to a neighbor's to call the police. If you have a cellular or cordless phone handy, take it with you and place the call after you've safely made it out. After you call 911, they'll dispatch an officer and give you instructions for what to do next.

Life Savers

If a criminal is in your bedroom and approaches you with a weapon, grab the weapon and don't let it go. Grab the barrel of the gun and step out of the way, grab the blade of the knife, grab the end of the club, and go animal. Do whatever it takes to win, and refuse to lose. Think like a survivor, not a victim. Believe me when I say this is a serious situation. You need to fight with everything you've got, so don't hold anything back.

handle the situation the same way. Turn around, run to a neighbor's, and call the police. The criminal might still be in your house. Because there's no way of knowing for sure without going in, let the police handle it. Besides, you don't want to disturb the crime scene until the police can make their report, so why go inside? You don't want to accidentally smudge important fingerprints.

Creating an Escape Route

One of the best things you can do to prepare for an intruder is create a plan of escape in advance. Having a criminal chasing you through your house or hearing someone fumbling downstairs in the middle of the night is not the best time to figure out how you're going to make your exit. I recommend that you choose a window in your bedroom. It needs to be rigged so it can be opened in a hurry without making a lot of noise. If your bedroom is on the second floor (or higher), you can purchase a fire-escape ladder (usually for less than $50) that is very compact until dropped out the window. This is a great item to have in case of a fire as well.

Bad Guys Beware!

If an intruder is chasing you through your house, run to the kitchen. In the kitchen, there often is a door, a phone, a knife, and sometimes all three.

Don't run to your bedroom unless you have prepared it in advance as your safety room. If you haven't prepared your bedroom with a weapon, a phone, or an escape route, you could be trapping yourself.

The Safety Room

Depending on the circumstances, exiting your home might not be possible without putting yourself in great danger. This is why having a safety room is a smart idea. Choose a room in your home as the designated spot to go and hide if an intruder enters your home and you can't leave. Your safety room should be equipped with the following items:

➤ A cell phone. (Emergency/911 cell phones now can be purchased for as little as $10 a month.)

➤ If you don't have a cell phone, keep a cordless phone nearby. A cell phone is a much safer option, though, because sometimes criminals cut the phone lines.

➤ A canister of pepper spray. (Buy the biggest one available for personal defense.)

➤ A towel to put over your face in case you need to cough or sneeze or if you have to spray the mace in a closed environment.

➤ A flashlight.

➤ If you have an alarm system, have a panic button installed in your safety room that will set off the alarm, summon the police, or both.

Stay on Your Toes

The main objectives of the safety room are to have a safe place to hide, to be able to call 911, and to be equipped to defend yourself if the intruder spots you. If possible, the best place to set up your safety room is in the bedroom.

Perception Is Everything

If you live alone or are going to be alone for several nights or weeks, you need to give the impression that your house is full of people. Thieves are clever. They'll listen to answering machine messages, read mailboxes, call you, or even ask around just to find out who's in the house and when. Burglars love targeting vacant homes, but the real sickos intentionally target homes occupied by one person. It makes their job a lot easier, which is why you need to learn to throw up a few smoke screens.

The Answering Machine

If you have an answering machine or voice mail and you live alone, don't let your message reveal this fact. Avoid messages like "Hi, this is Melissa. I can't come to the phone right now." If you're a woman living alone, have a male friend record your message for you. It should say "We can't come to the phone" instead of "I can't come to the phone." If you record your own message, use "we" instead of "I" as well. Try to get creative with your message. Do something fun like having a large dog barking in the background.

Bad Guys Beware!

Whether you live alone or are going to be alone for a short period of time, don't tell acquaintances and strangers. Telling your hairdresser that your husband is out of town on business for two weeks is a big no-no. You need to give everyone (except friends and family, of course) the impression that you're not staying in an empty house.

The Phone

Make sure not to let any callers you don't know in on the fact that you live alone. If you don't live alone but you just happen to be home alone at the time, don't give away this information either. If you don't know who the caller is and the person asks for someone who isn't home, just say they aren't available or they can't come to the phone. Don't say things like "He's not here" or "I don't know when she'll be back." If you have children that sometimes are home alone, be sure to teach them this rule.

The Mailbox

If you like to put your name on your mailbox but you live alone, you might want to consider conning the cons. If your last name is Brown, for example, I recommend that your mailbox read "The Browns." Even if you're not one to put your name on your mailbox, if you live alone, you might want to consider it. It's an easy and inexpensive way to turn off criminals looking for people who live by themselves. Mailboxes usually are out in the open for everybody to see, which is why this trick is so effective.

The Least You Need to Know

➤ You should never feel obligated to open the door to your home for anybody.

➤ If an intruder is in your home, it's best not to make your presence known.

➤ Planning an emergency exit in advance and creating a safety room take only a little time to do, but they can save your life.

➤ Giving the appearance that you don't live alone should be an important part of your safety plan.

Children: The World's Most Valuable Resource

What do you think is a parent's highest priority? Is it their money, their job, their health, or the safety of their children? You guessed it—the safety of their little ones has always ranked among the highest priorities for most parents and probably always will.

Today in the United States, there are approximately 40 million children under the age of 10. That's a lot of kids. What are we doing to keep them out of harm's way? If we are going to keep the bad guys away from our children, we are going to have to roll up our sleeves and work hard at it. It requires taking time out of our busy schedules to properly educate ourselves with up-to-date information and to spend quality time passing that information on to our children. All of this information must be delivered in an environment full of love and understanding, not fear and ignorance. By reading this chapter, you will have completed half your task because it is packed with some of the most current, practical, and effective information available today. Now all you have to do is put it to good use.

Some Helpful Statistics

The thing about numbers is that they aren't good and they aren't bad—they just are. They are completely unbiased and aren't partial to any person, place, or thing. Try to keep this in mind as I give you some important but uncomfortable statistics throughout this chapter. Remember that the purpose is not to create fear but to give you a better understanding of who and what you are up against so you can be victorious in the end.

Nearly 1,000 children are abducted daily in the United States, according to a recent study done by the U.S. Justice Department. This adds up to 360,000 child abductions per year, of which friends and family members commit more than 98 percent. This means that breaking up with your significant other can greatly increase the risk of your child being abducted. That still leaves nearly 5,000 annual abductions committed by people other than friends and family members. In other words, the problem of our children being abducted is a serious one. The good news is that well over 100,000 attempted kidnappings fail every year.

Stay on your Toes

Fewer than two percent of all child abductions are committed by strangers. Because of this, it's crucial that we teach our children to be prepared to deal with all people, including friends and family.

The Safety-Conscious Parent

Before we go any further, I'd like to take a moment to compliment you for taking the safety of your children seriously enough to carefully review this chapter. In doing so, you have placed yourself in the top few percentile of responsible, concerned, safety-conscious parents who refuse to sit idly and do nothing. If you have ever tried to find materials about this subject, you know how frustrating it can be. Most bookstores carry very little about child safety. My goal in writing this chapter is to equip you with enough solid information to properly educate your child for the worst of situations. I have found that, when it comes to this subject, you don't need a lot of information. You just need the *right* information.

The first thing you must realize is that, for the most part, your child's safety training ultimately is your responsibility. It's not up to police officers, schoolteachers, or day-care workers. These individuals cannot be expected to make up the difference or to pick up the slack if you choose to neglect your child's training. If you do your job properly by working with your child at home, however, these individuals can assist you by enforcing, encouraging, and supporting your efforts during your absence. (Also helpful is having your child fingerprinted and always keeping a recent photo on hand.)

Let the Training Begin

Prior to beginning the training process with your children, we need to lay down some solid ground rules. The first thing you need to know is that you must always strive to make the training fun. What kid is going to want to sit down with mom or dad and be yelled at or scared half to death? Try to make this a very special time for your child, one that he or she will always remember as a time of bonding and relationship building. Not only will this help open the doors to future communication between you and your children, it also will help them retain the information instead of forgetting it the moment you walk out the door.

Over the years, I have taught thousands of kids about safety, and it has been my experience that the best way to teach them is by role-playing. What kid doesn't love to play cowboys and Indians, dress-up, or cops and robbers? One of our children's greatest strengths is their imagination, so this is what we must build on. Knock on the door and pretend to be a salesman or get on the phone with them from another room and try to get them to tell you where they live. When they mess up, laugh a little and give them some encouragement before correcting them. Always be quick to reward them with praise for correct answers.

Bad Guys Beware!

Create realistic training scenarios for your children from time to time. Test them by having them be approached by someone that you know but your children don't.

Before starting the training, make a phone call to your local police department and ask whether any convicted child offenders are living in your neighborhood. This information is very valuable and should be taken into consideration when teaching your child. After all, if a convicted child offender is living next door to your child's best friend, wouldn't you want to know? For the most part, a parent's greatest concern is pedophiles. I don't mean to frighten or alarm you; this is simply a fact with which parents must deal. According to the U.S. Department of Justice, between 250,000 and 500,000 pedophiles currently are living in the United States. Each one will molest an average of 300 children during their lifetime. The worst part is that, nearly 80 percent of the time, children are molested by someone they already know. The majority of all child offenders are men. This doesn't mean there aren't women pedophiles out there, too; it just means the person is more likely to be a guy.

Responsible, Safe Children

The goal is to have responsible, safe children. The two go hand in hand like peanut butter and jelly, and you can't have one without the other. I recommend that you begin teaching your children responsibility at an early age for two reasons. First, their safety depends on it. Second, responsible kids are more pleasant to be around than irresponsible ones. Some great ways to teach your children responsibility include letting them do little things such as locating your vehicle in the parking lot, paying the cashier at the counter, and telling you where to turn on your way home. (I don't recommend you give them the steering wheel, however!)

Make sure your children know how to use 911 from both residential phones and pay phones and help them memorize their full name, address, and phone number. If they can say their ABCs, they are old enough to memorize their personal information. As soon as they memorize this information, teach them to never give it to a stranger for any reason.

What Is a Stranger?

A few years ago, I listened to a lecture by Steven Covey on audiocassette. During his lecture, he told a short story about the cost of poor communication, and I believe the story is very relevant to the subject of safety. He talked about a father who disciplined his son for riding his bicycle past the street corner. Later, the little boy approached his father with a puzzled look on his face and said, "Daddy, what's a corner?"

Because a lot of the safety issues you will be teaching your children relate to protecting them from strangers, the very first thing you should teach them is your definition of what a stranger is. It would be presumptuous for you to assume that they know what you mean every time you use the word "stranger." The definition I like is that a stranger is anyone whom you, the parent, have never met. This means that, just because a man in the park befriends your child over a period of time, he still is a stranger because *you* don't know him. Therefore, all rules regarding strangers apply, no matter how kind your child believes the person is.

The next thing you must teach your children is the definition of a safe stranger. If your children ever become lost or separated from you in a crowded place, they should begin looking for a safe stranger to help them. This also is someone to whom your children can give their personal information if they're lost or in trouble. To qualify as a safe stranger during a time of crisis, a person must fit the following criteria:

➤ The person must be someone your child chooses to approach, not vice versa.

➤ The person must be someone who is working and who is preferably wearing a name tag.

➤ The person must be a woman. (Remember, most pedophiles are men.)

Creating Passwords and Commands

Life Savers

While in the department store, you and your child become separated. First, find the manager. Ask the manager to give a description of your child to the employees and place an employee or two at each exit. Their job is to make sure your child doesn't exit the store, alone or with a stranger. Next, have the manager make an announcement over the loud speaker explaining the situation and giving clear instructions.

A family password is one of the most important tools you can implement to help ensure the safety of your children. It's easy to use, fun to practice, and nearly impossible for the bad guy to work around. The family password is a secret word that only the parents and children know. The rule is that this word must be spoken to the child by an adult prior to the child leaving with that adult or letting him or her into the house. There should be no exceptions to this rule. If the person doesn't know the word, your child doesn't cooperate! A good example would be if someone tried to pick your child up after school without your permission. Either your child or the teacher should ask the individual for the password. If you arranged for that person to pick up your child, you should have given him or her the password in advance. It's a good idea to change the word from time to time and to discipline your children if they spill the beans. This tool is effective only if it remains a secret.

It is very important for your children to know exactly what is expected of them if they are with you when a criminal approaches. Create a command word or phrase for them and let them know what their responsibilities are when you give the order. If a criminal tries to rob you at gunpoint when you're with your child, for example, you can yell "purple polka dot" to have your child run like Carl Lewis to the nearest phone and dial 911. This is a much more desirable situation than having your kid frantically screaming and holding onto your leg while you're trying to ward off an attacker.

A woman defending her-self while holding a child.

When You're Not There

Nearly 20 million children live in an environment in which they are left alone, by themselves and unsupervised, sometimes for hours at a time. This is largely due to the fact that many children are raised in single-parent homes in which the parent must work just to keep food on the table. In most cases, this means the parent doesn't get home from work until after the child gets home from school. In addition, many parents who live together both hold full-time jobs to try to make ends meet. This lifestyle causes a serious safety issue for our children.

The You Are Nevers

The "you are nevers" are steadfast guidelines that define what is and is not acceptable behavior when dealing with adults, especially strangers. The following guidelines should be obeyed at all times without exception:

➤ You are never allowed to do a favor for a stranger. If a stranger asks your child for help, he or she should say, "Please wait while I go get a grown-up."

➤ You are never permitted to get into a vehicle with a stranger.

➤ You are never permitted to go into a stranger's home.

➤ You are never allowed to keep secrets with strangers or with adults other than your parents.

Teach your children how to say "No!" with boldness and let them know that it's all right if they hurt the feelings of a stranger who makes them feel uncomfortable. Tell them that you won't punish them for being rude to an adult who is trying to make them do something they don't want to, but let them know that they will have to explain themselves afterward.

Discuss with your child the private parts of his or her body that no one is allowed to touch for any reason, especially close friends and family members. Also prepare your child in advance for adults who say, "If you tell your parents, I will hurt them." Explain to your kids that this is a big, fat lie.

Stay on your Toes

When a child withholds information from his or her parents pertaining to an adult who's been bad, it is almost always for one of two reasons. Either the child is afraid of being accused of lying and being punished, or the bad adult threatened to hurt the child's parents if he or she tattled.

Take Times

There are four "take times" you can do as a parent to help prevent any foul play from targeting your children. "Take times" earned their name by requiring that you take extra time to go the extra yard. In the long run, however, everybody wins.

➤ Before allowing your child to spend the night with a friend, take time to personally get to know the hosting adults.

➤ Anytime your children return home after being away overnight, take time to have a quality conversation with them. Ask if they had a good time and if it was something they would like to do again in the future.

➤ Before leaving your child with a baby-sitter, take time to know with whom you are dealing. If it's an adult, take time to run a background check. These cost around $50 and are worth every cent.

➤ When picking up your child, take time to get out of the car and go inside for a moment. Your instincts as a parent are invaluable, but they're worthless if you're in the car honking your horn.

Fighting Back

One of the most effective weapons your child has is his or her set of pipes. Very few noises will get an adult's attention faster than a child's scream. Make sure you teach your children not to yell "Help!" though. Some adults will just think it's kids playing or being disciplined by their parents. Teach your child to yell "Stranger, stranger,

Safety Alert!

Teach your children to run from a stranger instead of staying and fighting, unless it's their only option. If they must fight, teach them to bite, poke eyes, and kick the groin. (The groin area is that sensitive area between a man's legs.)

911!" There aren't too many things that phrase can mean when yelled by a child, and it can get a bad guy to go away in a hurry!

Most children are slower runners and worse fighters than adults, but there's a good chance most adults won't chase a kid for too long for fear of drawing attention to themselves and getting caught. Because of this, tell your children to only fight back as an absolute last resort and to run whenever possible. Like adults, the best time for your child to try to get away is right away. Teach them not to wait for the right time. Instead, tell them to go for it as soon as they are approached. Believe me, it's their best chance of escaping. If they can't run and must stay and fight, teach them to "go animal." There are only three things they need to know how to do while screaming "Stranger, stranger, 911!" They are bite, poke eyes, and kick the groin really hard. Remember that there are no rules when it comes to survival. When running, your child needs to head for the nearest car and begin running around it in circles while screaming. Do you know how difficult it is to catch a child running around a vehicle? It's equivalent to trying to gargle peanut butter while standing on your head—sticky business.

If someone tries to knock your child off his or her bike, teach your child to quickly wrap both arms and legs tightly around the bike and begin screaming "Stranger, stranger, 911!" It's nearly impossible to throw a screaming child attached to a bike into a vehicle.

A boy avoids abduction by wrapping his arms and legs around the bike.

Here is a tough scenario to have to think about, but I'm sure you will agree that it's an important one, so bear with me as I walk you through it. If your child is ever thrown into the trunk of a vehicle, here is what he or she should do. Instruct your child to pull out every wire he or she can get his or her hands on. Most vehicles that get pulled over are for minor traffic violations, and there's a good chance your child will get a brake light, a tail light, or a turn signal wire. If your child is successful, the driver will be unaware until he sees flashing red lights in the rearview mirror. Again, I know this sounds terrible, but think of the alternative.

Home Safety for Kids

Here is some good advice for your children if they are ever home alone. If they think someone is trying to enter the home, teach them to dial 911, leave the phone off the hook, and sneak out the back door. By leaving the phone off the hook, the police will send an officer to your home. This is where having a neighbor you can trust comes in really handy. Having a trustworthy friend next door could save your child's life one day, so get that grill fired up and invite 'em over.

You should map out in advance your children's emergency escape route so they don't have to make one up when they're scared and in a hurry. This isn't just for bad guy insurance; it's also invaluable if there ever is a fire in the middle of the night. Teach your children that hiding in the house isn't a good idea. To prove your point, have them hide in the house and show them how long it takes you to find them.

You also might want to take the time to secure their room from any unwanted late-night guests. A few good window locks at about $1 each should do the trick.

Stay on your Toes

Unless taught otherwise, children almost always will run to their room and hide if a stranger tries to enter the house or if a fire breaks out. This is why it is so important for you to teach your children the importance of exiting the home quickly in both situations.

Teach your child the three "never tells" of telephone safety when talking to strangers. They are

1. Never tell the caller who you are.

2. Never tell the caller where you live.

3. Never tell the caller you are home alone.

Finally, nearly 50 million homes in America are equipped with deadly firearms, many of which are easily accessible.

Unfortunately, this translates into the tragic deaths of hundreds of kids every year—more than one a day, every day. If there is a firearm in your home, make sure there is no way your child could ever get to it, regardless of how hard he or she tried. Spend quality time educating your child about the dangers of firearms and set strict guidelines that you enforce. Your child's friend might have parents who aren't quite as careful about where they hide their gun, so your child better know the rules in advance.

Safety Alert!

If you have children in your home and own a firearm, it is your responsibility to make sure it cannot be accessed. It should be well hidden, locked up, and unloaded with the ammo hidden in another location.

Tips Worth Remembering

Last but not least, here is a list of easy-to-do, hard-to-forget tips that should be discussed with your child a few at a time. There's no rush in trying to push all this information onto your child at once, so take your time and just go through a few each week. Thirty minutes here and there quickly adds up over the course of a few months, so take your time and have fun.

➤ Teach your children to never leave with a police officer unless *two* uniformed officers are present. Any good police officer will honor your child's request.

➤ Encourage your children to practice staying in groups and to never stray off alone.

➤ Never allow your children to be alone in a parking lot while waiting for their ride to pick them up.

➤ If your children are going to be walking or riding their bikes somewhere, discuss with them what route they are going to take. This is extremely valuable information if they wind up missing.

➤ Don't let your children wear clothes or name tags that reveal their names to a stranger. The stranger could call out their names and then act like a friend of the family.

➤ Make calling to check in a rule in your home and thank your children every time they do.

➤ If you can afford it, invest in a pager for your child.

➤ Teach your children to walk in the direction of oncoming traffic. If they are being followed by a vehicle, teach them to run in a direction the vehicle can't follow.

I know we've covered some pretty sensitive material in this chapter, and I am proud of you for being a trooper and sticking it out. The truth is that, if parents don't take the time to sit down with their children and teach them about these issues, who will? As long as you keep a positive attitude and a gentle spirit, you will be great at this. What are you waiting for?

The Least You Need to Know

➤ The responsibility of your children's safety rests on your shoulders. If you don't take it seriously, no one will.

➤ For safety training to be effective, it must be fun and must always be done with love and understanding.

➤ When teaching children, you must remain consistent with your discipline, your encouragement, and your praise—without compromise.

➤ Spread the safety training out over a few months to make it easier for your children to retain. This also will help prevent them from becoming over-whelmed or intimidated.

Good-Old-Fashioned Safety for Seniors

An elderly man accepts an offer to have his roof inspected for free after a major storm tears through his county. The repairman tells him that a few small areas need to be repaired soon; otherwise, rain will begin leaking into the house. The elderly man takes the repairman's advice and tells him to do the work. The next day, the repairman presents a bill for $3,800, which is the man's entire life savings. He thought the repairs were minor and were only going to cost a few hundred dollars.

What started off as a free inspection turned into a home repair scam. To make matters worse, the roof wasn't fixed correctly because it was worked on by a con man instead of a roofer. In the United States, the elderly hold a large share of our country's wealth—and con artists know it. Senior citizens are targeted for every type of scam imaginable because they are viewed as easy prey by professional scum seeking to take advantage of anyone they can. If you are in your golden years, the information in this chapter is a must. Learn how to protect yourself from these rogues and enjoy the best years of your life while staying safe and secure. You don't have to be a victim of these crimes, and you don't have to live in fear.

Protecting Yourself from Scams

For a con artist, the weapons of choice are a million-dollar smile, a nice suit, a wonderful personality, and an ear to listen. Con artists are attracted to the elderly and their money like bumblebees are to honey. There is no better way to protect yourself and your money from scams than to set forth some strict rules and guidelines and to stay current on the scams in circulation. By reading this section, you will be brought up to speed about what's going on, you will learn how these criminals operate, and you will be equipped with practical guidelines that should help you avert financial disaster.

Bad Guys Beware!

If you want to make a financial investment, go to a reputable company.

Investments

When it comes to investing, if a deal sounds too good to be true, it usually is. Think about it. If it was such a hot, money-making idea, why would a total stranger take time out of his or her day to call you on the phone or pay you a visit, just so you can get a piece of the pie? That's an awful kind thing for someone to do, especially someone you have never met. Don't you think?

Never invest through a stranger who approaches you by telephone, mail, or your front door. The best investments are made with people you approach, not vice versa. A favorite technique of these con men is to try to rush you into making a quick decision. They will tell you that you have to decide whether you're going to invest money right now, or you will lose this wonderful opportunity. They do this because they don't want you to get any counsel from friends or family, they don't want you to have time to check them out, and they definitely don't want you to have time to think about it. Being rushed to make an investment is a sure sign that you are dealing with a crook. A legitimate investment professional always gives you time to think about the investment and to look the prospectus over carefully. If someone's trying to rush you, just say no.

Here are a few things you can do to check the legitimacy of an individual or company that wants you to invest money:

➤ Call the Better Business Bureau.

➤ Ask the person for a list of references.

➤ Call their place of employment to verify that they really work there.

➤ Ask to review their qualifications and credentials.

➤ Ask to see their driver's license to make sure they are who they say they are (and be suspicious of an out-of-state license).

Stay on Your Toes

According to the U.S. Office of Consumer Affairs, fraud in America is about a $100 billion a year business.

Remember, your money is a big deal. Before you let go of it, especially on an investment-type level, you need to be absolutely sure that everything is on the up and up. Some of these crooks go as far as to get a beautiful office with nice furniture, and they even have fancy brochures printed to impress you. Some will even let you earn money on a small investment in an attempt to earn your trust and to get you to invest larger sums of money.

Two things you can do are make sure they are incorporated and take a look at their offering memorandum, which should give you information about the investment and let you know what kind of risks are involved. To verify that a company is incorporated, call the Secretary of State where you live.

Home Inspections and Repairs

Another popular scam is to offer someone a free home inspection or to offer a special price on repairs due to leftover materials from another job. Bad news usually comes with a free inspection, usually in the form of a list of what needs to be fixed immediately. They take your money up front and then don't do the job at all, don't finish it, or don't do it correctly. You also can expect to be charged an arm and a leg for the work, whether it was done or not.

The following are just a few home-repair scams to watch out for:

➤ Spraying for termites and other insects

➤ Paving or repairing your driveway

➤ Inspecting or repairing your heating or air conditioning unit

➤ Inspecting or repairing your roof

Bad Guys Beware!

Be sure to agree on a price in writing before allowing any work to be done.

You must get references in advance from anyone who works on your home. A reputable businessperson in the home-repair profession will not have a problem giving you the references you need. A con, however, might not be so cooperative. When you do get a list, be sure to call the people on it and don't assume they're all satisfied customers. In fact, they might not be customers at all but people randomly pulled out of the phone book. You also should call the Better Business Bureau and ask about the company you are considering to do the work.

Finally, it's important to make sure the work they say has been done actually has been done. If you hire someone to fix your furnace, for example, turn it on and let it run for a little while to make sure it works—even if it's the middle of July.

Always agree on a price before allowing any work to be done on your home. If you don't, you might be sorry.

You Win!

"Congratulations, you have just won an all-expenses-paid cruise to the Bahamas! All you have to do to claim your prize is give me your credit card number so I can process your information and mail you your package. There's also a $50 processing fee, which must be paid up front."

Stay on Your Toes

If someone tells you that you've won something but you have to give your credit card number or pay some money up front, it's probably a scam.

Never give out your credit card number to a stranger who asks you for it, especially one who calls you on the phone. Also avoid giving out your calling card number, bank account number, or social security number. These numbers are as good as cash to a con artist, who can either sell your number or purchase items with the card, and they need to be protected.

Donations Accepted

"Would you like to donate money to the Arthritis Foundation? We are close to finding a cure, and with your help, we might be able to heal millions of sufferers. Can we count on your support?"

Don't be taken in by one of these calls—they could be a scam in disguise. If you want to give money to one of these organizations, place a call to one of their offices (they should be listed in the phone book) and ask a representative to mail you information so you can look it over. When it comes to strangers calling you and rattling off their name, their cause, and their need, be sure to proceed with caution. Tell whoever is calling to mail the information and to leave their name and phone number with you. If they don't want to do this for any reason, hang up the phone and be thankful you didn't get burned. Reputable organizations will be happy to oblige, and the cons will have 10 reasons why they can't.

Lost Inheritances

Beware of companies or individuals that tell you someone has left you an inheritance. These scammers try to get you to pay them a fee for telling you who has left you money or for instructing you about what steps you need to take to obtain your newly acquired cash. This is a very popular scam, with the elderly as a common target.

Recoup Owed or Lost Money

The preceding rules also apply to people who want to help you recoup lost or owed money. If someone calls you and says records show that Social Security has been underpaying you for six years and that you are entitled to a bunch of money, don't believe it. The next thing the person probably will tell you is that, for a fee, he or she will help you collect it. A good rule of thumb is to make people perform before paying them. This separates the crooks from the honest with very little effort.

> **Bad Guys Beware!**
>
> If someone tries to talk you into paying a fee in advance for getting you money, tell the person you will pay the fee after you have collected your money and then see what he or she says. Don't be surprised if the person suddenly disappears from your life.

Out of the House

So you've decided that the best way to avoid crime and violence is to stay inside and lock your doors. This way of thinking is called "Camp Mentality," and it's very unhealthy. There's a fine line between living life and merely existing, and staying inside your home definitely falls into the "merely existing" category. Getting out and staying active are the best things you can do for your mental and physical health; however, you do need to know some basic safety tips to keep you safe.

Safety in Numbers

When it comes to getting out of the house, nothing you can do will improve your overall safety more than being with a friend. Whether you're going for a brisk walk, driving to the store, or going to the bank, taking a friend along is the best way to stay safe and to be left alone by a criminal. One elderly person walking out of a bank might be a desirable target for a robber, but two seniors walking out of the bank looks like trouble. Find a buddy you can trust and get into the habit of going out together.

Try to do as much as you can during daylight hours and definitely take a friend if you're going out at night. It's a safe idea that works.

Stay on Your Toes

If you are mugged by an experienced thief, he or she more than likely will try to knock your glasses off so you can't get a good look and to help make the getaway easier.

If you wear glasses, be sure to wear them when you're out of the house. If you are mugged by an experienced thief, he or she more than likely will try to knock your glasses off so you can't get a good look and to help make the getaway easier.

Have a chain connected to your glasses to keep them from hitting the ground and being stomped on if they get knocked off by a criminal. You're in trouble without your vision. Don't use chords for your glasses, though, because chords won't break if pulled by a criminal, and you can be choked or dragged. Chains are better because they break if pulled, but they'll keep your glasses from hitting the ground if they get knocked off.

Getting Some Exercise

When walking and exercising, you should be aware and alert but relaxed. Try not to look paranoid or fearful because it will draw the criminal's attention. If you have a purse, be sure to carry it correctly to avoid a purse snatching (see Chapter 8, "Playing It Safe When Out of the House"). Twelve percent of all crimes against senior citizens are robberies on the street and purse snatchings. Men should carry their billfold in their front pocket to avoid pickpockets.

I recommend carrying a fanny pack to hold your money and ID because criminals don't like fanny packs. Fanny packs are the little carrying cases that strap around your waist and can be closed securely with snaps, zippers, or Velcro. They can't be grabbed off your body quickly, and they act as a deterrent to a thief looking for a quick score.

Be sure to carry some pepper spray with you—it's a great non-lethal weapon that is easy to use, inexpensive to buy, and can save your life (see Chapter 23, "Weapons and Gadgets: What Really Works").

You might want to consider carrying a personal alarm with you as well. I suggest that you carry the type you wear around your neck and pull in an emergency. When you pull the alarm away from the chord, it goes off automatically.

Bad Guys Beware!

If you walk with a cane, you can use it as a weapon to defend yourself (if you learn a few moves in advance). Taking big swings with a cane is not a good idea because they are too slow and too easy to block. Learn one or two short, simple, and quick moves that can buy you a few valuable seconds and give you time to get away.

Here are a few more practical tips that will help keep you safe:

➤ Avoid carrying a lot of cash.

➤ Don't carry a credit card unless you plan to use it.

➤ Anytime you approach your vehicle or the door to your home, be sure to have your key ready to unlock instead of waiting until the last moment.

Driving

The following are some precautions you should take when driving:

➤ Keep all doors locked whenever you're in the vehicle.

➤ Keep your windows rolled up and your vehicle in gear when in slowed or stopped traffic.

➤ Keep a car length's distance between you and the vehicle in front of you when in stopped or slowed traffic. (This gives you room to drive off and escape in the event of a carjacking.)

➤ Never let your fuel tank get below one quarter of a tank.

➤ Keep your vehicle properly maintained (scheduled oil changes, tune-ups, tire rotations, and so on).

➤ Choose the route you will be traveling in advance and with safety in mind. (Take well lit, well traveled roads.)

➤ Don't keep valuables on the seat where they can be seen.

➤ Never give rides to strangers.

➤ If you become stranded, stay in your vehicle and wait for help to arrive, but don't accept a ride from a stranger (see Chapter 18, "Roadside Assistance for the Stranded Driver").

Also, if you ride the bus, train, or subway, be sure to always sit near the driver or near an exit.

Shopping

Here are some practical tips you can use when out shopping:

➤ Don't lay your purse or checkbook in your shopping cart.

➤ Don't carry cash to shop with if you can use a checkbook, ATM card, check card, or credit card instead.

➤ Don't flash cash out in the open.

➤ Be careful where you set bags down (this includes purses).

➤ Park in well lit areas.

➤ Don't be afraid to ask for security or a store employee to escort you to your car if leaving the store at night.

➤ Avoid wearing flashy or expensive jewelry that gives the impression you're a person of means.

Banking

Millions of elderly people depend on monthly checks from the government. Unfortunately, criminals are aware of this, and they make it a point to know what day the checks come each month. This is why I strongly suggest that you set up direct deposit with your bank. This means no more waiting by the mailbox, not as many trips to the bank, and no risk of getting your check stolen. Setting up direct deposit with your bank is simple and usually is a free service.

Avoid withdrawing large amounts of cash at the front counter of the bank. If you must make a large withdrawal, wait to see someone who can help you in an office and let this employee bring the cash to you discreetly. Also avoid withdrawing large amounts of money from ATM machines. If you go to the bank regularly, don't get into a habit of going on the same day every month or every week. Switch up the times. Finally, take advantage of your bank's safe deposit boxes and store your valuables there.

Stay on Your Toes

Not only is using direct deposit safer, you probably will get your check a day or two early because it doesn't have to go through the mail. This means there's a smaller chance of it getting lost in the mail.

Bad Guys Beware!

Call your local police department for assistance in starting a neighborhood watch program. More than likely, the department will assign a police officer to your community to assist you with the startup process.

Bad Guys Beware!

Here is what the www.ncpc.org Web site has to say about the Triad Program: "It's sponsored on a national level by the American Association of Retired Persons (AARP), the International Association of Chiefs of Police, and the National Sheriffs' Association (NSA). Triad promotes partnerships between senior citizens and the law enforcement community, both to prevent crime against the elderly and to help law enforcement benefit from the talents of older people. If you're interested , contact your chief of police, sheriff, or AARP chapter or call Triad at NSA, 703-836-7827."

Your Community

Your community is an extension of your home, and whether it's a safe place to live depends greatly on the people who live there and their level of involvement.

Securing Your Home

Securing your home is the first step to safeguarding your community. The fewer desirable targets in your community, the more likely it is the thieves will go away. Keep your doors and windows locked and make your home look occupied even when it's not. Invest in proper lighting and quality locks (see Chapter 13, "Fortifying Your Castle") and keep an eye on your neighbor's home and vehicle. A watchful neighbor is a great deterrent to crime.

Neighborhood Watch

Get involved with a neighborhood watch program in your community. If you don't have one, start one. Someone has to do it, and it might as well be you. The elderly are great candidates for starting neighborhood watch programs because they usually are retired and have time to properly organize events and do things right. As retirees, you and your neighbors also can take turns keeping an eye on things throughout the day.

Who to Contact

If you've been scammed, robbed, harassed, or even just suspect that someone is up to no good, it's your responsibility to report the incident to the proper authorities. If someone tries to con you out of your life's savings, for example, and you are fortunate enough to catch on to the con before it's too late, you still have a responsibility to try to prevent that person or company from victimizing someone else. If you see someone suspicious hanging out in your neighborhood, don't just shut your blinds. Report your suspicions to the police.

The following is a list of places you can contact, depending on how serious the problem is or to what it relates:

➤ **Better Business Bureau:** To report a person or a business that is less than honorable.

➤ **Police Department:** To report someone suspicious or to file a report for a fraud or crime.

➤ **Attorney general or prosecuting attorney:** To report scams, cons, and frauds.

Getting involved is not only your responsibility, it's your privilege.

Stay on Your Toes

The elderly can make a huge impact on crime and violence in this country simply by voting. Voting is not trivial. It is very powerful, and your single vote can make a difference.

The Least You Need to Know

➤ When it comes to making investments, if it sounds too good to be true, it probably is.

➤ Investing your hard-earned money is a serious matter. You should take your time making a decision and should get counsel from friends and family.

➤ When out and about, nothing protects you better than having a friend with you.

➤ Direct deposit for monthly checks greatly reduces the chance of theft and robbery and is easy to set up.

➤ It's important to contact the proper authorities when things go wrong.

Self-Defense for the Physically Challenged

Several teenagers who are bored and looking for trouble decide to harass a handicapped woman for some cheap entertainment. The wheelchair convinces them that she is an easy target. The leader of the group walks up to the woman and begins to make fun of her, but she ignores him and continues on her way. He then begins to push her wheelchair in an attempt to upset her, but that doesn't work either.

Finally, the teenager decides he is going to take her purse, which is sitting on her lap, and help himself to whatever money she is carrying. The moment he touches the woman's purse, she instinctively grabs his hand and twists it 180 degrees as she bends it backwards. Before he knows what's happening, he is lying on the ground in excruciating pain and is begging for the woman to please let him go. The other teenagers laugh at their friend, but they aren't going near the woman after what they've just witnessed. She finally releases her aggressor, and he quickly gets up and flees the scene. The only thing that's been hurt is his pride, but she could really have hurt him if she thought her safety was in danger. Just because she's physically challenged doesn't mean she's not prepared to defend herself against an attacker.

In this chapter, I am going to teach those of you who are physically challenged how to effectively defend yourselves from the criminals of this world. Although I wrote the majority of this information for people confined to a wheelchair, some of this material might also be useful for people whose circumstances are somewhat different, depending on their physical limitations.

I will teach you how to block, throw handstrikes, and perform control and restraint techniques that can hold down even the biggest of thugs if performed correctly. I'm also going to teach you how to guard your valuables, and I'll discuss some personal protection items you might want to carry with you in case of an emergency.

Blocks

Just because you're confined to a wheelchair doesn't mean you can't throw strong, effective blocks. In some cases, you should be able to throw better blocks because the lower you are to the ground when performing a block, the more stable you become.

Stay on Your Toes

Being low makes the block stronger and greatly improves your overall balance. It's easy to knock someone over who is standing up and trying to block, but when someone gets really low and drops his or her center of gravity, it's almost impossible to push the person off balance.

The X Block

X blocks are great because they're strong enough to stop the force of a baseball bat and are quick enough to stop a fast punch. Many Korean styles of martial arts systems use the X block to defend against something with a great deal of force behind it as well as to block overhead attacks.

To properly execute an X block, overlap both forearms in front of your forehead or over your head (depending on the angle of the strike being thrown) and form an X. Both fists should be pointing up at 45-degree angles. This block gets its strength and stability from the entire upper body. It utilizes the chest, shoulders, and arms—unlike one-handed blocks that have only half the strength of an X block. Another good thing about this block is that it gives the defender a large margin for error because the X created with the arms is more than one-foot wide, which means your aim doesn't have to be perfect.

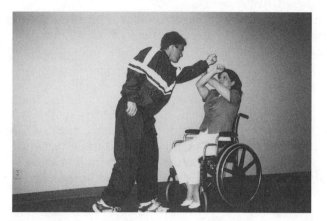

An X block.

The Inward Block

The best self-defense techniques are the ones that already are comfortable and instinctive motions for the student. Inward blocks are one of my favorites because, for most people, the movement is very natural. If you've ever swatted at a fly buzzing around your face, you've probably performed an inward block without even knowing it.

Here's how the inward block is done. Simply take your right or left hand (whichever one you prefer) and push it across your face with your palm facing the direction your hand is moving. If you're using your right hand, for example, open your hand and push it across your face until your hand is resting directly in front of your left

Bad Guys Beware!

A great self-defense technique is to quickly roll your wheelchair forward into the shins of your attacker just as he is trying to assault you. This will cause him to stop his assault in mid-flight to reach down with his hands and stop the chair from banging his shins.

An inward block.

315

shoulder when it's finished. It's that simple. This block is great for deflecting anything coming straight toward your face or your chest area such as a punch, a choke, a push, or a knife being thrust forward.

The Hat Block

A hat block is one of the easiest blocks in self-defense to learn, and it is one of the most versatile. It's designed to stop anything and everything directed toward your face or head region. If you are caught off-guard and need to protect yourself in a hurry, the hat block is the way to go. If you see a hook punch heading toward the side of your head really fast, call on the faithful hat block. In short, it's a great multi-purpose and practical block that everyone should know.

A hat block.

To perform this block, take your right or left hand (whichever one you prefer) and place it on top of your head like you would a hat. (Have your hand in the open position, grabbing your head.) By doing this, you place your elbow in front of your face. This is a great defense against a straight punch, especially if your attacker hits your elbow with his fist. Your forearm, biceps, triceps, and shoulder muscles will protect the side of your head and jaw area from any punches that might be coming at you from the side.

Handstrikes

With most handstrikes, the majority of power comes from the legs, footwork, and hip rotation. The handstrikes taught in this section are specifically designed to generate a great deal of power without having to shuffle in, drop body weight, or twist. This means you can throw these strikes from a sitting position and still generate enough power to make even the biggest of attackers think twice about coming back for seconds.

The Back Fist

Back fists are as quick as lightning and can really throw your attacker off-guard.

Stay on Your Toes

If you're in the sitting position and your hands are resting on your lap, you're in the perfect position to throw a handstrike because it won't be noticeable and will catch your attacker off guard.

To properly throw a back fist, it's important that you first know what part of the hand to use and what your target is. The part of the hand that does the striking is the large knuckles (the knuckles of the index and middle fingers) on the back of your hand. (Avoid using your backhand because you will cause damage to it.) The knuckles are nice and pointy and will do significant damage without hurting your hand in the process. The target is your attacker's face. This includes his jaw, cheek, eyes, or nose. These all are great targets that really hurt when hit, and they'll definitely get someone's attention in a hurry. Just make a fist and hit your target with the backs of your large knuckles as quickly and as hard as you can.

A back fist.

The Sword Hand

This block got its name because the hand looks like the blade of a sword when held properly. The sword hand has one purpose—to strike the attacker's groin area with

Bad Guys Beware!

When you throw a handstrike, it's very important that you return the strike as soon as possible. If you don't return your handstrike back to your body fast enough, you run the risk of having it grabbed by your attacker. If you snap your strikes back quicker than you throw them, you won't run into this problem.

both speed and accuracy. The part of the hand that you strike with is the front edge. The thumb should be tucked in toward your palm to protect it from being broken. This handstrike is perfect for someone who is sitting down because his or her hand already is positioned at groin level and only needs to move a short distance to hit its target. The shorter the distance a strike has to travel, the less time the person being hit has to react. This means they are more likely to be hit.

To throw a good sword hand, hang your hand down at your side or, if you're in a wheelchair, down the side of the chair. Swing it upward as quick as you can and into the groin of your attacker. Because of the positioning of the hand, you should be able to come up underneath the attacker's groin even if his legs are together. Strike your target with the part of your hand between your thumb's lowest knuckle and the top of your wrist. This is one strike that can cause a lot of pain to an unsuspecting attacker.

A sword hand.

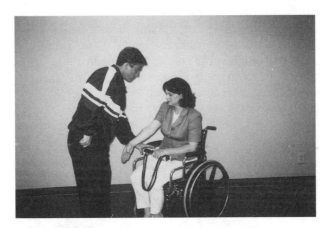

The Heel Palm

If you really want to stop someone in a hurry, hit him or her in the head or face with a heel palm. The heel palm was designed to be thrown at an attacker without causing injury to your hand while, at the same time, generating a great deal of force.

To throw a heel palm, open your hand and strike your target with the palm of your hand. This strike has the same mechanics as a normal punch, but you're using the open part of your hand instead of your fist. These strikes need to be thrown in a straight line and directly at your target (the same way a boxer throws a jab or a cross at his opponent's face). Just before making contact, however, be sure to snap the palm of your hand toward your target. This gives it a little extra oomph.

Safety Alert!

Avoid hitting someone in the nose with the heel palm. You can accidentally take someone's life if you don't know what you're doing when throwing this strike at someone's nose. Just to be on the safe side, don't throw a heel palm at someone's nose unless you've earned a Black Belt.

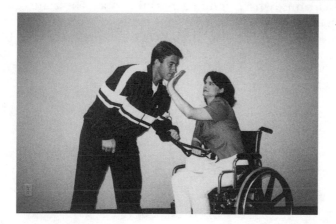

A heel palm.

The Snap Strike

A snap strike is one of the most powerful handstrikes in self-defense. This strike hits your attacker from the side and has more power than a hook punch (a punch that is thrown from the side, like a large hook or circle). It also is quicker than a hook and protects your hand at the same time.

This strike is designed to hit only the head or face area of your opponent, never the body. (Openhanded strikes are not effective when used on the body.) These strikes resemble heel palms because you strike your target with the palm of your hand, but snap strikes attack from the side while heel palms attack straight ahead. Just remember that heel palms are openhanded linear strikes and snap strikes are openhanded circular strikes. This should help prevent you from confusing the two.

A snap strike.

Control and Restraint

Have you ever watched a movie in which actor Steven Segal ties the bad guys into knots while using their arms, wrists, and fingers as the rope? These are called *control and restraint* techniques because they control your opponent by bending appendages and extremities in the opposite direction of how they are supposed to be bent. Not only do these techniques really hurt, they also can bring a grown man to his knees in a hurry with very little effort.

Stay on Your Toes

When it comes to controlling and restraining, size and strength aren't important. Fulcrum (the point of support on which a lever turns), leverage, and proper technique are what makes this work, and manipulating joints and bones are what make it hurt. The great thing about this type of self-defense is that you can control your opponents by inflicting a great deal of pain, but you don't have to injure them in the process.

The Wristlock

A wristlock is a technique in which you take the attacker's wrist and bend it back, way back, opposite its normal direction. If done correctly, a good wristlock will take the fight right out of even the biggest opponent. If executed poorly, however, your opponent probably will just give you a funny look. As with all control and restraint moves, technique is vital to success, so practice, practice, practice!

The following are the steps for performing a good wristlock:

➤ Grab one of your opponent's wrists with both hands.

➤ Place your thumbs on the backside of your opponent's hand with your thumbs slightly below the person's knuckles and with his fingers pointed upward.

➤ Bend the person's wrist straight back as you twist his hand toward the outside of his body at the same time.

➤ Don't let up on your pressure until the person goes down to one knee or falls back. It is important that they drop to one knee because it's an act of surrender or helplessness, and it shows that you have the advantage.

➤ After you have the person where you want him, maintain a constant amount of pressure and yell for help.

This is the proper hand position for executing a wristlock.

The Arm Bar

The arm bar is an awesome technique. It got its name because it enables you to use the attacker's arm as a bar that can effectively control him or her. It does this by bending the arm back at the elbow and causing excruciating pain. This limits the arm's range of motion so that the attacker no longer is a threat.

The following are the steps for performing an arm bar correctly:

➤ Tightly wrap your hand around your opponent's wrist. (If you're grabbing your opponent's left wrist, use your left hand and vice versa.)

➤ Place your forearm bone into the back of your opponent's elbow and push down really hard until your opponent drops to the ground.

➤ While you're pushing down on your attacker's elbow with your forearm, pull up on their wrist at the same time with your hand. (Push down with your left forearm and pull up with your right hand or vice versa.)

An arm bar.

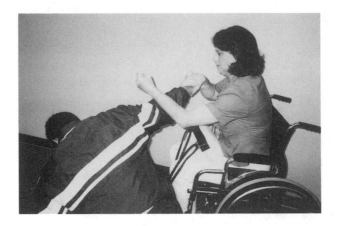

The Hair Sweep

There is only one requirement to perform a good hair sweep: your opponent has to have hair. To perform this technique, grab your opponent's bangs (or the front of the person's hair) and pull straight back. Don't pull the hair to the side, or the person will roll out of this hold with little effort. By pulling the bangs straight back, you will put your opponent on his or her backside in a hurry. Make sure not to grab any hair other than the bangs for this move, though, because directly over the forehead is where it's the most sensitive and where it hurts the most.

A hair sweep.

Digit control.

Digit Control

Digit control is taking your attacker's fingers or thumbs and bending them back until your attacker succumbs to the pain. Nobody wants their fingers broken, and when they think they're about to snap, they become cooperative really fast. The best time to use digit control is when someone tries to grab you. Just grab a finger and start bending.

Other Good Stuff

This section covers some great information for protecting any valuables you might be carrying with you. I'm also going to take the liberty of recommending a few safety products that you might want to consider carrying around with you for added protection. If you have a child confined to a wheelchair, I have a few practical pointers for you as well. You'll learn a few effective techniques for protecting your child when a criminal strikes.

Protecting Your Belongings

If you're in a wheelchair, you might carry large items with you from time to time such as a backpack, a purse, a briefcase, or a laptop computer. If you carry any of these items with you, you need

Life Savers

I was jumped by several attackers once, and I came out of the situation without a scratch thanks to digit control. I grabbed the fingers of one of the four guys who jumped me in a parking lot and told him to instruct his friends to back off. They wouldn't listen to me, but they did listen to their friend. Every time one of them took a step toward me, I cranked on one of their friend's fingers until he yelped in pain. It didn't take long for them to figure out they were hurting their friend by getting near me. Within a few minutes, the police arrived and I let the guy go. I was outnumbered four to one, and they had been drinking. The situation could have gotten ugly really fast, but thanks to digit control nobody got hurt.

to know how to protect them from thieves. The following are some things you can do to reduce your chances of getting ripped off:

➤ Secure the strap of your bag to the wheelchair.

➤ Keep the opening of the bag securely closed whenever it's not in use.

➤ If possible, cover the bag up or keep it out of sight.

➤ If you're going to hang the bag on the back of your chair, rig it so that if someone touches it you will feel it.

Protecting a Child in a Wheelchair

If you are out with a child confined to a wheelchair and you are confronted by a criminal, do the following to help protect the child:

➤ Place yourself between the child and the criminal and continue pivoting to maintain this position.

➤ Point the child in a safe direction and give the chair a good push while commanding the child to keep going.

➤ If the criminal tries to hurt the child, sit in the chair on the child's lap. (This enables you to fight back while shielding the child from the attack.)

➤ Create a command word to be used only in an emergency situation and let the child know what his or her responsibility is when the word is spoken.

For Extra Protection

For extra protection, I recommend that the following items be carried with you when in your wheelchair:

➤ A small container of mace that is easily accessible

➤ Enough change to make two phone calls

➤ Identification

➤ A whistle, an air horn, or a personal alarm that can summon help in case of an emergency

➤ A cellular phone

The Least You Need to Know

➤ People in wheelchairs have a lower center of gravity, which makes them good at defense.

➤ The best blocks are ones that already are natural and instinctive movements.

➤ Handstrikes can deter attackers from continuing with their assault.

➤ Control and restraint techniques can bring large attackers to their knees.

➤ When performing control and restraint techniques, be sure to apply as much pressure as possible and don't let up until help arrives or the criminal flees.

➤ Learn to guard your valuables carefully when out in public.

Glossary

aggravated assault   A physical and violent attack on another person.

assailant   An attacker.

burglary   Breaking into a home or business with the intent to steal.

carjacking   The use of force or a threat to steal someone's vehicle.

chop shop   An illegal garage where stolen vehicles are taken to be disassembled.

digital certificate   Software that can be purchased to provide your personal computer with extra security while you surf the Internet.

digit control   Taking your attacker's fingers or thumbs and bending them back as far as you can until your attacker succumbs to the pain.

dojo   A school where martial arts are taught.

domestic violence   Violence that occurs in the home, usually between family members.

encryption   A way of scrambling important computer information into symbols so it is difficult for a hacker to understand.

felony   A serious crime usually punished by a fine and/or a prison term of more than one year.

force continuum   A process every police officer must go through when using force to detain someone.

forensic   The application of scientific or medical knowledge to assist in the investigation of a crime.

gap insurance   Vehicle insurance that covers the difference between what you owe the bank and what your vehicle is worth (if it is ever stolen or totaled).

Harris Self-Defense System   A self-defense system founded by Chris Harris in 1993 that combines only the most practical and realistic martial arts techniques to complete a well-rounded system of defending oneself.

hay maker   Another name (slang) for a hook punch.

homicide   When one person kills another person; murder.

internet service provider (ISP)   A company that provides access to the Internet for its users.

kata   A martial arts term used to describe the use of choreographed offensive and defensive movements for practice or meditation.

kiai   The loud, intimidating noise that martial artists yell when kicking, blocking, or punching. This term means "energy harmony" in Japanese.

kubotan   A self-defense device used for joint manipulation, striking, and key flailing. It is about the size of a magic marker.

larceny   Taking someone's property without their permission with the intent of keeping it.

martial arts   An all-encompassing term used to describe most all of the arts of self-protection and self-perfection. The name is derived from the ancient Roman god of war, Mars.

miranda rights   These rights read as follows: "You have the right to remain silent; anything you say can and will be held against you in a court of law. You have the right to an attorney; if you cannot afford an attorney, one will be appointed to represent you prior to any questioning."

misdemeanor   A minor criminal offense usually punished by a fine and/or a short jail term of less than one year.

MO   Stands for *modus operandi* and refers to a criminal's pattern of behavior.

no-bill   A legal term used when the reason for defending yourself appears to be self-evident, and no arrests or charges need to be made.

OSHA   Stands for Occupational Safety and Health Administration. This government agency is responsible for regulating workplace environments.

parry   A self-defense block that is thrown to deflect or redirect an opponent's attack.

pedophile   A person who has developed an abnormal sexual desire toward children.

pepper spray   Also known as mace, this spray contains a mixture of cayenne pepper and other chemicals that cause pain and irritation to whomever is sprayed.

perpetrator   Someone who has committed a crime.

Phone Butler   A product that helps take care of annoying sales calls by playing a recording that tells the sales person you're not interested.

recidivist   A criminal who is a repeat offender.

restraining order   A document declaring that, by law, a person is not allowed within a certain physical distance of the plaintiff.

road rage   When one driver gets angry at another driver and decides to take revenge.

robbery   Taking personal property that is in the possession or presence of the victim by using violence or intimidation.

Solar plexus   A network of nerves in the abdominal area just above the stomach and below the sternum that is very sensitive and hurts badly when struck.

strike plate   The metal plate screwed into the door frame that encases the dead bolt when the door is shut. It helps prevent the door frame from giving in when force is used.

voyeur   A peeping Tom.

World Wide Web   Millions of pages of information networked and arranged into sites by specific addresses that can be accessed from a computer with Internet capabilities by using a browser.

Books

Here is a list of personal safety and self-defense books for further reading:

101 Ways to Save Your Life
by Chris Harris
Simple precautions to keep you safe from crime.

101 Ways to Protect Your Children
by Chris Harris
Simple precautions to safeguard your children from crime.

Before He Takes You Out: The Safe Dating Guide for the '90s
by Scott Lindquist
An informative guide for preventing date rape and other dating disasters.

The College Student's Complete Guide to Self-Protection
by D'Arcy Rahming
Preparing the college student for dangerous situations.

Come Back Alive: The Ultimate Guide to Surviving Disasters, Kidnappings, Animal Attacks and Other Nasty Perils of Modern Travel
by Robert Young Pelton
A how-to guide for surviving disasters while traveling.

The Complete Idiot's Guide to Martial Arts
by Cezar Borkowski and Marion Manzo
A complete overview of martial arts and their origins.

The Domestic Violence Sourcebook: Everything You Need to Know
by Dawn Bradley Berry
A comprehensive look at the issues surrounding domestic violence.

The Gift of Fear
by Gavin de Becker
Using fear as a warning sign to avoid danger.

How to Fight Back and Win: The Joy of Self-Defense
by Judith Fein
Step-by-step lessons illustrating the basics of physical self-defense.

Life and Death on the Internet: How to Protect Your Family On the World Wide Web
by Keith A. Schroeder and Julie Ledger
A complete guide for protecting yourself and your children from online indecencies.

Obsession
by John Douglas
Understanding the criminal's mindset and ways to avoid becoming a victim.

Promoting Health and Safety: Skills for Independent Living
by Martin Agran, Nancy E. Marchand-Martella, and Ronald C. Martella
Strategies to help the physically challenged learn essential safety skills.

Safe Not Sorry
by Tanya K. Metaksa
A self-defense manual for you and your family.

A Senior's Guide to Personal Safety
by Janee Harteau
Educates senior citizens about self-protection.

The Seven Steps to Personal Safety: How to Avoid, Deal With or Survive the Aftermath of a Violent Confrontation
by Richard B. Isaacs and Tim Powers
A step-by-step guide explaining what you should do during a violent confrontation.

Smart Parents, Safe Kids
by Robert Stuber and Jeff Bradley
Teaching your kids to think for themselves when in danger.

Stop Being a Victim
by Junius Podrug
Provides practical advice about protecting your home, surviving at home, and personal and travel safety.

Street Sense for Women: How to Stay Safe in a Violent World
by Louis R. Mizell, Jr.
Teaches women how to achieve maximum safety and security.

Streetwise: A Complete Manual of Security and Self-Defense
by Peter Consterdine
A complete guide to becoming your own bodyguard.

Strong on Defense
by Sanford Strong
Survival rules to protect you and your family from crime.

Tough Target
by J. J. Bittenbinder and William Neal
How to reduce your chances of being a victim.

Violence in the Workplace
by Raymond B. Flannery, Jr.
An instructional guide for dealing with workplace violence.

When In Doubt Check Him Out
by Joseph J. Culligan
How to get to know someone before getting involved.

When Seconds Count: Everyone's Guide to Self-Defense
by Sammy Franco
A step-by-step approach that explains the various aspects of self-defense.

Workplace Violence: Before, During, and After
by Sandra L. Heskett
A comprehensive source for preventing and managing violent incidents in the workplace.

The World's Most Dangerous Places
by Robert Young Pelton
How to survive in the world's most dangerous places.

You, Too, Can Find Anybody
by Joseph J. Culligan
How to track down anyone, anywhere.

Travelwise: A Guide to Safety, Security, and Convenience When You Travel
by John F. Delaney
Illustrates the ins and outs of safe travel.

Dating Violence: Young Women in Danger
by Barrie Levy
Informs young women about the dangers of violent relationships.

When Violence Begins at Home
by Karen Wilson
How to cope with violence in your own home.

Videos

Here is a list of self-defense and personal safety videos I recommend:

Basic Guide to Self-Defense
An instructional personal safety program focused toward the deaf.

Basic Personal Self-Defense
by Emory Morris
Covers the three basics needed to increase your personal safety.

Defend Yourself! Instinctive Self-Defense for Men
by Hee Cho
Ten basic moves of self-defense for men.

Defend Yourself! Instinctive Self-Defense for Women
by Hee Cho
Ten basic moves of self-defense for women.

Fight Back: Emergency Self-Defense for Women
Equips women with skills to protect themselves.

Fight Back: Your Family Guide to Self-Defense
by Don Wilson
An instructional self-defense video for the whole family.

Instant Self-Defense Guide for Women
by John Deblasio and Robert MacEwen
Life-saving techniques in personal safety for women.

Karate and Self-Defense
Effective tactics to help you escape an attacker.

Martial Arts Series—Self-Defense
by Steve Powell
How to discover your strong points and your opponent's weak points.

Practical Self-Defense
by Bob Klein
Step-by-step instructions for how to control your attacker.

Protect Yourself: A Women's Guide to Self-Defense
by Robin Cooper
Precautions and instructions for how to overcome your opponent.

React! A Women's Guide to Safety and Basic Self-Defense
Provides women with basic skills to outsmart their attackers.

Self-Defense for Children
Classroom instruction for how to overcome a stronger attacker.

Trust Your Instincts: Don't Let Yourself Become a Victim
Illustrates the importance of instincts to detect potential dangers.

Tae Bo Workout
by Billy Blanks
Learn to defend yourself while getting a work-out.

Women's How To of Self-Defense
How to deal with bullies, drunks, rapists, flashers, and degenerates.

Web Site Addresses

Here is a list of self-defense and personal safety Web sites I recommend:

www.ncpc.org
The National Crime Prevention Council

www.mararts.org/index.htm
An explanation of various styles of martial arts

www.net-link.net/~swillo/wsd.htm
An outline for developing a personal safety program for yourself

www.loyola.edu/maru/slfdfens.html
Ways to protect yourself and how to fight back

www.allstate.com/safety/personal/danger.html
Safety precautions to remember while in danger zones

www.antistalking.com
A resource for anyone interested in preventing the crime of stalking

www.jetlink.net/~jgarner/index.shtml
Tips to help you avoid becoming a victim of crime and violence

www.armchair.com/info/netinfo.html
A guide to becoming a safe traveler

www.inform.umd.edu/UniversityHealthCenter/HealthEd/SexualAssualt/
A resource for personal safety advice that contains tips for safer dating

www.campussafety.org/STATS/
A guide to staying safe on college campuses

wysiwyg://12http://www.members.aol.com/endwpv/index.html
What you need to know about workplace violence

www.getsafe.com
How to make your home safer

www.antitelemarketer.com
How to protect yourself from unwanted phone calls

www.safeinternet.com
A guide to staying safe on the Internet

www.abanet.org/domviol/home.html
The American Bar Association's commission on domestic violence

www.fosters.com/autos/pages/safety_antitheft.htm
A guide to protecting your automobile

http://members.aol.com/itlind/main.htm
Tips for the stranded driver

www.geocities.com/CapitolHill/5355/
A guide to getting around safely in your city

www.harrispersonalsafety.com
Practical self-defense seminars for businesses and individual groups, as well as personal safety products

www.4safety.com
Safety information for all aspects of life

www.familydefense.com
Products to purchase for defending yourself and your family

www.crime-free.org/forum.html
Statistics on crime trends for the future

www.namca.com/English/inf-lkey.htm
Questions parents can ask children to test their knowledge about safety

www.cigna.com/personal/child.html
How to become a safety-conscious parent

www.police.nsw.gov.au/help/menu2/st_seniors.htm
Safety tips for senior citizens

www.KempoKarate.com/defense.html
Self-defense for the physically challenged

References

The following is a list of books I used for research and to assist me in writing this book:

101 Ways to Save Your Life
by Chris Harris

101 Ways to Protect Your Children
by Chris Harris

The College Student's Complete Guide to Self-Protection
by D'Arcy Rahming

The Complete Idiot's Guide to Martial Arts
by Cezar Borkowski and Marion Manzo

The Domestic Violence Sourcebook: Everything You Need to Know
by Dawn Bradley Berry

The Gift of Fear
by Gavin de Becker

Obsession
by John Douglas

Safe Not Sorry
by Tanya K. Metaksa

Street Sense for Women: How to Stay Safe in a Violent World
by Louis R. Mizell Jr.

Strong on Defense
by Sanford Strong

Tough Target
by J. J. Bittenbinder and William Neal

Violence in the Workplace
by Raymond B. Flannery Jr.

When In Doubt Check Him Out
by Joseph J. Culligan

Workplace Violence: Before, During, and After
by Sandra L. Heskett

The World's Most Dangerous Places
by Robert Young Pelton

You, Too, Can Find Anybody
by Joseph J. Culligan

Legal Forms

DURHAM POLICE DEPARTMENT
DURHAM, NORTH CAROLINA
ORI NC0320100

OFFENSE INCIDENT REPORT

Page ____ of ____

FORM
IR-1
Rev. 8/90

INCIDENT	IR #	Occurrence Date: From / To	Occurrence Time: From / To	Date Reported	Time Reported	Day of Week	Beat/Patrol Area	Map Ref Area	District

Common Name of Location of Incident | Incident Location Address | Apt/Suite

Location Type □ 1-Hwy, Pkg lot, etc. □ 2-Commercial □ 3-Service Station □ 4-Convenience Store □ 5-Residence □ 6-Bank □ 19-Other | Dept Classif Incident Type (Primary/1st Offense) | Case □ 1-Further Investigation Status □ 2-Inactive □ 3-Closed | Offender Under Alcohol: □ 1-Yes □ 2-No □ 3-Unk □ 4-NA Influence of... Drugs: □ 1-Yes □ 2-No □ 3-Unk □ 4-NA

VICTIM

Person/Business Name (If rape, leave blank and complete Involved Persons Rpt) (Last, First, Middle) | Address | Apt/Suite | Date of Birth | Employer

Occupation | Oper. Lic. # | State | Phone/Residence | Phone/Business | Sex: □ 1-Male □ 2-Female □ 3-Unk | Race: □ 1-White □ 2-Black □ 3-AmericanIndian/AlaskaNative □ 4-Asian/PacificIslander □ 5-Race Unknown | Age | Age Max | Ethnic Org: □ 1-Hispanic □ 2-NonHispanic □ 3-Unknown

Hgt ft in | Hgt Max ft in | Wgt b | Wgt Max b | Victim □ 1-Adult □ 2-Juvenile □ 3-Business □ 4-Financial Inst Type: □ 5-Govt □ 6-Law Off □ 7-Relig Org □ 8-Society/Public □ 9-Other | Residency: □ 1-City □ 2-County □ 3-Other □ 4-Unknown | Will Victim File Charges: □ 1-Yes □ 2-No □ 3-Unk | Can Identify/Describe Offender: □ 1-Yes □ 2-No □ 3-Unk | Extent of Injury: □ 1-Minor □ 2-Serious □ 3-Fatal □ 4-Unk □ 5-No Injuries | Hospitalized: □ 1-Yes □ 2-No □ 3-Unk Hosp Name:

RPT PARTY

□ 1-Person Reporting (if different than victim) □ 2-Complainant (if different than victim) (Last, First, Middle) | Address | Apt/Suite | Date of Birth

Employer | Oper. Lic. # | State | Phone/Residence | Phone/Business | Sex: □ 1-Male □ 2-Female | Race: □ 1-White □ 2-Black □ 3-AmericanIndian/AlaskaNative □ 4-Asian/PacificIslander □ 5-Race Unknown | Ethnic Org: □ 1-Hispanic □ 2-NonHispanic □ 3-Unknown

ARRESTEE

Suspect/Arrestee Instructions: Check one □ Arrestee - Officer complete ARRESTEE Section. □ Unknown Suspect - Records enter Suspect/Arrestee as "UNKNOWN" for Rape, Assault, Homicide. □ Suspect Named - Officer complete SUPPLEMENTAL Suspect Report. □ Suspect can be ID'ed or described - Officer complete SUPPLEMENTAL Suspect Report.

Arrestee #1 (Last, First, Middle) | Date of Birth | Sex: □ 1-Male □ 2-Female | Race: □ 1-White □ 2-Black □ 3-AmericanIndian/AlaskaNative □ 4-Asian/PacificIslander | Ethnic Org: □ 1-Hispanic □ 2-NonHispanic □ 3-Unknown | Status: □ 1-Arrestee □ 2-Escapee | Arrest Case No.

Arrestee #2 (Last, First, Middle) | Date of Birth | Sex: □ 1-Male □ 2-Female | Race: □ 1-White □ 2-Black □ 3-AmericanIndian/AlaskaNative □ 4-Asian/PacificIslander | Ethnic Org: □ 1-Hispanic □ 2-NonHispanic □ 3-Unknown | Status: □ 1-Arrestee □ 2-Escapee | Arrest Case No.

OFFENSE #1

Offense #1 | Records □ 1-Attempt □ 2-Commit | Type of Weapon/Force Used □ 1-Handgun □ 2-Rifle □ 3-Shotgun □ 4-Other Firearm □ 5-Knife, etc. □ 6-Hands, fist, feet □ 7-Fictitious Gun □ 8-BB Gun, etc. □ 9-Blunt Obj. □ 10-Pry Tool □ 11-Hammer, etc. □ 12-Key Bypass □ 13-Chemicals/Drugs □ 19-Other | Struct Occup (Arson): □ 1-Occupied □ 2-Unoccupied □ 3-Abandoned | Evidence □ 1-Yes Collected: □ 2-No

UCR □ 1-Open □ 2-Cleared by Arrest-Adult □ 3-Cleared by Arrest-Juv | Date of Dispo | Exc Clr Type: □ 1-Death of Offender □ 2-Prosecution Declined □ 3-Extradition Declined □ 4-Lack of Cooperation □ 5-Juv, No Custody | Drug Activity □ 1-Buy/Rec'v □ 2-Cultivate/Mfr □ 3-Sell/Distr. □ 4-Opers/Assist □ 5-Possess w/int Sell □ 6-Possess □ 7-Import □ 8-Use | Drug Type:

Dispo: □ 4-Except Cleared-Adult □ 5-Except Cleared-Juv □ 6-Unfounded

Assault/Homicide Information | Victim is (Relationship to Suspect) | Circumstances | Officer Involved: □ 1-Yes □ 2-No | Justifiable Homicide Circumstance Killed By: □ 1-Citizen □ 2-Officer | Justif Hom □ 1-Attacked Off □ 2-Attacked Other Off □ 3-Attacked Ofc □ 4-Flight Code □ 5-Commission of Crime □ 6-Resisting Arrest □ 7-Undetermined

Officer Assaulted | Empl No. | Off was... □ 4-Asslt-Minor Injury □ 5-Asslt-No Injury | Case Type: □ 1-Killed - Fleonious Act □ 2-Killed-Negl/Accid □ 3-Asslt-Serious Injury | Officer Activity: □ 1-Disturbance □ 2-Burglary □ 3-Robbery □ 4-Arrest □ 5-Civil Disorder □ 6-Prisoner □ 7-Investigate Suspicious Person/circumstance □ 8-Ambush □ 9-Mental □ 10-Traffic Pursuit/Stop □ 11-All Other | Officer | Assignment: □ 1-Two-Ofr Veh □ 2-Ofr Alone □ 3-Ofr Assisted □ 4-MenuPatrolOfrAlone □ 5-Non-Patrol Ofr Assisted □ 6-Other Alone □ 7-Other Assisted

OFFENSE #2

Offense #2 | Records □ 1-Attempt □ 2-Commit | Type of Weapon/Force Used □ 1-Handgun □ 2-Rifle □ 3-Shotgun □ 4-Other Firearm □ 5-Knife, etc. □ 6-Hands, fist, feet □ 7-Fictitious Gun □ 8-BB Gun, etc. □ 9-Blunt Obj. □ 10-Pry Tool □ 11-Hammer, etc. □ 12-Key Bypass □ 13-Chemicals/Drugs □ 19-Other | Struct Occup (Arson): □ 1-Occupied □ 2-Unoccupied □ 3-Abandoned | Evidence □ 1-Yes Collected: □ 2-No

UCR □ 1-Open □ 2-Cleared by Arrest-Adult □ 3-Cleared by Arrest-Juv | Date of Dispo | Exc Clr Type: □ 1-Death of Offender □ 2-Prosecution Declined □ 3-Extradition Declined □ 4-Lack of Cooperation □ 5-Juv, No Custody | Drug Activity □ 1-Buy/Rec'v □ 2-Cultivate/Mfr □ 3-Sell/Distr. □ 4-Opers/Assist □ 5-Possess w/int Sell □ 6-Possess □ 7-Import □ 8-Use | Drug Type:

Dispo: □ 4-Except Cleared-Adult □ 5-Except Cleared-Juv □ 6-Unfounded

PROPERTY INFO

Item #	Property Heading (See Property Report for Codes)	Description of Stolen or Damaged Property	Color	Serial No./Account No.	Make, Issuer, etc.	Model/Type	UCR Prop. Type	Dept Prop. Type	$ Amt of Damage	Value $ Stolen	Prop Damage	Doc Type
	□ 1-Stolen □ 6-Damaged										□ 1-Arson □ 2-Other	
	□ 1-Stolen □ 6-Damaged										□ 1-Arson □ 2-Other	

VEHICLE INFO

Vehicle # ___ of ___ | Vehicle □ 1-Stolen (Only) □ 4-Suspect □ 6-Damaged □ 7-Theft From Heading □ 19-Other (Use Vehicle Report for Recovered, Seized, Towed Vehicle) | UCR □ 4-Locally Stolen Type □ Other Type | Vehicle □ 1-Auto □ 2-Truck/Van □ 3-Bus □ 4-RV □ 6-Motorcycle, etc. Type □ 12-Other (ATV, Golf Carts, Dune Buggies, etc.) | Year | Make | Model

Style (Codes - See Veh Rpt) | Color (Top) (Codes - See Veh Rpt) | Color (Bottom) (Codes - See Veh Rpt) | License No. | State | VIN | Vehicle Damage □ 1-Arson □ 2-Other Fire □ 3-Vandalism □ 4-Wreck □ 5-Strip/Theft From □ 6-Other

Stolen Value $ | Amt Damage $ | Vehicle Feature/Oddlty | Keys In □ 1-Yes □ 2-No Veh? □ 3-Unknown | Vehicle □ 1-Yes □ 2-No Locked? □ 3-Unknown | Stolen Location | NCIC # | Enter Date

CASE REFERRAL □ CID □ OCD □ JUV □ FD □ FRAUD □ OTHER _____
ID Tech. □ Yes Name:
Called? □ No

NARRATIVE

□ Check if Narrative Continued | Warrant Advised? □ Yes □ No | Complainant's Signature

Reporting Officer's Signature	Date	Empl. No.	Supervisor's Signature	Empl. No.	Review Date	Records Emp Initial	Empl. No.	Entry Date

Offense Incident Report. This general form is used to report most offenses except property crimes and domestic violence crimes. It provides a full description of the incident, the victim, the arrestee, and the type of offense that occurred.

DURHAM POLICE DEPARTMENT DURHAM, NORTH CAROLINA	DOMESTIC VIOLENCE SUPPLEMENTAL REPORT		PAGE____ OF ____

IR #	OCCURRENCE DATE: FROM	TO	OCCURRENCE TIME: FROM	TO	DATE REPORTED	TIME REPORTED	PATROL AREA
	DAY OF WEEK: M T W TH F S SU						

INCIDENT LOCATION	NATURE OF CALL

VICTIM'S NAME (LAST, F, M)	DOB	RACE: ☐B ☐W ☐H ☐A	SUSPECT'S NAME (LAST, F, M)	DOB	RACE: ☐B ☐W ☐H ☐A
VICTIM'S ADDRESS	PHONE # (H): (W):		SUSPECT'S ADDRESS	PHONE #(H) (W)	

SPONTANEOUS UTTERANCES BY VICTIM	STATEMENTS BY SUSPECT

VICTIM	RELATIONSHIP BETWEEN VICTIM AND SUSPECT (ALL THAT APPLY)	LENGTH OF RELATIONSHIP: ____YEARS ____MONTHS DATE ENDED:	ALCOHOL OR DRUGS INVOLVED? Y / N
CONDITION OF VICTIM WHEN OFFICER ARRIVED		PRIOR HISTORY OF DOMESTIC VIOLENCE? Y / N VIOLENCE DOCUMENTED? Y / N	TYPE: BY WHOM?
☐ANGRY ☐COMP. OF PAIN	☐SPOUSE ☐FORMER SPOUSE		
	☐COHABITANTS ☐FORMER COHAB.	CASE #: INVESTIGATING AGENCY:_____	MEDICAL TREATMENT? ☐NONE ☐FIRST AID
☐APOLOGETIC ☐BRUISE(S)	☐DATING/ENGAGED ☐FORMER DATING	# OF PRIOR INCIDENTS:____ ☐MINOR? ☐SERIOUS?	☐OWN DOCTOR ☐REFUSED MEDICAL AID
☐CRYING ☐ABRASION(S)	☐SAME SEX ☐EMANCIPATED MINOR	DVPO EVER ISSUED? Y / N ☐CURRENT ☐EXPIRED	☐PARAMEDIC ↓ ☐HOSPITAL ↓
☐FEARFUL/ AFRAID ☐MINOR CUT(S)	☐PARENT OF CHILD FROM RELATIONSHIP	CONFIRMED BY: ☐WARRANT ☐VICTIM'S ☐OTHER CONTROL COPY AGENCY	UNIT #_____ NAME:_____
☐HYSTERICAL ☐LACERATION(S)	**EVIDENCE**		**WITNESSES**
☐CALM ☐FRACTURE(S)	EVIDENCE COLLECTED? Y / N FROM? ☐CRIME SCENE ☐HOSPITAL ☐OTHER		STATEMENTS TAKEN Y / N NAME: ADDRESS PHONE
☐IRRATIONAL ☐CONCUSSION(S)	PHOTOS? Y / N NUMBER:___ ☐35MM ☐POLAROID TAKEN BY:		#1:
☐NERVOUS ☐OTHER (EXPLAIN	PHOTOS OF VICTIM'S INJURIES? Y / N DETAILS:		#2:
☐THREATENING IN NARRATIVE)	PHOTOS OF SUSPECT'S INJURIES? Y / N DETAILS:		CHILDREN PRESENT? Y / N NUMBER PRESENT:_____ STATEMENTS TAKEN? Y / N
SUSPECT	PHOTOS OF CRIME SCENE? Y / N DETAILS:		NAMES: #1 AGES: #1
CONDITION OF SUSPECT WHEN OFFICER ARRIVED	WEAPONS USED DURING INCIDENT? Y / N DETAILS:		#2 #2
☐ANGRY ☐COMP. OF PAIN	WEAPON TYPE?: SEIZED? Y / N PHOTO? Y / N FIREARM IMPOUNDED FOR SAFETY? Y / N		#3 #3
☐APOLOGETIC ☐BRUISE(S)	DISPOSITION: ☐ARREST ☐FURTHER INVESTIGATION ☐WARRANTS → ☐SERVED ☐PENDING		
☐CRYING ☐ABRASION(S)	☐IF NO ARREST GIVE REASON:		
☐FEARFUL/ AFRAID ☐MINOR CUT(S)	NARRATIVE: DESCRIBE ALL CONDITIONS OBSERVED (PHYSICAL, EMOTIONAL, CRIME SCENE)		
☐HYSTERICAL ☐LACERATION(S)			
☐CALM ☐FRACTURE(S)			
☐IRRATIONAL ☐CONCUSSION(S)			
☐NERVOUS ☐OTHER (EXPLAIN			
☐THREATENING IN NARRATIVE)	REPORTING OFFICER: EMPLOYEE #: ASSISTING OFFICER: APPROVED BY: DATE:		

Domestic Violence Supplemental Report. This form is used to report any domestic violence incident and to gather general information about the victim, the suspect, and the relationship between the victim and the suspect. It is used to document any evidence gathered from the case.

DURHAM POLICE DEPARTMENT
DURHAM, NORTH CAROLINA

INFORMATION FOR VICTIMS OF DOMESTIC VIOLENCE
(Information para las victimas de violencia domestica)

PAGE____ OF ____

IF YOU HAVE BECOME THE VICTIM OF DOMESTIC VIOLENCE, YOU HAVE CERTAIN RIGHTS AND PRIVILEGES UNDER THE LAW.

• You may make a private citizen's arrest for any crimes committed against you by filing a warrant at the Magistrate's Office located at the Durham County Jail, 217 South Magnum Street.
• You may file a petition for a protective order with the Civil Clerk of Courts on the 3rd floor of the Durham County Courthouse, 201 East Main Street (on the corner of Roxboro and Main Streets). The order can grant any of the following:
  --Restrain your abuser from abusing you or any other family members, and from purchasing or possessing a firearm.
  --Prevent your abuser from entering your residence, school, business or place of employment.
  --Grant you possession of the residence or household, and direct your abuser to leave.
  --Award custody of or visitation rights to your minor child or children.
  --Direct the party not granted custody to pay support of minor children, if there is a legal obligation to do so.

If the abuser violates the order by trespassing, harassing or assaulting you, the abuser will immediately be arrested by the police. You can file an Order to Show Cause with the Civil Clerk of Courts for any violation of the order when an arrest is not made by the police. The order is usually valid for one year and can be renewed for an additional year.

• You have the right to file civil suit for losses suffered as a result of abuse, including medical expenses, loss of earnings, and other expenses for injuries sustained and damage to property, and any other related expenses incurred by the victim or by any agency that shelters you.
• Call the Magistrate's Office to find out when your abuser will be released from jail.

SI USTED HA SIDO VICTIMA DE VIOLENCIA DOMESTICA TIENE DERECHOS Y PRIVILEGIOS ANTE LA LEY.

• Usted puede hacer cargo de acuerdo con los delitos que se han cometidos a la oficina del magistrado (magistrate). Esta oficina se situa en la carcel de Durham (Durham County Jail), 217 South Magnum Street.
• Usted puede establecer una peticion para una orden protectiva con la corte (Civil Clerk of Courts) en el tercer piso del tribunal judicial (Durham County Courthouse), 201 East Main Street (en la esquina de Roxboro y Main Streets). Esta orden puede ortorgar cualquiera de lo siguiente:
  --No permite que el abusador la abuse a usted o su familia, o que tenga o compre una arma de fuego.
  --Le ortorga a usted posesion de su residencia o casa, y obliga a su abusador que se retirer.
  --No permite que el abusador entre a su residencia, escuela, negocio, o lugar de empleo.
  --Le ortorga a usted custodia o derecho de visitar a su hijo o hijos menores de edad.
  --Obliga a una persona que no tiene custodia de su nino o ninos, a que pague para mantener a esos hijos.

Si el abusador infringe la orden por trapasar o por asaltaria, el sera encarcelado inmediatamente por la policia. Si la policia no hace un arresto inmediatamente, usted puede establecer una orden (Order to Show Cause) con la corte (Civil Clerk of Courts). La order protectiva es valida por un ano y puede renovada por un ano mas.

• Usted tiene derecho a entablar una demanda civil por perdidas sufridas causadas por maltrato y abuso. Esto incluye gastos medicos, perdida de sueldo y otros gastos que resultaron en danos y perjuicios. Tambien incluye gastos contraidos por la victima y las agencias que la protegieron.
• Llame por telefono a la oficina del magistrado (magistrate) para saber cuando el abusador sera liberado.

SERVICES OF THE ORANGE/DURHAM COALITION FOR BATTERED WOMEN
(Servicios de Organisacion Para las Mujeres Abusadas)

• free, confidential services 24 hours everyday	• gratis, servicios confidenciales 24 horas al dia
• individual victim counseling and support	• apoyo individual para la victima
• shelter for women and children	• albergue para la mujer y los ninos
• answers to questions	• respuestas a cualquiera pregunta
• court advocacy	• asistencia en la corte
• support groups	• grupos de apoyo

SAFETY PLAN

Make a plan for what you will do the next time your batterer assaults you.

• Decide NOW where you will go and how you'll get there the next time he becomes violent. Do this even if you really don't think there will be a next time.
• Leave some money, extra sets of car and house keys, extra clothes, special medications and sentimental valuables and photos with a neighbor or with someone you trust.
• Keep important documents (birth certificates, social security cards, medical records, insurance policies, bank account numbers, checkbook, marriage license) and a list of important phone numbers hidden at a neighbor's or friend's house.
• Develop a code word with your children, neighbor and friends that lets them know that you need to get out now.
• If you leave, ALWAYS try to take your children with you.
• If beaten or abused, get medical attention and have pictures taken for evidence of physical abuse. Keep ripped clothing for evidence as well. File a report with police.
• Tell someone you know and trust what is happening to you in case you have to leave in a hurry so that you will have someone you can ask for help.

PLAN DE SEGURIDAD

Plannee lo que va a hacer la proxima vez que su agresor la ataque.

• Decida AHORA MISMO donde ira usted y como va a llegar alli, la proxima vez que el se ponga violento. Haga esto aunque usted piense que no habra una proxima vez.
• Deje algun dinero, llaves de repuesta para su auto y casa, ropa, medicaciones especiales y los objetos y fotos sentimentales en la casa de un vecino o con alguien en que usted confie.
• Mantenga documentos importantes (certificados de nacimiento, documentos medicos y financieros, certificado de matrimonio, tarjetas de seguro social, documentos de seguros, chequera, numeros de cuentas banqueras) y una lista de numeros de telefono importantes en casa de un vecino o amigo.
• Pongase de acuerdo con sus hijos, vecinos y amistades sobre una palabra clave que indique cuando usted tenga que marcharse inmediatamente.
• Si usted se marcha, SIEMPRE trate de llevarse a sus hijos con usted.
• Si golpeada o abusada, reciba atencion medica y tome fotos para tener evidencia de abuso fisico. Mantenga ropa rota tambien. Haga un reporte confidencial con la policia.
• Cuentele a alguien que usted conozca y en quien confie de lo que le esta ocurriendo para que en caso que usted tengo que marcharse de su hogar apresuradamente, usted tengo a alguien a quien pedirle ayuda.

IMPORTANT PHONE NUMBERS (los numeros de telefono importantes)

• Orange/Durham Coalition for Battered Women   --crisis line: 688-2372
  (Organisacion para las Mujeres Abusadas)   --office: 688-4015

• Durham Police   560-4427
  Victim/Witness Assistance (Asistencia para la Victima)   560-4404

• Magistrate's Office   560-6826   • District Attorney's Office   560-6044

• Change--A Treatment Program for Batterers (Una Programa para Abusadores)   286-3757

• Child Protection Services   560-8424

• Child and Parent Support Services (CAPSS)   286-7112
  --Parenting Education classes, Parent Support groups and Therapeutic Children groups
  (Clases Educativas y Grupos de Apoyo para Padres, y Grupos de Apoyo para Ninos)

In an emergency, dial 911
(En caso de emergencia, marque 911)

343

STATE OF NORTH CAROLINA

File No.

_____ County

In The General Court Of Justice
District Court Division

Name Of Plaintiff

VERSUS

**DOMESTIC VIOLENCE
PROTECTIVE ORDER**

Name Of Defendant

G.S. 50B-2, -3

FINDINGS

This matter was heard by the district court judge named below after due notice to the defendant. The Court makes the following findings of fact:

1. Present at the hearing were: ☐ the plaintiff, represented by _____
   ☐ the defendant, represented by _____

2. The parties: ☐ are married. ☐ are divorced.
   ☐ are persons of the opposite sex who are not married but live together or have lived together.
   ☐ have a child in common.
   ☐ are parent and child or grandparent and grandchild.
   ☐ are current or former household members.
   ☐ are persons of the opposite sex who are in or have been in a dating relationship.

☐ 3. The defendant has attempted to cause or has intentionally caused bodily injury to the plaintiff or has threatened the plaintiff or a member of plaintiff's family or household with immediate serious bodily injury; or has committed a sexual offense against the plaintiff; the last act of violence occurred on or about _____ *(give date)* .

☐ 4. The defendant has attempted to cause or has intentionally caused bodily injury to the child(ren) living with or in the custody of the plaintiff, has threatened immediate serious bodily injury to the child(ren) or has sexually abused the child(ren); the last act of violence occurred on or about *(give date)* _____ .

☐ 5. The parties are the parents of the following children under the age of eighteen. The children are presently in the physical custody of the ☐ plaintiff. ☐ defendant. The plaintiff has submitted an "Affidavit As To The Status Of The Minor Child." **(Note To Judge:** *A copy of AOC-CV-609 must be attached to the order.)*

Name	Date Of Birth	Name	Date Of Birth

☐ 6. The ☐ defendant ☐ plaintiff is presently in possession of the parties' residence at the address listed below:
Address Of Residence

☐ 7. The ☐ defendant ☐ plaintiff is presently in possession of the parties' vehicle described below:
Describe Vehicle

☐ 8. Other: *(specify)*

AOC-CV-306, Rev. 5/98
© 1998 Administrative Office of the Courts   (Over)

Domestic Violence Protective Order. *This form is used when a victim of domestic violence wants to receive a protective order against the suspect.*

CONCLUSIONS

Based on these facts, the Court makes the following conclusions of law:

☐ 1. The defendant has committed acts of domestic violence against the plaintiff.

☐ 2. The defendant has committed acts of domestic violence against the minor child(ren) residing with or in the custody of the plaintiff.

☐ 3. There is danger of serious and immediate injury to the ☐ plaintiff. ☐ minor child(ren).

☐ 4. The Court has jurisdiction under the Uniform Child Custody Jurisdiction Act, and it is in the best interests of the minor child(ren) of the parties that temporary custody of them be given to the plaintiff.

☐ 5. The plaintiff has failed to prove that the defendant has committed acts of domestic violence.

ORDER

It is ORDERED that:

☐ 1. the defendant shall not assault, threaten, abuse, follow, harass by telephone, visiting the home or workplace or other means, or interfere with the plaintiff. A law enforcement officer shall arrest the defendant if the officer has probable cause to believe the defendant has violated this provision. **[C51]**

☐ 2. the defendant shall not assault, threaten, abuse, follow, harass by telephone, visiting the home or workplace or other means, or interfere with the child(ren) named in Finding No. 5. A law enforcement officer shall arrest the defendant if the officer has probable cause to believe the defendant has violated this provision. **[C52]**

☐ 3. the defendant shall not threaten a member of the plaintiff's family or household. **[C53]**

☐ 4. the plaintiff is granted possession of, and the defendant is excluded from, the parties' residence described above and all personal property located in the residence except for the defendant's personal clothing, toiletries and tools of trade. **[C54]**

☐ 5. the law enforcement agency named below shall evict the defendant from the residence and shall assist the plaintiff in returning to the residence. **[C55]**

Name And Address Of Law Enforcement Agency

☐ 6. the ☐ plaintiff **[C56a]** ☐ defendant **[C56b]** is entitled to get personal clothing, toiletries, and tools of the trade from the parties' residence. A law enforcement officer shall assist the ☐ plaintiff ☐ defendant in returning to the residence to get these items. **[C56]**

☐ 7. the defendant shall stay away from the plaintiff's residence or any place where the plaintiff receives temporary shelter. A law enforcement officer shall arrest the defendant if the officer has probable cause to believe the defendant has violated this provision. **[C57]**

☐ 8. the defendant shall stay away from the following places:

  ☐ (a) the place where the plaintiff works. **[C58a]**   ☐ (b) the child(ren)'s school. **[C58b]**

  ☐ (c) the place where the child(ren) receives day care. **[C58c]**   ☐ (d) the plaintiff's school. **[C58d]**

  ☐ (e) Other: *(name other places)* **[C58e]**

☐ 9. the plaintiff is granted possession and use of the vehicle described on reverse. **[C59]**

☐ 10. *(Check this block only if Block No. 4 in Conclusions is checked.)* the plaintiff is awarded temporary custody of the child(ren) named in Finding No. 5. **[C60]**

☐ 11. the defendant is ordered to make payments to the plaintiff for support of the minor child(ren) as required by law. **[C61]**

☐ 12. the defendant is prohibited from ☐ possessing **[C62a]** ☐ purchasing a firearm for the effective period of this Order **[C62b]** ☐ and the defendant's concealed handgun permit is suspended for the effective period of this Order. **[C62c]**

☐ 13. the defendant shall attend and complete an abuser treatment program offered by the following agency, which is approved by the Department of Administration and held within a reasonable distance of defendant's residence: **[C63]**

☐ 14. Other: *(specify)* **[C64]**

☐ 15. this Order is effective for ☐ one year from the date below. ☐ other:

☐ 16. this action is dismissed and as of this date, any ex parte order issued on this case is null and void.

☐ 17. the costs of this action are taxed to the ☐ plaintiff. ☐ defendant.

Date	Name Of District Court Judge (Type Or Print)	Signature Of District Court Judge

CERTIFICATE OF SERVICE WHEN DEFENDANT NOT PRESENT AT HEARING

I certify that this Order has been served on the defendant named by depositing a copy in a post-paid, properly addressed envelope in a post office or official depository under the exclusive care and custody of the United States Postal Service.

Date	Signature Of Clerk	☐ Deputy CSC ☐ Assistant CSC ☐ Clerk of Superior Court

NOTE TO CLERK: *A copy of this Order shall be mailed or given to each party, to your sheriff, and to the police department of the plaintiff's residence, if any.*

AOC-CV-306, Side Two, Rev. 5/98, © 1998 Administrative Office of the Courts

A protective order ensures the victim that, by law, the suspect cannot have future contact with the victim.

STATE OF NORTH CAROLINA

_____ County

	File No.
	In The General Court Of Justice
	District Court Division

Name Of Defendant

Street Address Of Defendant (Not P.O. Box)

City   State   Zip

IDENTIFYING INFORMATION
ABOUT DEFENDANT
DOMESTIC VIOLENCE ACTION

G.S. 50B-3(d)

INSTRUCTIONS: *In order to assist law enforcement agencies in serving and enforcing this Order, if issued by the Court, the following information is requested. It is not required for the issuance of this Order, but may allow law enforcement agencies to locate and more quickly identify the persons involved in this case and to enforce the provisions of this Order more effectively. Answer these questions accurately and honestly.*

If you do not know the answer to any of the following questions, leave the question blank.

INFORMATION ABOUT DEFENDANT

Date Of Birth

Race: ☐ White ☐ Black ☐ Indian ☐ Asian/Pacific Islander ☐ Other   Sex: ☐ Male ☐ Female

Height   Weight   Hair Color   Eye Color

Identifying Marks (List any marks, scars, tattoos)

Does the defendant have a driver's license or state-issued identification card from any state? ☐ Yes ☐ No

If yes, provide the state and number if possible: State: _____ Number: _____

Vehicle description and license plate: _____

Social Security No. Of Defendant   Telephone No. Of Defendant

The defendant's current work information:

Employer's Business Name

Business Address

Business Telephone No.   Defendant's Work Hours (List Work Start Time And Work Stop Time)

Does the defendant have a permit to purchase a handgun or crossbow? ☐ Yes ☐ No

If yes, state which law enforcement agency issued the permit, if known: _____

Does the defendant have a permit to carry a concealed handgun? ☐ Yes ☐ No

If yes, state which law enforcement agency issued the permit, if known: _____

Is there any reason that a law enforcement officer should consider the defendant a potential threat *(i.e., carries concealed weapons while drinking alcohol, has threatened an officer, etc.)*? ☐ Yes ☐ No

If yes, specify the circumstances:

_____

_____

PLAINTIFF

Date Of Birth

Race: ☐ White ☐ Black ☐ Indian ☐ Asian/Pacific Islander ☐ Other   Sex: ☐ Male ☐ Female

Date   Name Of Plaintiff (Type Or Print)   Signature Of Plaintiff

NOTE TO CLERK OR MAGISTRATE: *If an order is issued, a copy of this form should be attached to the appropriate order and forwarded to the sheriff of the issuing court county.*

AOC-CV-312
New 4/96
©1997 Administrative Office of the Courts

Original - Court File   Copy - Sheriff

Identifying Information About Defendant—Domestic Violence Action. This form is used to gain information about the suspect to assist law enforcement agencies in identifying the victim and enforcing the order for the victim more quickly.

DURHAM POLICE DEPARTMENT
DURHAM, NORTH CAROLINA
ORI NC0320100

PROPERTY INCIDENT REPORT

☐ CONTINUATION   ☐ SUPPLEMENTAL

Page _____ of _____   **FORM**
IR-3
Rev. 8/90

Notes: Do not mix property from different locations on same form.

IR #	Occurrence Date: From	To	Occurrence Time: From	To	Date Reported	Time Reported	Day of Week	Beat/Patrol Area	Map Ref Area	District

INCIDENT

Common Name of Location | Incident Location/Address | Apt/Suite

Location Type ☐ 1-Hwy, Pkg lot, etc. ☐ 2-Commercial ☐ 3-Service Station ☐ 4-Convenience Store ☐ 5-Residence ☐ 6-Bank ☐ 19-Other

Dept Classif Incident Type (Primary/1st Offense)

Case ☐ 1-Further Investigation   Status ☐ 2-Inactive ☐ 3-Closed

Offender Under Alcohol: ☐ 1-Yes ☐ 2-No ☐ 3-Unk ☐ 4-NA   Influence of... Drugs: ☐ 1-Yes ☐ 2-No ☐ 3-Unk ☐ 4-NA

VICTIM, ETC.

Name ☐ 1-Person Reporting ☐ 2-Complainant ☐ 3-Victim ☐ 5-Missing Person ☐ 7-Other (Last, First, Middle) | Address | Apt/Ste | Date of Birth

Employer | Phone/Residence | Phone/Business | SEX: ☐ 1-Male ☐ 2-Female ☐ 3-Unk | Race: ☐ 1-White ☐ 2-Black ☐ 3-AmericanIndian/AlaskaNative ☐ 4-Asian/PacificIslander ☐ 5-Race Unknown | Ethnic Org: ☐ 1-Hispanic ☐ 2-NonHispanic ☐ 3-Unk | Victim Type: ☐ 1-Adult ☐ 2-Juv. ☐ 3-Bus ☐ 4-Fin Inst ☐ 5-Govt ☐ 6-Law Ofr ☐ 7-Relig Org ☐ 7-Society/Pub. ☐ 9-Other | Residency: ☐ 1-City ☐ 2-County ☐ 3-Other ☐ 4-Unknown

OFFENSE

Offense | Records ☐ 1-Attempt ☐ 2-Commit | Type of Weapon/Force Used ☐ 1-Handgun ☐ 2-Rifle ☐ 3-Shotgun ☐ 4-Other Firearm ☐ 5-Knife, etc. ☐ 6-Hands, fist, feet ☐ 7-Fictitious Gun ☐ 8-BB Gun, etc. ☐ 9-Blunt Obj. ☐ 10-Pry Tool ☐ 11-Hammer, etc. ☐ 12-Key Bypass ☐ 13-Chemicals/Drugs ☐ 19-Other | Struct Occup (Arson): ☐ 1-Occupied ☐ 2-Unoccupied ☐ 3-Abandoned | Evidence ☐ 1-Yes Collected: ☐ 2-No

UCR ☐ 1-Open ☐ 2-Cleared by Arrest-Adult ☐ 3-Cleared by Arrest-Juv   Dispo: ☐ 4-Except Cleared-Adult ☐ 5-Except Cleared-Juv ☐ 6-Unfounded | Date of Dispo | Exc Clr Type: ☐ 1-Death of Offender ☐ 2-Prosecution Declined ☐ 3-Extradition Declined ☐ 4-Lack of Cooperation ☐ 5-Juv, No Custody | Drug ☐ 1-Buy/Rec'v ☐ 2-Cultivate/Mfr ☐ 3-Sell/Distr. ☐ 4-Operate/Assist Activity ☐ 5-Possess w/Int Sell ☐ 6-Possess ☐ 7-Import ☐ 8-Use | Drug Type:

SUSP.

Suspect/Arrestee (Last, First, Middle) ☐ -Unknown | Date of Birth | Sex: ☐ 1-Male ☐ 2-Female ☐ 3-Unk | Race: ☐ 1-White ☐ 2-Black ☐ 3-AmericanIndian/AlaskaNative ☐ 4-Asian/PacificIslander ☐ 5-Race Unknown | Ethnic Org: ☐ 1-Hispanic ☐ 2-NonHispanic ☐ 3-Other | Status: ☐ 1-Arrestee ☐ 2-Escapee ☐ 3-Suspect | Arrest Case No.

LOCATION

Location Stolen/Lost | Recovered By | Date | Time

Recovered/Found Location | Controlling Officer | Empl. No.

CODES

Property Heading: 1-Stolen (Only) 2-Recovered (Only) 3-Stolen & Recovered 4-Recovered Other Jurisdiction 5-Found 6-Damaged 7-Lost 8-Evidence/Seized 9-Counterfeited/Forged 10-Counterfeited/Forged 11Other/Unknown

Document Type: 1-US Currency 2-Personal Check/Draft 3-Company Check/Draft 4-Fin Inst. Check/Draft 5-Govt Check/Draft 6-Money Order 7-Travel Check 8-Credit card 9-ATM/Debit card 10-Stock Cert 11-US Bond 12 State Bond 13-Municipal Bond 14-Corp Bond 15-Other Security 16-Bank Cert of Dep 17-Other Bank Instr 18-Will 19-Deed 20-Prescription 21-Driver's Lic 22-ID Card 23-IOU/Prom Note 24-Airline Ticket 25-Bus Ticket 26-Train Ticket 27-Coupons 28-Food Stamps 29-Postage Stamps. 30-Motor Vehicle Title 31-Motor Vehicle License 32-Foreign Currency 98-Other Documents 99-Unknown

Drug Type: 1-Crack Cocaine 2-Cocaine 3-Hashish 4-Heroin 5-Marijuana 6-Morphine 7-Opium 8-Other Narcotic 9-LSD 10-PCP 11-Other Halucinogen 12-Amphetamine 13-Methamphetamine 14-Other Stimulant 15-Barbiturate 16-Other Depressant 19-Other Drugs 20-Unknown 21-Drug precursors, chemicals 22-Drug manufacturing equipment 83-Drug use paraphernalia

Unit Code/Abbrv: 1-GM (gram) 2-KG (kilogram) 3-OZ (av. ounces) 4-LB (pound) 5-ML (milliliter) 6-LT (liter) 7-FO (fluid ounces) 8-GL (gallon) 9-DU (dosage units, pills, items) 10-NP (no. of plants)

PROPERTY INFO

ITEM #	Prop Head	Description	Color	Serial No./Account No.	Make, Issuer, etc.	Model/Type	UCR Prop. Type	Dept. Prop. Type	$ Amt of Damage	Value $ Stolen	Value $ Recovered	Prop Damage	Doc Type	Drug Type	Drug Quantity	Units of Measurement Abbv. Code
												☐ 1-Arson ☐ 2-Other				
												☐ 1-Arson ☐ 2-Other				
												☐ 1-Arson ☐ 2-Other				
												☐ 1-Arson ☐ 2-Other				
												☐ 1-Arson ☐ 2-Other				
												☐ 1-Arson ☐ 2-Other				
												☐ 1-Arson ☐ 2-Other				
												☐ 1-Arson ☐ 2-Other				

CASE REFERRAL ☐ CID ☐ OCD ☐ JUV ☐ FD ☐ FRAUD ☐ OTHER

I.D. Technician Called? Name: ☐ Yes ☐ No

NARRATIVE

☐ Check If Narrative Continued   Complainant's Signature

Reporting Officer's Signature	Date	Empl. No.	Supervisor's Signature	Empl. No.	Review Date	Records Emp Initial	Empl. No.	Entry Date

Property Incident Report. *This form provides information about all property crimes. The information includes the type of incident, the location at which it occurred, and a description of any damaged or stolen property dealing with the occurrence. This form is also used to document any victim and suspect information.*

347

```
 ┌──────────────────────────────────────────────────────────────────────┐
 │       RALEIGH POLICE DEPARTMENT SUSPECT/ARRESTEE DESCRIPTION           │
 │ Offense:_____Date/Time:_____/_____  Case No:_____ │
 │ Offense Location:_____  Victims Name:_____ │
 └──────────────────────────────────────────────────────────────────────┘
```

(Last Name, First Name, Middle Name/Initials) ADDRESS (No. & Street, City, State, & Zip)

Suspect/Arrestee # 1:_____
   AKA/Ethnicity   :_____   ☐ H-Hispanic ☐ N-Non Hispanic ☐ U-Unknown
Suspect/Arrestee # 2:_____
   AKA/Ethnicity   :_____   ☐ H-Hispanic ☐ N-Non Hispanic ☐ U-Unknown

RACE   SEX   AGE   DOB   M   PB   O.L. STATE & NO.   SSN
1 2   MIN MAX
      1 Unk.   1   1
      2 Asian   2   2
      3 Black   CA
      4 Indian   HANDED
      5 White   1   2
      99 Other:

HGT   WGT   EYE COLOR   HAIR COLOR   FACIAL HAIR
MIN MAX MIN MAX   1 2   1 2   1 2
                        1 Black   1 Black   1 Beard
                        2 Blue   2 Blond/Strawberry   2 Clean Shaven
                        3 Brown   3 D.Brown   3 Goatee
                        4 Gray   4 L.Brown   4 Long Side Burns
                        5 Green   5 Gray   5 Moustache, Bushy
                        6 Hazel   6 Red/Auburn   6 Moustache, Fu Manchu
                        99 Other: 7 Salt & Pepper   7 Moustache, thin/light
                                           8 Sandy   8 Pork Chop Side Burns
                                           99 Other: 99 Other:

COMPLEXION   SPEECH
1 2   1 2
   1 Dark   1 Deep Voice   INJURIES   DESCRIBE CLOTHING
   2 Light   2 Eastern US   1   1
   3 Medium   3 English   2   2
   4 Olive   4 Fast
   5 Pale   5 French
   6 Red   6 High Voice   TRANSPORTED TO/BY   WEAPONS USED
   7 Yellow   7 Hispanic   1   1
   99 Other: 8 Northern US   2   2
BODY   9 Slang
1 2   10 Southern US
   1 Heavy   11 Stutter
   2 Medium   99 Other: DESCRIBE ANY SCARS, MARKS, OR TATOOS
   3 Muscular EYES   1
   4 Thin   1 2   2
   5 Obese
   99 Other: 20 Blinking
                  21 Bulging
TEETH   22 Close Set
1 2   23 Crossed
   70 Braces   24 Glasses   FACIAL SHAPE   FACIAL ODDITIES   HAIR TYPE
   71 Buck   25 L.Eye Miss. 1 2   1 2   1 2
   72 Chipped   26 R.Eye Miss.   30 Broad   40 Birthmark   50 Afro
   73 Decayed   27 Squints   31 Heart   41 Freckles   51 Bald
   74 Gaps Bottom 299 Other: 32 Hi Cheeks   42 Moles   52 Bushy
   75 Gaps Top   33 Long   43 Pimples   53 Crew Cut
   76 Gold Bottom   34 Round   44 Pocked   54 Curly
   77 Gold Top   OTHER   35 Square   499 Other: 55 Kinky
   78 Silver Bottom PHYSICAL   36 Thin   56 Long
   79 Silver Top ODDITIES   399 Other: NOSE   57 Part.Bald
   80 Very White 1 2   1 2   58 Straight
   899 Other: 110 Smells bad   90 Blood Veins   59 Receeding
                   111 Dirty   91 Broad   60 Thin
   OCCUP./EMPLOYER 112 Jewelry: 92 Crooked   61 Toupee
                   113 Neat/well dressed   93 Flat   62 Wavy
1   114 Mod/unusual: 94 Hooked   63 Wig
2   115 Uniformed: 95 Long   699 Other:
                   119 Other: 96 Small
                                                    97 Thin
Officer: Code No: Assignment: 98 Upturned
                                                    999 Other:
```

```
 ┌──────────────────────────────────────────────────────────────────────┐
 │              CASE STATUS CHANGE              Inv:_____ Date:_____│
 │  ☐ - Unfounded   ☐ - Death of Offender  ☐ - Prosecution Declined        │
 │                                              Supv:_____ Date:_____│
 │  ☐ - CBA  ☐ - Juvenile/No Custody  ☐ - Extradition Declined             │
 │                                              Entry:_____ Date:_____│
 │  ☐ - CBA by Another Agency  ☐ - Refuse to Cooperate  ☐ - Inactive       │
 │                                              Page    of                 │
 └──────────────────────────────────────────────────────────────────────┘
```

Suspect/Arrestee Description. *This form is dedicated to giving a detailed description of the suspect or arrestee involved with or connected to a crime. It provides information about the suspect's appearance, the clothing worn by the suspect during the crime, and any unusual identification marks the suspect might have.*
```

STATE OF NORTH CAROLINA
COUNTY OF WAKE

IN THE GENERAL COURT OF JUSTICE
DISTRICT COURT DIVISION

STATE OF NORTH CAROLINA
VS

_____

SUBPOENA
AND
INSTRUCTIONS
FOR PROSECUTING WITNESS

TRIAL DATE: _____   **TIME:** _____ **DAY:** _____

1. This is a SUBPOENA. You are <u>commanded</u> to appear and testify in the WAKE COUNTY COURTHOUSE, Room 4-B, on the trial date above and <u>each time thereafter the case is set.</u> If you fail to appear, the charges will probably be dismissed and you may be charged with contempt and bear the penalties attached thereto.

2. If you change your address before this case is tried, you must notify the Clerk of Superior Court of such new address.

3. If you learn that the defendant or any witness you have named has a change of address, you must notify the Clerk of Superior Court of such new address.

4. <u>Before</u> you swear out this Warrant, you may decide that you would like to try MEDIATION. If you decide to try MEDIATION and it is unsuccessful, you still have two years to swear out a Warrant on this complaint.
    <u>Once a warrant is sworn out:</u>

5. ONLY THE DISTRICT ATTORNEY CAN DROP THE CHARGES.
    If you change your mind and want to request that the District Attorney drop the charges, you may make this request to the Assistant District Attorney ONLY ON THE DAY AND TIME OF THE TRIAL. You will be required to pay the court costs, in cash, on the trial date.

6. On the day of the trial you may also request that the case be referred to Mediation. If you desire to try to resolve this matter through Mediation, you will need to make that request to the Assistant District Attorney only on the day and time of the trial. If the case is successfully mediated, you will not have to pay court costs if the Assistant District Attorney honors the request for the case to be dismissed.

7. The Assistant District Attorney can dismiss the charges even if you disagree. The Assistant District Attorney can refuse to dismiss the charges even if you disagree.

8. To verify that your case has been served and docketed for the assigned date, call the Clerk of Superior Court at 755-4110, on the last working day prior to your court date, between the hours of 8:30a.m. and 5:00p.m.

_____
(MAGISTRATE)

I have received a copy of this SUBPOENA. I have read it, or the Magistrate has explained it to me. I understand it and agree <u>to appear in court on the trial date and each time thereafter that the case is on the docket.</u>

Date:_____   _____
(Prosecuting Witness)

Subpoena. *This form is used by the courts to summon individuals who might be involved in a particular incident so that they can provide testimony pertaining to the case on trial. If the recipient of the subpoena fails to appear in court on the scheduled day, the individual can be charged with contempt of court.*

349

ARREST REPORT

AGENCY INFO.	Agency Name			ORI NC		Date/Time of Arrest Mo Date Year Hrs.		OCA	
	☐ Taken Prints ☐ Photos	Fingerprint Card Check Digit # (CKN)		Arrest Tract		Residence Tract	Arrest Number		

ARRESTEE INFORMATION	Name (Last, First, Middle)				D.O.B.	Age	Race	Sex	Place of Birth	Country of Citizenship
	Current Address			Phone		Occupation		☐ Resident ☐ Non-Resident	☐ Unknown	
	Employer's Name			Address					Phone	
	Also Known As (Alias Names)			Hgt	Wgt	Hair	Eye	Skin Tone	Consumed Drug/Alcohol ☐ Yes ☐ No ☐ Unk	
	Scars, Marks, Tatoos			Social Security # — —		OLN and State		Misc. # and Type		
	Nearest Relative Name			Address				Phone		

ARREST INFO.

If Armed, Type of Weapon — ☐ On-View ☐ Criminal Summons ☐ Order for Arrest ☐ Citation ☐ Warrant — Place of Arrest

Charge #1	☐ Fel ☐ Misd	Counts	DCI Code	Offense Jurisdiction (If not arresting agency)	Statute #	Warr. Date Mo Date Yr
Charge #2	☐ Fel ☐ Misd	Counts	DCI Code	Offense Jurisdiction (If not arresting agency)	Statute #	Warr. Date Mo Date Yr
Charge #3	☐ Fel ☐ Misd	Counts	DCI Code	Offense Jurisdiction (If not arresting agency)	Statute #	Warr. Date Mo Date Yr

VEH. INFO.

VYR	Make	Model	Style	Color	Lic/Lis	Vin

Vehicle: 1. ☐ Left at Scene ☐ Secured ☐ Unsecure Date/Time_____ Hrs._____
2. ☐ Released to other at owners request ☐ Name of Other_____
3. ☐ Impounded ☐ Place of storage_____ Inventory on File?_____

CONFINED BOND INFO.

Date/Time Confined Hrs.	Place Confined		Committing Magistrate
Type Bond ☐ Written Promise ☐ Unsecured ☐ Secured ☐ No Bond ☐ Other	Amt. Bond	Trial Date	Court of	City
Assisting Officer Name/ID Number	Released By: Name/Dept/ID		Date/Time Released Hrs.

Status Codes
L – Lost   S – Stolen   R – Recovered   D – Damaged   Z – Seized   B – Burned   C – Counterfeit / Forged   F – Found
(Check "OJ" column if recovered for other jurisdiction)

DRUGS AT TIME OF ARREST

					Check up to 3 types of activity for each					
DCI	Status	Quantity	Type Measure	Suspected Type	Possess	Buy	Sale	Mfg.	Importing	Operating

COMPLAINANT

Name: Complainant ☐ Victim ☐   Address: Phone:

NARRATIVE

STATUS

Arresting Officer Signature/ID #	Date/Time Submitted Mo Date Yr Hrs.	Supervisor Signature
Case Status: ☐ Further Inv. ☐ Inactive ☐ Closed	Case Disposition: ☐ Cleared By Arrest / No Supplement Needed ☐ Arrest/No Investigation	Arrestee Signature

DCI-608F   Rev. 3/92

Arrest Report—Campus Safety. *This is an example of a form used by college campus security, or the public safety department, to record information about an initial arrest and to provide descriptive information about the arrestee.*

Index

H

I-J-K-L

M-N-O